PCs
for Grown-Ups

Getting the Most Out of Your Windows 8 Computer

Paul McFedries

800 East 96th Street,
Indianapolis, Indiana 46240 USA

PCs for Grown-Ups
Getting the Most Out of Your Windows 8 Computer

Copyright © 2013 by Que Publishing

ISBN-13: 978-0-7897-4961-1
ISBN-10: 0-7897-4961-0

Library of Congress Cataloging-in-Publication data is on file.

First Printing: February 2013

Trademarks

All terms mentioned in this book that are known to be trademarks or service marks have been appropriately capitalized. Que Publishing cannot attest to the accuracy of this information. Use of a term in this book should not be regarded as affecting the validity of any trademark or service mark.

Warning and Disclaimer

Every effort has been made to make this book as complete and as accurate as possible, but no warranty or fitness is implied. The information provided is on an "as is" basis. The author and the publisher shall have neither liability nor responsibility to any person or entity with respect to any loss or damages arising from the information contained in this book.

Bulk Sales

Que Publishing offers excellent discounts on this book when ordered in quantity for bulk purchases or special sales. For more information, please contact

U.S. Corporate and Government Sales
1-800-382-3419
corpsales@pearsontechgroup.com

For sales outside the United States, please contact

International Sales
international@pearsoned.com

Editor-in-Chief
Greg Wiegand

Executive Editor
Rick Kughen

Development Editor
Rick Kughen

Managing Editor
Sandra Schroeder

Project Editor
Seth Kerney

Copy Editor
Chuck Hutchinson

Indexer
Cheryl Lenser

Proofreader
Debbie Williams

Technical Editor
Karen Weinstein

Publishing Coordinators
Cindy Teeters
Romny French

Book Designer
Anne Jones

Compositor
TnT Design, Inc.

Table of Contents

About the Author

Paul McFedries is full-time technical writer and passionate computer tinkerer. He is the author of more than 80 computer books that have sold over four million copies worldwide. His recent titles include the Sams Publishing books *Windows 7 Unleashed* and *Windows Home Server 2011 Unleashed* and the Que Publishing books *Windows 8 In Depth* (co-authored with Brian Knittel), *Formulas and Functions with Microsoft Excel 2013, Using iPhone,* and *Using the Microsoft Office Web Apps.* Paul is also the proprietor of Word Spy (www.wordspy.com), a website devoted to tracking new words and phrases as they enter the English language. Paul's web home is at www.mcfedries.com, and he can be followed on Twitter at twitter.com/paulmcf and twitter.com/wordspy.

Dedication

For my parents.

Acknowledgments

I've been writing computer books for more than 20 years now (ouch!), which is a long time to do *anything*, much less something that exercises the old noodle the way researching and writing a computer book does. Despite that, however, I still leap out of bed most mornings and can't wait to get my hands on the keyboard once again and start tapping away.

Maintaining enthusiasm for your job is never easy, but it sure helps when you get to work with some amazingly smart, talented, and nice people. I speak, of course, of the bright lights who populate the Que editorial department, who are as awesome a collection of Hoosiers as you're ever likely to meet (assuming you come across Hoosier collections regularly). In particular, I'd like to extend my heartfelt and profuse thanks to the editors I worked with directly on this book, including executive editor and development editor Rick Kughen; project editor Seth Kerney; copy editor Chuck Hutchinson; and technical editor Karen Weinstein. Thanks to all of you for the excellent work.

We Want to Hear from You!

As the reader of this book, *you* are our most important critic and commentator. We value your opinion and want to know what we're doing right, what we could do better, what areas you'd like to see us publish in, and any other words of wisdom you're willing to pass our way.

We welcome your comments. You can email or write to let us know what you did or didn't like about this book—as well as what we can do to make our books better.

Please note that we cannot help you with technical problems related to the topic of this book.

When you write, please be sure to include this book's title and author as well as your name and email address. We will carefully review your comments and share them with the author and editors who worked on the book.

Email: feedback@quepublishing.com

Mail: Que Publishing
           ATTN: Reader Feedback
           800 East 96th Street
           Indianapolis, IN 46240 USA

Reader Services

Visit our website and register this book at quepublishing.com/register for convenient access to any updates, downloads, or errata that might be available for this book.

In most households these days, the joke is that it's the kids who run the show, at least as far as the technology goes. They provide the specs for new PCs, suggest peripherals and gadgets to buy, configure the router, perform routine Windows tasks, handle computer maintenance and repairs, and go inside the PC when the hard drive or the memory needs upgrading. And even if the kids are all grown up with families of their own, they probably still perform all these tasks whenever they drop by for a visit; that, or their kids— yes, the *grandkids*—take over these duties.

That's all well and good, but it leads to an important question: Why are parents and grandparents—why are *you*— letting the kids and grandkids have all the fun? The basics of the PC—including how to buy a PC, how to use Windows, how to get online, and how to maintain and repair a PC— are accessible to anyone of any age who is curious and motivated to learn. It might seem that tasks such as deciding on a computer, configuring a router, and replacing the hard drive are too advanced for older adults, but nothing could be further from the truth. That's because working with a PC doesn't require any advanced skills or knowledge, so it can be done by any beginner:

- All the needed parts are readily available online or from big-box retailers or electronics stores.

- All the tools you need are part of most people's toolkits or can be easily obtained.

- All the techniques you need are simple and straightforward.

Add to this the important fact that buying, using, maintaining, and repairing one's own PC gives the average grown-up an extra level of independence because he or she no longer has to rely on others or wait until a child or grandchild has time to perform these tasks.

PCs for Grown-Ups aims to be your guide on this independent, do-it-yourself path. With a friendly, knowledgeable tone, this book shows you everything you need to know to understand, use, and maintain a PC.

How This Book Is Organized

To help you learn about PCs in the easiest and most straightforward way, I've organized this book into four reasonably sensible parts that include related chapters. Here's a summary:

- **Part 1, "Understanding PC Basics,"** helps you understand PCs, including the various parts that make up a typical PC, purchasing a PC, setting up a PC, and taking the initial steps.

- **Part 2, "Understanding Windows,"** gives you a quick tour of some Windows basics, from getting around the screen to creating documents to installing applications. This part of the book also teaches you basic digital media literacy, including importing and organizing digital photos, setting up and maintaining a digital music library, and viewing digital video.

- **Part 3, "Working, Learning, and Playing Online,"** gets you online, with information on setting up a router and making wireless connections. From there, you learn about the Web, email, online shopping, researching, social networking, and the all-important topic of Internet security and privacy.

- **Part 4, "Maintaining and Repairing Your PC,"** is the biggest section of the book with eight chapters devoted to basic PC maintenance, troubleshooting, and repair. You learn not only the Windows tools that are most useful for maintaining and troubleshooting the system, but also step-by-step techniques for replacing the hard drive, replacing the DVD drive, adding memory, and more.

This Book's Special Features

PCs for Grown-Ups is designed to give you the information you need without making you wade through ponderous explanations and interminable technical background. To make your life easier, this book includes various features and conventions that help you get the most out of the book and your PC:

- **Steps**—Throughout the book, each task is summarized in step-by-step procedures.

- **Things you type**—Whenever I suggest that you type something, what you type appears in a **bold** font.

- **Commands**—I use the following style for menu commands: File, Open. This means that you pull down the File menu and select the Open command. I also have placed names of menus, commands, and anything you click on screen in a **bold** font.

This book also uses the following boxes to draw your attention to important (or merely interesting) information.

Note

The Note box presents asides that give you more information about the topic under discussion. These tidbits provide extra insights that give you a better understanding of the task at hand.

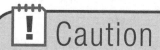Caution

The all-important Caution box tells you about potential accidents waiting to happen. There are always ways to mess things up when you're working with computers. These boxes help you avoid at least some of the pitfalls.

Tip

The Tip box tells you about methods that are easier, faster, or more efficient than the standard methods.

Chapter 1

Getting to Know the PC

The great science fiction writer Arthur C. Clarke once said that "any sufficiently advanced technology is indistinguishable from magic." That maxim no doubt rings true whenever you ponder your PC. Consider: You press the PC's power switch, and the machine spends a minute or two whirring and clicking impenetrably until at last the Windows screen makes its appearance. You then tap away on your keyboard or jiggle and click your mouse, and somehow the PC translates these obscure movements into apparently purposeful onscreen action. Along the way, you might even get some useful things done. "If that's not magic," you might mumble to yourself, "then I don't know what is."

In your heart of hearts, of course, you know that it isn't magic that's afoot, but rather an example of a "sufficiently advanced technology." On the surface, PCs *do* seem inordinately mysterious, but it's my goal in this book to remove some of that mystery and to make your PC if not exactly transparent, then at least a lot less opaque.

This chapter gets you well started toward that goal by taking you on a tour of the various bits and pieces that comprise the inside and outside of a typical PC. This will stand you in good stead when we turn our attention to buying and setting up a PC in the next couple of chapters, and especially a bit later in the book when we talk about PC maintenance and repair.

It's What's Inside That Counts

All that internal buzzing and ticking would seem to indicate that your PC is up to *something* in there, but what exactly is happening under your PC's hood? A full explanation of the complexities of how PCs work internally would require several books the size of this one, so you're not going to get the full scoop from me. That's fine, because in any case you don't need to know the gory details of how computers work to be able to buy, use, or maintain a PC. Instead, the next few sections merely hit the highlights to give you a basic understanding of what your PC is up to when the power switch is in the "on" position.

The Central Processing Unit

The heart of a PC's innards is a device called the *central processing unit*, also known as the *CPU*, the *microprocessor*, or simply the *processor*. In keeping with the "central" portion of its name, the CPU, with just a few exceptions, has a hand in everything that goes on within your PC. Press a key on your keyboard, for example, and the signal goes straight to the CPU, which then passes along the pressed key to Windows. Similarly, if a program you're using needs to send data to a printer, it hands off that data to Windows, which sends it to the CPU, which then routes the data to the printer. The only major exception to the CPU's micromanaging is with most of today's graphics cards (see "Expansion Cards" a bit later in this chapter), which usually have a dedicated *graphics processing unit* (GPU) that handles most of the graphics chores so the CPU can work on other things.

Given all that the CPU must do, you'd expect it to be a massive hunk of technology, but you'd be surprised. A typical CPU (I'm holding one between my fingers in Figure 1.1) fits easily into the palm of your hand and is just a fraction of an inch thick.

Figure 1.1 *Your average CPU isn't as large as you might think.*

Hard Drive

The *hard drive* (or *hard disk*) is the main storage area inside your PC. What does it store? Lots of things, actually:

- **Windows**—When you purchased your PC, it came with Windows already installed, and all the Windows bits and pieces reside full-time on the PC's hard drive.

- **Programs**—Any programs that came preinstalled with your PC or that you install on your PC yourself are also stored on your hard drive.

- **Data**—Any information required by Windows or your programs—this information is called *data*—is stored on the hard drive, too. This is also true of another type of data: those documents and files that you either create yourself while working with your PC or that you add to your PC (for example, photos that you take or music that you buy).

Every hard drive has an inherent *capacity*, which is a measure of the maximum amount of program code and data that it can store. The capacity is usually measured in *gigabytes* (GB), which means a billion (more or less) bytes. What's a *byte*? It's a unit of storage equal to a single character, such as a letter or number. So a 500GB hard drive can store the equivalent of about 500 billion characters. These days, *terabyte* (TB) hard drives are becoming common, and a terabyte is equal to about a *trillion* bytes. That's a lot of bytes.

A typical hard drive is a metal box that looks suspiciously like the one shown in Figure 1.2. Newer hard drives—called *solid-state drives* or *SSDs*—are smaller, but they're not as popular because they're more expensive. Amazingly, SSDs have no moving parts!

Figure 1.2 *A typical hard drive.*

Memory

The basic purpose in life for your computer's *memory* (short for *random access memory* or *RAM)* is to be used as a work area for your programs and data. These things normally slumber peacefully on your hard drive, but when you need them, Windows rouses them from their spacious beds and herds the program code and data into the relatively cramped confines of memory. From there, different bits of code and data are swapped in and out of memory, as needed. Why not just work with everything from the hard drive itself? One word: *speed*. Even the highest of high-tech hard drives is a tortoise compared to the blazing memory chips.

Entire books can be (and, indeed, have been) written about the relationship between your computer and its memory. What it all boils down to, though, is quite simple: The more memory you have, the happier your computer (and Windows and the programs you run on it) will be.

This all sounds well and good, but a fundamental problem underlies everything. Most hard drives can store hundreds or even thousands of gigabytes of data, but the memory capacity of a typical computer is limited to a measly few gigabytes.

Think of your computer as a carpenter's workshop divided into two areas—a storage space for your tools and materials (the hard drive) and a work area where you actually use these things (memory). The problem is that your computer's "work space" is much smaller than its "storage space." For a carpenter, a small work space limits the number of tools and the amount of wood that can be used at any one time. For a computer, it limits the number of programs and data files you can load.

Why not simply have as much RAM as you have hard drive space? The problem is that, although there's no theoretical reason hard drives can't keep increasing their capacities (other than certain laws of physics, which might come into play in 10 or 15 years), the amount of RAM you can put into your computer has a maximum that can't be exceeded on most systems. On systems that for geeky reasons are called "32-bit," that maximum value is 4GB, which is far smaller than any modern hard drive. So-called "64-bit" systems can use up to 256GB of RAM if they're running Windows 8, but that's still smaller than today's typical hard drive.

Your computer's memory is actually a collection of tiny memory chips, but these days all those chips are combined into a single piece called a *memory module* (or sometimes a *memory stick*). Figure 1.3 shows a typical memory module. Your PC likely has between one and four of these modules.

Figure 1.3 *A memory module.*

DVD Drive

Any PC worthy of the name will come with a DVD drive (see Figure 1.4), which is a device that reads (and in some cases can create) DVDs and CDs.

Among many other uses, the optical drive enables your system to play audio CDs, watch DVD movies and high-definition video (you need a Blu-ray drive for that), install programs, store data, and make backups.

Memory Card Reader

Most modern PCs come with a built-in *memory card reader*, which is a device for reading various types of memory cards. Each reader typically offers multiple slots for different types of cards (see Figure 1.5), such as CompactFlash, Secure Digital, MultiMediaCard, Memory Stick, and so on.

Note

A Little Geek-Speak

Many people prefer the phrase *optical drive*, a catchall term that includes every type of CD and DVD drive, as well as the latest Blu-ray drives. The *optical* part tells you that these drives use light—specifically, a semiconductor laser—to read data from and write data to the disc. (For example, the *Blu* in Blu-ray comes from the fact that it uses laser light with a wavelength in the blue section of the spectrum.)

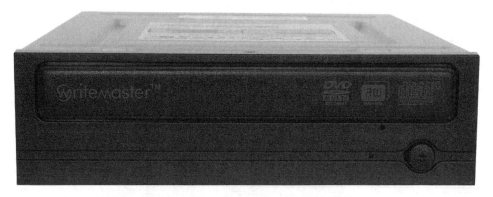

Figure 1.4   *A DVD drive.*

Figure 1.5   *An internal memory card reader lets you read the contents of multiple memory card formats.*

Expansion Cards

An *expansion card* is a circuit board that gets inserted into a special slot inside your PC. As the name implies, you use an expansion card to expand the capabilities of your PC. There are many different types of expansion cards, but the two most common are the video card and the sound card.

The Video Card

A *video card* (sometimes called a *video adapter* or *graphics card*) is an expansion card (see Figure 1.6) that enables software to display text or an image on the monitor. How images appear on your monitor is a function of two measurements: the color depth and resolution.

Figure 1.6 *A sample video card.*

The *color depth* is a measure of the number of colors available to display images on the screen. In general, the greater the number of colors, the sharper your screen image appears—and the more processing power required to display those colors.

Table 1.1 lists the bit values for the most common color depths.

Table 1.1   Bit Values for Some Standard Color Depths

Bits	Colors
4	16
8	256
15	32,268
16	65,536
24	16,777,216
32	16,777,216

The *resolution* is a measure of the density of the pixels used to display the screen image. The pixels are arranged in a row-and-column format, so the resolution is expressed as *rows × columns*, where *rows* is the number of pixel rows and *columns* is the number of pixel columns. For example, a 1,024 × 768 resolution means screen images are displayed using 1,024 rows of pixels and 768 columns of pixels. The higher the resolution, the sharper your images appear, although individual screen items also get smaller. So when you're selecting a resolution, it's usually a trade-off between sharpness and being able to read what's on the screen!

The key point to bear in mind about all this discussion is that there's usually a trade-off between color depth and resolution, and that trade-off is based on the memory installed on the video card. That is, depending on how much video memory is installed on the card, you might have to trade off higher color depth with lower resolution, or vice versa.

The Sound Card

The *sound card* is an expansion card that enables your PC's programs to make some noise. Although most PCs have a relatively barebones sound system built-in, adding a sound card can improve the audio quality by offering features such as Dolby Digital surround sound and multiple output channels. If you are a music lover, you like to play games, or you want to Skype with family in glorious surround sound, you might want to consider adding a sound card.

A Horse of a Different Color

On some systems, the color depth value isn't listed as a specific number of bits or colors. Instead, the color depth is listed as either "Medium" or "Thousands," both of which refer to the 16-bit, 65,536-color depth; or as "Highest" or "Millions," both of which refer to the 32-bit, 16,777,216-color depth.

The Skinny on Pixels

A *pixel* is a tiny element that displays the individual dots that make up the screen image (*pixel* is short for "picture element"). Each pixel consists of three components—red, green, and blue—and these components are manipulated to produce a specific color.

Judging a PC by Its Cover

Now that you've had a good look around the inside of the PC, it's time to turn your attention to the outside. The following sections are a little less abstract and a little more comprehensible because now we are dealing with those parts of the PC that you can see and, more importantly, that you can manipulate (by poking them, plugging things into them, and so on). This discussion focuses on the desktop PC, but most of the principles also apply in a general way to laptop PCs and to tablets (both of which I talk about in more detail in Chapter 2, "Buying a PC.").

The Case

The external shell of the PC is called the *case,* and the combination of the case and what's inside it is called the *system unit* (because all the most important parts of the PC system—especially the CPU, hard drive, and memory—reside within). The purpose of the case is to keep dust and other debris away from the PC's sensitive insides, as well as to expel the hot air generated by the CPU and other components through the use of strategically placed fans and openings.

Besides keeping the internal components safe from harm, the case also serves as the home of various slots, switches, buttons, and bays that serve a wide variety of uses. I go into these in some detail in the next couple of sections.

Finally, I also want to point out that cases come in a number of different shapes and sizes, or *form factors* as the know-it-alls say. In order of biggest to smallest, the most typical form factors are the full-tower, the mid-tower (see Figure 1.7), the micro-tower, and the small form factor (SFF; see Figure 1.8). Generally speaking, tower-type cases can only sit vertically, whereas SFF cases can sit either vertically or horizontally.

Note

The Full Meal Deal

I would be remiss if I didn't mention yet another type of PC form factor that's becoming quite popular these days: the *all-in-one* PC. This machine doesn't come with a separate system unit and monitor. Instead, it comes with a single piece that has a screen in front, the internal components (CPU, memory, and so on) crammed behind the screen, and the various ports and connectors on the back.

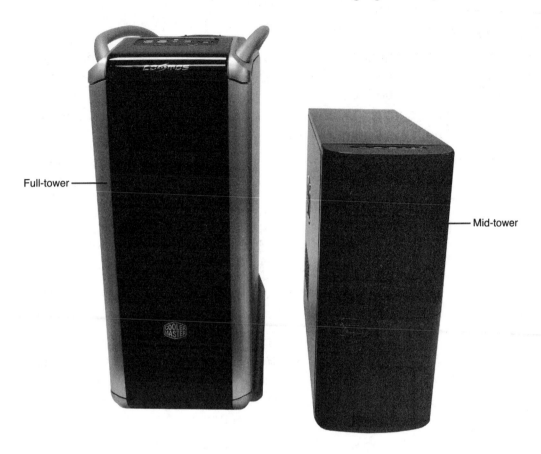

Figure 1.7   *The full-tower and mid-tower case styles.*

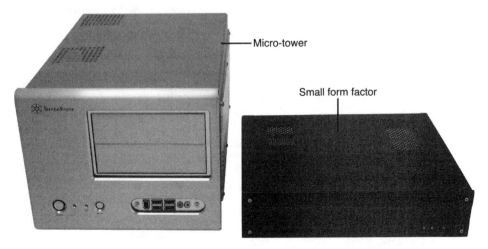

Figure 1.8   *The micro-tower and small form factor case styles.*

What's Up Front

Like snowflakes and fingerprints, no two computer models have the same external design or layout. However, most PCs these days have a similar overall configuration and a similar collection of features, so we can make some generalizations. As pointed out in Figures 1.9 and 1.10, the front of a typical computer case offers the following widgets:

Power button	This button turns on the computer's power if it's currently off, or it turns off the power if the machine is currently on.
Reset button	This button shuts off the computer briefly and then turns it back on. Note that many PCs don't come with a Reset button these days.
Activity lights	These lights glow when the computer's power is turned on and when the hard drive is active.
Front ports	These ports are connectors for things such as a headphone, a microphone, one or more Universal Serial Bus (USB) devices, and a FireWire device. They are usually more convenient to use than the computer's rear ports (which I talk about in the next section).
Drive bays	These slots hold the PC's DVD drive and usually a memory card reader. Many PCs come with one or two empty drive bays to enable you to add another device (such as a second optical drive).
Front panel	This door swings open to reveal the case's drive bays, so you can insert a disc into a DVD drive or insert a memory card into a card reader.
Front bezel	This access panel comprises the front of the case (and includes the front panel). You remove the front bezel to insert a device into or remove a device from a drive bay.

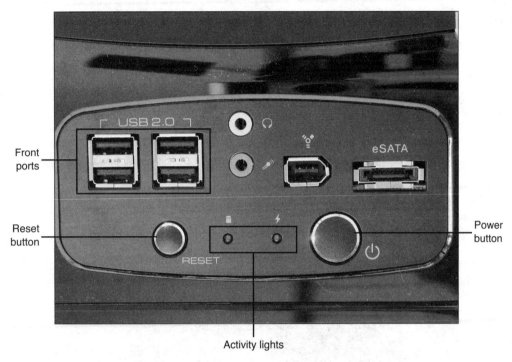

Figure 1.9 *Typical buttons and ports and things on the front of a PC.*

Ports, Ports, and More Ports

In PC parlance, a *port* is a connection point on the computer, meaning that you use it to connect something to the machine. As you saw in the preceding section, most modern PCs come with a collection of ports on the front of the case, but the real port action happens at the back, which, as you can see in Figure 1.11, is loaded with ports of all different shapes and sizes.

Figure 1.10 *More frontal PC parts.*

Let's knock some sense into these knickknacks:

Power outlet	You use this port to plug in your PC's power cord.
Keyboard/ mouse port	You use this port to plug in your keyboard or mouse. Bear in mind, however, that your typical modern keyboard and mouse plug into a USB port instead.
Monitor ports	You use one of these ports to connect your monitor.
USB ports	You use these ports to plug in devices that use the Universal Serial Bus connector. Keyboards, mice, printers, digital cameras, and many other devices use USB connectors.

Network port	You use this port to connect your PC to a wired network or to an Internet modem.
Sound ports	You use these ports to connect sound devices to your PC. If you have external speakers, they connect to the Line Out (green) port; if you have a microphone, you connect it to the Mic In (pink) port.
Wi-Fi connector	You use this port to connect a Wi-Fi antenna for accessing a wireless network.

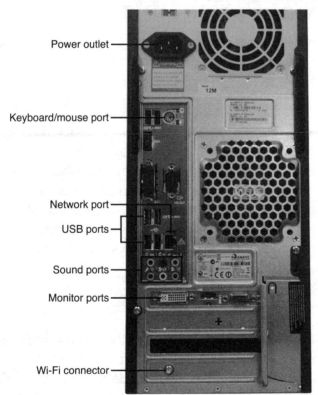

Figure 1.11   *The back of a typical computer case.*

I know this is a lot to digest, but here are three reasons not to worry too much about any of this back-of-the-case stuff right now:

• As you saw in Figure 1.10, the front of most computer cases comes with a few access ports—particularly USB and sound ports—so you may rarely have to use these back ports.

- You learn a lot more about each type of port and making these physical connections in Chapter 3, "Setting Up Your PC," so if the details are a bit fuzzy right now, things should clear up considerably in that chapter.

- Although there are perhaps a couple of dozen ports shown in Figure 1.11, the vast majority of computer setups use only a fraction of these: the power outlet, the monitor port, a USB port or three, and the speaker port.

A Sideways Look at Peripherals

Let's close this chapter by taking a quick look at some of the most common PC *peripherals*, which are external devices that you connect to the PC.

Monitor

The term *monitor* refers to the TV-like device that your PC uses to show you what's happening inside the machine using a combination of text, graphics, and other data. Some folks also call it the *video display,* and the rectangular part that shows the data is called the *screen*. The monitor is connected to the PC using a cord that connects to the monitor port in the back of the PC (although, as I mentioned in a note a few pages back, the relatively new all-in-one PC form factor combines the monitor and system unit, so no connection is necessary).

Keyboard

You use the typewriter-like device, or *keyboard,* to enter information (such as a letter or a list). In some cases, you also use the keyboard to type instructions for the computer to follow. Most keyboards connect to a USB port instead of the old-style keyboard port. However, lots of keyboards these days are *wireless*, meaning that they beam their keystrokes to a device called a *transceiver* that connects to the PC.

Mouse

You use the mouse device as a kind of hand-operated pointing tool that you use to select things on the screen that you want to work with, as well as to move things here and there on the screen. Most mice connect to a USB port instead of the old-style mouse port. However, just like the keyboard, many modern mice are wireless.

Printer

You use a printer to take something inside your computer—it might be a text document or a photo—and transfer it to paper. So-called *ink-jet* printers are loaded with various colors of ink to print in full color, whereas *laser* printers use a substance called *toner* to transfer text and images to paper. Modern printers either connect to a USB port or can operate wirelessly.

Sound System

The term *sound system* typically refers to a set of speakers that you connect to the Line In port in the back of the PC. Other sound system components you might come across are subwoofers (for extra bass output), headphones (for listening to system sounds without disturbing your neighbors), and microphones (for recording audio or even controlling your PC using voice commands).

Chapter 2

Buying a PC

If you're in the market for a new PC, I feel your pain. Whoops, I mean how exciting for you! I jest because purchasing a PC is probably more complicated than actually using one. There are tons of manufacturers, each offering umpteen models with impenetrable names such as "ET2600SFX" and "597D3i." Then there are the specifications for each machine, which toss around head-scratch-inducing terms such as "dual core" and "DDR3" and "L3 cache." Without knowing the meaning of these and other examples of PC-buying geek speak, how can you be sure not only that you're buying the right PC, but that you're buying the right PC *at the right price*?

That's where this chapter rides to the rescue. My goal here is to demystify the whole PC purchasing process, from deciding what you need to deciphering the specs to making the purchase. By the time we're done, you'll be able to waltz into any computer store—whether it's made of bricks or bits—and make your best deal.

Choosing a Computer Type

The first item you have to check off your "PC Buying Guide" checklist is the type of computer you want. There are four main types—tower, all-in-one, laptop, and tablet—and I take you through the pros and cons of each type in the next few sections.

Tower PC

The tower PC is a common type of PC, and as you learned in Chapter 1, "Getting to Know the PC," it comes in many different shapes and sizes, from tall full-tower models to relatively puny small form factor PCs. There are three reasons why you might consider going the tower route:

- **Selection**—Because tower PCs are quite common, there's a vast selection available from just about every PC manufacturer. This makes it easy to find the computer you need and the price you prefer.

- **Customizability**—No matter which type of computer you decide to buy, most manufacturers offer a number of options for customizing your purchase, but by far the biggest number of options is available with any of the tower models.

- **Upgradeability**—With the exception of some of the tinier models, tower PCs come with lots of ports for connecting things and lots of room inside for adding things. The ability to upgrade a PC down the road can give an old PC an extra year or two of service.

The biggest drawback to tower PCs is the sheer size of the things, particularly the behemoth full-tower models. This isn't a big deal if you're fortunate to have a large den or office, but smaller spaces might argue against a tower choice (or lead you toward an SFF model). Tower PCs also tend to be noisy because they usually have a number of fans whirring away inside to keep the interior cool. They also use up the most energy of any of the PC types, although you can minimize energy use by putting the PC to sleep when you're not using it.

All-In-One PC

An *all-in-one PC* combines the monitor and the system unit into a single package with the monitor in front and the system unit behind (see Figure 2.1). There are two main reasons to go for an all-in-one:

- **Space considerations**—An all-in-one PC doesn't take up much more room than a monitor on its own, so if space is tight, it's nice not to have to worry about finding a spot to put a separate system unit.

- **Aesthetic considerations**—All-in-one PCs are generally nice-looking machines, so they add a bit of eye candy to your desk. Buying one also means you do without the aesthetic horrors of a separate system unit (which is usually an ugly black box) and the extra cables (one for power and one to connect the monitor and the unit) that this entails. Most all-in-ones have few moving parts inside, so they require fewer cooling fans than a tower, making them much quieter.

Figure 2.1   *All-on-one PCs combine a monitor with the system unit.*

On the downside, all-in-one PCs don't have as many ports as towers, you generally can't upgrade their insides with extra hard drives or circuit boards, and they also tend to be slightly more expensive than tower/monitor combinations. Another consideration is that when you need to replace an all-in-one, you're really replacing both the system unit and the monitor at the same time, compared to a tower where if the system unit goes (or becomes obsolete), you only have to replace the unit and you still keep the monitor (which tends to last a few years longer than a typical system unit).

Laptop PC

A *laptop PC* (also sometimes called a *notebook PC*) goes the all-in-one two steps further by combining not only the monitor and the system unit in a single package, but also the keyboard and the mouse. This *everything-in-one* design means that laptops offer four significant advantages:

Note

All-In-One Portability

One other factor in the all-in-one's favor is its relative portability compared to its tower cousin. These models are not all that light—they typically weigh in at around 20–25 pounds—but that's much more luggable than the 35–40 pounds that a garden variety tower weighs. Plus, you only have to hump a single unit to another room, whereas relocating a tower means two trips: one for the system unit and one for the monitor.

- **Ease of setup**—When it's time to set up your new laptop PC, you don't have to do much else besides plug in the power cord. As you see in Chapter 3, "Setting Up Your PC," setting up a tower and even an all-in-one requires quite a few more steps.

- **Low space usage**—Laptop PCs are small. Even the bigger laptops are usually no more than about 16 inches by 11 inches, which is still a pretty compact package. If you have a small desk in a small room, a laptop might be the way to go.

- **Portability**—Laptop PCs are light. These babies usually weigh between three and six pounds, but are available even lighter. This makes it a breeze to take a laptop to any other room in the house at a moment's notice or to take with you on the road.

- **Unpluggability**—Laptop PCs become even more ridiculously portable when you add in the fact that they all come with batteries inside that can power them without AC for several hours. So not only can you unplug the power cord and whisk your laptop to any other room in your house, but you can also whisk it *outside* your house, should the mood strike you.

On the con side of the ledger, laptops do tend to be slightly more expensive than tower PCs. They also have fewer ports, so you're limited in the number of peripherals you can attach. Laptops also generally have relatively small system units, so most of their internal components aren't as powerful as those in a typical tower or all-in-one. For example, they often have smaller hard drives and poorer graphics performance. (That said, some manufacturers are creating high-end laptops that have correspondingly high-end components. They're super-expensive, but they pack as much punch as a powerful desktop PC.) You also have to be careful of the built-in keyboard, which can be a bit chintzy in some laptops, and the trackpad that replaces the mouse can be hard to get used to.

Tablet PC

A *tablet PC* is a laptop PC with a special screen that you can pivot so that it lies flat on the keyboard and trackpad. How on earth do you make anything happen if the keyboard and trackpad are hidden? The tablet PC's screen is touch sensitive, so instead of clicking things, you tap them with your finger or with a special pen-like device called a *stylus* (also called a *digital pen*). It also has an on-screen keyboard that you can call up when you need to type things. You can even use the stylus to write directly on the screen, and special software converts your handwriting into regular computer text. You can also get devices just called *tablets* that do away with the keyboard and trackpad altogether and rely exclusively on touch input.

Tablets (meaning tablet PCs in the touch-only configuration and tablet devices) bring three main advantages to the table:

- **Ease of use**—Using your finger to manipulate onscreen objects sounds odd, but getting the hang of it is amazingly easy. Most people find that a touch interface is the most natural way to interface with a PC. Even better, Windows 8 is designed with tablets in mind, so using your tablet is even easier than before.

- **Flexibility**—Tablets enable you to provide the device with many different kinds of input. For example, at a meeting you can jot notes, draw diagrams, annotate documents, and input handwritten messages. By contrast, regular PCs can only accept keyboard input (unless you add special equipment).

- **Ultra-portability**—Although tablet PCs weigh about the same as laptop PCs, pure tablets tip the scales at only 1.5 to 2 pounds, so you can take them anywhere you want to go. Also, their batteries tend to last for six or seven hours, so they're perfect for a plane ride or just getting out of the office for an afternoon.

A tablet PC's drawbacks are the same as those for a laptop PC. The biggest drawback of a tablet is that it's expensive (typically about the same as a regular PC). Also, a tablet tends to have very few ports (usually just a single USB port), so you can't add many peripherals (although most support a technology called Bluetooth that enables you to connect devices wirelessly). Finally, because a tablet doesn't come with a physical keyboard, using it for real work is hard, so don't count on using a tablet as a replacement for a regular PC.

Selecting a CPU

In computer ads, a description of a PC always begins with the manufacturer's name, followed by the PC's model name (or, really, number). You almost always see the CPU description, which looks something like one of the following two items:

Intel Core i7-2700K (3.50GHz) 8MB L3 cache

AMD FX-Series FX-8120 (3.1GHz) 4MB L3 cache

There are five bits of information in this seemingly impenetrable prose:

- **Company name**—This is *Intel* in the first line and *AMD* in the second. These are the two major CPU manufacturers, and because they both make top-notch processors, you can't go wrong with either one.

- **Processor family**—This is *Core* in the first item and *FX-Series* in the second item. The processor's family (or class) name is kind of an umbrella term that encompasses a series of related processors that use the same underlying architecture. For our purposes, the family name doesn't mean a whole lot, so it can be safely ignored.

- **Processor model number**—This is *i7-2700K* in the first item and *FX-8120* in the second item. The processor's model number actually has lots of info about the CPU, but we don't need to get that geeky about things. As a general rule, however, the higher the numbers, the more powerful the processor. So for Intel, an i7 processor is more powerful than an i5 processor, and an i7-2700K processor is more powerful than an i7-2600K processor. For AMD, an FX-8120 processor is more powerful than an FX-6120.

- **Processor speed**—This is *3.5GHz* in the first item and *3.1GHz* in the second item. The *processor speed* (sometimes called the *clock speed*) is a measure of how fast the processor operates internally. With each "tick" (which is called a *cycle*) on the clock, the processor performs an operation; therefore, the more ticks per second, the faster the processor, and the better performance your computer will have. Note that clock speeds are now measured in gigahertz (GHz), where 1GHz is one billion cycles per second. That's fast!

- **Processor cache memory**—This is *8MB L3 cache* in the first item and *4MB L3 cache* in the second. The *cache memory* is a memory area that the CPU uses to store frequently accessed bits of data. Generally speaking (and assuming the other CPU features are equal), the bigger the cache, the better the performance. Cache sizes are measured in megabytes (MB).

How Much Memory Do You Need?

Recall from Chapter 1 that your PC's memory is its work area. When you launch a program or open a document, the data is peeled off the hard drive and loaded into memory so that you can go about your business. So you might think that the answer to the not-so-musical question "How much memory do you need?" would be, simply, "As much as possible!" However, that turns out not to be true. To understand why, think of the restraints you might face in the real world when deciding how big of a work area you need. Clearly, it can't be too small; otherwise, it just won't be practical. On the other hand, if you lease too big of a building, you'll overpay for space you don't need.

PC memory works the same way. For starters, you definitely want to avoid getting too little memory. For one thing, all versions of Windows have a minimum amount of memory that they require just to get off the ground. Beyond that, however, this minimum amount (or even an amount slightly more than the minimum) usually means your PC will feel sluggish and slow, and you don't want that, believe me. As a general (but not universal) rule, the more memory your PC has to work with, the faster and more sprightly your programs will feel.

However, like the too-large work space, there is definitely such a thing as too much memory. Installing, say, 10 or 20 times the minimum memory requirement would probably cost you an extra $1,000 or $2,000 on your purchase price, but the vast majority of the time your PC would only use a fraction of that vast memory space.

Okay, so what's the right number? The answer depends on what you're going to be using your PC for and how much you have to spend. Here are five levels to consider:

- **Bare minimum**—This is the level of the minimum memory requirement for Windows. For both Windows 7 and Windows 8, the minimum is 1GB of memory. (Recall from Chapter 1 that a gigabyte is equal to about a billion characters.) If your budget is very tight, you can get away with just 1GB in your PC, but don't expect anything to happen quickly on your machine.

- **Real-world minimum**—For real day-to-day work on a PC, you really should have at least 2GB of memory installed. This gives you acceptable performance for most programs, allows you to run several programs at once, and doesn't cost very much money.

- **Sweet spot**—These days, I think the ideal amount of memory for most folks is 4GB. This gives you great performance for almost every program you might want to run, enables you to open many programs at once without slowing things down, and doesn't break the bank. Note, however, that for technical reasons we don't need to go into here, to get the most out of 4GB of memory, you need to get the 64-bit version of Windows (*not* the 32-bit version).

- **Performance**—If you're going to be using your PC for serious pursuits—I'm talking about video editing, big-time photo manipulation, or high-end gaming—you'll be much happier in the long run if you go for 8GB of memory. These activities place maximum demands on a

PC and so will be happiest if they have a good chunk of memory to roam around in. Note that this amount of memory requires a 64-bit version of Windows.

- **Over-the-top**—Many PC manufacturers and vendors are only too happy to try to sell you systems that come with 12, 16, or even 24GB of memory, and are also happy to charge you big bucks for the privilege. Just say, "Thanks, but no thanks" to these offers because you really do not need this much memory in your PC unless you are a gamer or run powerful graphics apps, such as Photoshop or Illustrator.

As a final note on memory, when you're shopping around, you'll see PC ads and listings that look something like this:

All-in-One PC Intel Core i5 2400S (2.50GHz) 4GB DDR3

Note

Saving Money on Memory

You can save yourself a lot of money by getting only a small amount of memory when you purchase your PC and then installing more memory yourself. This is particularly true if you're buying from a PC manufacturer, which might charge you $100 to $150 to go from 2GB of memory to 4GB. By contrast, you can purchase 4GB of memory online for $25 to $30. See Chapter 22, "Adding More Memory," to learn how to add memory to your PC.

You already know that *All-in-One PC* is the computer type and *Intel Core i5 2400S (2.5GHz)* is the CPU type and speed. The *4GB* here refers to the amount of memory. What about that mysterious *DDR3* business? That tells you the type of memory, and its details are too arcane to be of interest to us here. On the odd chance that you also see systems that come with DDR2 memory, know that DDR3 memory is about twice as fast as DDR2, so always go for DDR3.

Selecting Data Storage Options

Your PC needs to store data, which mostly means choosing a hard drive. However, you also should add in an optical drive for reading CDs and DVDs, as well as a memory card reader.

Selecting a Hard Drive

Hard drives are relatively simple devices, at least from the point of view of choosing one for your new PC. However, in your PC research excursions, you might still come across hard drive descriptions that look something like this:

Seagate ST310005N1A1AS 1TB SATA 6.0Gbps 7200rpm

As is so often the case, these descriptions are pure gobbledygook if you're not used to seeing them. The good news is that not only is it possible to translate this apparently foreign language without much fuss, but you'll also see that the translation itself offers tons of useful information that will help you make an informed choice. Here's a quick summary of what each item in the previous description represents:

Seagate	This is the name of the hard drive manufacturer.
ST310005N1A1AS	This is the hard drive's model number.
1TB	This is the capacity of the hard drive, which is a measure of how much data it can store. You won't find many hard drives with capacities less than 500GB these days, and 1TB (a terabyte is about 1,000 gigabytes) and 2TB drives are now common.
SATA	This is the hard drive's interface. SATA stands for Serial Advanced Technology Attachment; it's the current gold standard for PCs, and it's the only standard you should really consider for the hard drive on your PC because it's three to six times faster than the old Parallel Advanced Technology Attachment (PATA) drives. You might also see solid-state drives (SSDs), which are very fast, but they're also quite expensive.
6.0Gbps	This is the hard drive's throughput, which is a measure of how much data the drive can transfer per second. The higher this number is, the better.

7200rpm	This is the speed of the hard drive, which is a measure of how fast the drive's internal platters spin, measured in revolutions per minute (rpm). In general, the higher the rpm value, the better the drive's performance. Most SATA hard drives spin at 7,200rpm. If money is no object, SATA drives are available that spin at 10,000rpm, which offers a substantial performance boost.

Other than making sure you get a SATA drive (which is by far the most common type these days), the only important consideration when choosing a hard drive is what capacity to get. A PC with a 500GB drive costs a bit less than one with a 1TB drive, so you might be tempted to go for the smaller drive. However, the general trend with PCs is to store more and more data on our systems. We're ripping and downloading audio CDs and DVDs, recording TV shows, making digital video movies, and taking digital camera images by the thousands. So how do you know how much storage you need?

One way to get some idea is to examine your storage needs, particularly for media. To help you calculate this, look at how much 100GB can store for various types of media:

- 6,800 minutes of VHS-quality video
- 1,700 minutes of DVD-quality video
- 300 minutes of HDTV-quality video
- 1,800 hours of MP3 music (ripped at 128Kbps)
- 700 hours of MP3 music (ripped at 320Kbps)
- 30,000 digital photos (12 megapixels, JPG format)
- 2,800 digital photos (12 megapixels, BMP format)

As a result, 500GB might fill up awfully fast, so if your budget can afford it, I recommend purchasing at least a 1TB hard drive. On the other hand, if all you'll be using your PC for is a bit of web surfing, emailing, and word processing, 500GB is plenty of room, so no need to spring for the more expensive hard drive.

Selecting an Optical Drive

Any PC worth its processor should have an *optical drive,* a catchall term that includes every type of CD and DVD drive, as well as the latest Blu-ray drives. The *optical* part tells you that these drives use light—specifically, a semiconductor laser—to read data from and write data to the disc. (For example, the *Blu* in Blu-ray comes from the fact that it uses laser light with a wavelength in the blue section of the spectrum.) Among many other uses, adding an optical drive enables your system to play audio CDs, DVD movies, and high-definition video (you need a Blu-ray drive for that); install programs and device drivers; store data; and make backups.

Here's a quick look at the types of optical drives you're likely to come across when shopping for a PC:

- **CD-ROM drive**—This stands for *compact disc read-only memory*. A CD-ROM drive is one in which you insert a CD-ROM disc that might contain data, software, or music. The *ROM* part of the drive name means that your computer can only read the disc's contents; it can't change the contents.

- **CD-R drive**—This stands for *compact disc-recordable*. A CD-R drive allows you to record, or *burn*, data to a CD-R disc. Keep in mind that you can record data to the CD-R disc only once. After that, you can't change the disc's contents. CD-R drives can also read data from previously recorded CD-R discs, as well as from CD-ROM discs.

- **CD-RW drive**—This stands for *compact disc-rewritable*. A CD-RW drive allows you to record data to a CD-RW disc. You can add data to and erase data from a CD-RW disc as often as you want. CD-RW drives can also read data from CD-R and CD-ROM discs.

- **DVD-ROM drive**—This stands for *digital versatile disc–read-only memory.* A DVD-ROM drive allows you to use a DVD-ROM disc, which might contain data or software. The *ROM* part of the drive name means your computer can only read the disc's contents; you cannot change the contents. All DVD drives can also read all CD-ROM, CD-R, and CD-RW discs.

- **DVD-R, DVD+R, or DVD±R drive**—This stands for *digital versatile disc-recordable.* A DVD-R, DVD+R, or DVD±R drive allows you to record data once to a DVD-R, DVD+R, or DVD±R disc. The ± symbol means the drive supports both the DVD-R and DVD+R formats. DVD-R, DVD+R, and DVD±R drives can read data from previously recorded DVD-R, DVD+R, or DVD±R discs, as well as from DVD-ROM discs.

- **DVD-RW, DVD+RW, or DVD±RW drive**—This stands for *digital versatile disc-rewritable*. A DVD-RW, DVD+RW, or DVD±RW drive allows you to record data to a DVD-RW, DVD+RW, or DVD±RW disc. You can add data to and erase data from the disc as often as you want.

- **BD-ROM**—This stands for *Blu-ray disk–read-only memory*. A BD-ROM drive allows you to use a Blue-ray disc, which might contain data or high-definition video. The *ROM* part of the drive name means your computer can only read the disc's contents; you cannot change the contents. All Blu-ray drives can also read all CD and DVD discs.

- **BD-R**—This stands for *Blu-ray disc-recordable*. A BD-R drive allows you to record data once to a BD-R disc. BD-R drives can read data from previously recorded BD-R discs, as well as from Blu-ray discs.

- **BD-RE**—This stands for *Blu-ray disc-recordable erasable*. A BD-RE drive allows you to record data to a BD-RE disc. You can add data to and erase data from the disc as often as you want.

Note

DVD-R and DVD+R

After the DVD-R format was released, a group called the DVD+RW Alliance released the DVD+R format, which is a bit more robust than the earlier format. The two formats aren't compatible, unfortunately, but you shouldn't have to choose between the two. Almost all drives support DVD±R, a hybrid format that supports both DVD-R and DVD+R.

Note

Dealing With Dual Layer

The phrase *dual layer* means that an optical drive writes data on both sides of the disc. If the optical drive supports dual-layer recording, you see *DL* added to the supported formats. For example, if a DVD±RW drive supports dual-layer recording, you see the format listed as DVD±RW DL.

Besides the supported formats, probably the most important consideration when choosing an optical drive is the speed at which it operates. Optical drive performance is generally measured by how fast it is in three categories:

Write speed	This determines how fast a recordable drive (CD-R, DVD-R, DVD+R, DVD±R, BD-R) records data.
Rewrite speed	This determines how fast a rewritable drive (CD-RW, DVD-RW, DVD+RW, or DVD±RW, BD-RE) rewrites data.
Read speed	This determines how fast the drive reads a disc's contents.

In all cases, the speed is measured relative to a baseline amount, which is the audio CD rate of 150KBps. This speed is designated as 1x, and all optical drive speeds are a multiple of this amount. For example, a read speed of 52x means the drive reads data 52 times faster than a music CD player.

Note that you sometimes see the drive speed shown like this:

DVD+RW 16X8X18

You interpret the numbers as *writeXrewriteXread*, so in this example the write speed is 16x, the rewrite speed is 8x, and the read speed is 18x.

The following observations are generally true regarding optical drive speeds:

- CD drives are faster than DVD drives, which are faster than Blu-ray or HD DVD drives.

- Read speeds are faster than write speeds, and write speeds are faster than rewrite speeds.

- ROM drive read speeds are faster than burner read speeds.

Selecting a Memory Card Reader

Most PCs don't require more than a hard drive and an optical drive. However, for the sake of storage completeness, you should also consider getting a memory card reader. If you use various types of memory cards— CompactFlash, Secure Digital, MultiMediaCard, Memory Stick, and so on— you should consider adding an internal memory card reader to your system.

Most readers support multiple card formats, so just make sure that the reader you choose supports the card format (or formats) you use.

Choosing a Monitor

Because you look at the monitor all day long, you should get a good monitor/video card combination that is easy on your eyes and does not break your budget. Of course, this advice applies only if you're buying a desktop PC because all-in-ones, laptops, and tablets come with the monitor built in. (That's not to say that you should ignore the monitor component of a laptop or all-in-one. Screen sizes vary, so you need to choose a screen that suits your needs. Also, larger screens add weight to a laptop, so bear that in mind when you're selecting a screen size.)

The good news about choosing a monitor is that there is only one type to consider: a *liquid crystal display* (LCD, also called a *flat panel*). *Light emitting diode* (LED) monitors also are available, but they're too expensive.

Note

Energy-Efficient Displays

Although full LED monitors are too expensive, many LCD monitors use LEDs as backlights (because LCDs need some source of illumination to produce an image). These backlights use much less power than regular LCD light sources, so look for "LED backlight" in the monitor specifications if you want to get an energy-efficient display.

The most important consideration for a monitor is the size of the screen. Put simply, a large monitor allows you to display more elements on the screen than a small monitor. You can determine the size of a monitor by measuring diagonally from corner to corner. Keep in mind that if you see a computer ad that says "19-inch monitor (18.5-inch *viewable image size,* or v.i.s.)," this means that although the monitor has a full 19 inches of glass, only 18.5 inches of that glass are actually used to display the image.

When choosing a monitor, you really don't need to delve much deeper than that. However, if you want to get into it, or if you're just wondering what those weird monitor specs are all about, here's a quick summary:

- **Resolution**—To create an image onscreen, monitors activate small dots (these dots are liquid crystals on an LCD) that are called *pixels*.

The resolution tells you the number of pixels the monitor can display horizontally and vertically. For example, if a monitor listing says it supports a "native resolution" of 1,920 × 1,080, it means the monitor can display rows with 1,920 pixels each, and columns with 1,080 pixels each. In general, the higher the resolution, the more items you can fit on the screen and the sharper those objects will appear.

- **Connections**—This refers to the ports that appear on the back or bottom of the monitor, and they determine how it connects to your PC. The three most common connection types are VGA, DVI, and HDMI. The only real concern here is to make sure your get a monitor that has at least one connection port that matches the monitor connection port on your PC.

- **Dot pitch**—The distance between each pixel is called the *dot pitch* (or *pixel pitch*). This is a measure of the clarity of the monitor's image: the smaller the dot pitch, the sharper the image. Look for a monitor with a dot pitch of 0.26 millimeters (mm) or less.

- **Brightness**—This tells you how bright the screen appears, and it's measured in candelas per square meter (cd/m^2). For most uses, 200–250 cd/m^2 is fine.

- **Contrast ratio**—This is a measure of the difference between the light intensity of the brightest white and the darkest black. Most monitors offer a contrast ratio of around 1,000:1. However, you might see monitors advertising "dynamic" contrast ratios on the order of 10,000,000:1. This is hype and should be ignored.

- **Other features**—Some monitors come with built-in speakers, which is handy because it means you don't have to put separate speakers somewhere on your desk. Many newer monitors also come with several USB ports, which is useful for plugging in desktop devices such as your keyboard, mouse, smartphone, or digital camera.

Purchasing Additional Software

Your computer comes with a number of programs that are part of the operating system. For example, Windows 8 comes with programs for working with photos and videos, playing music, sending and receiving email, surfing the Web, and more. However, many of these programs have only minimal features, so you might want to upgrade to specialized applications. Here are some suggestions:

- **Productivity suite**—A productivity suite (also called an office suite) is a collection of programs that usually includes a word processor, spreadsheet, presentation graphics program, and a database. The most popular, as well as the most expensive, is Microsoft Office. Less expensive alternatives are Microsoft Works and WordPerfect Office.

- **Graphics**—If you want to create your own images, you might want to use a different graphics program than the one that ships with Windows 8. For example, you can choose graphics software such as Corel PaintShop Pro or Adobe Illustrator. If you want to work with digital photos, consider photo-editing programs such as Adobe Photoshop Elements and Serif PhotoPlus.

- **Security**—Although Windows 8 has built-in Internet security, you might want to upgrade to a more advanced security program. Some popular security programs are Microsoft Security Essentials, Norton Internet Security, AVG Internet Security, and McAfee Internet Security Suite.

- **Educational**—The personal computer is an excellent learning tool when you combine it with educational programs such as Celestron Sky Maps or Encyclopedia Britannica.

Note that Windows 8 comes with a feature called the Windows Store, which offers thousands of apps in these and many other categories. This means that you can download and install apps right from the comfort of home with just a few mouse clicks. Even better, many of these apps are free, so you can stock up without straining your budget.

Some Final Purchase Considerations

Before you purchase a computer, you have a few other factors to consider before making your decision:

- **Where to buy**—Always purchase your computer from a reputable store or online vendor, such as a well-known chain or smaller outlet that other people have recommended to you. Disreputable retailers abound in the computer business, so it's not worth taking a chance simply to save a few dollars.

- **Price**—When you are buying your first computer, it's a good idea to avoid the low end and the high end of the price range. Low-priced computers are often too slow for day-to-day use and are made with cheap parts that may not last very long. High-priced computers are usually more powerful than what you need. Mid-priced computers generally have the best combination of quality and performance.

- **Promotions**—You can often save money by watching for special promotions offered by computer dealers. For example, a dealer may offer extra memory or an upgrade to a DVD burner free with the purchase of a new computer. Similarly, a retailer may include brand-name printers or other peripherals in the purchase at very low prices.

- **Warranty**—Although all computers come with a standard manufacturer's warranty, many computer retailers will ask if you want to upgrade to an extended warranty. Doing so is almost always a waste of money because if you're buying a mid-priced computer from a reputable dealer, your PC will almost certainly give you years of trouble-free service. Besides, if a PC is a lemon (and, although it's rare, it can happen), you'll usually find out within a few days or weeks of purchase, so you'll still be well within the manufacturer's warranty.

- **Installation**—Many computer dealers offer to install your new system for a fee. However, setting up a basic computer system is easy, so you might want to save your money and set up the computer yourself. For more information about getting started with your computer, see Chapter 3.

Setting Up Your PC

Now that you've got your PC, you're probably chomping at the bit waiting to get it up and running. I can't blame you! A new computer is always an exciting addition to the family, but this is the time to slow down just a bit and get things right. In this chapter, I show you the best way to get your PC set up, from choosing a location to setting up your work area to connecting all the components.

Setting Up Your Work Area

The short answer to the question "Where should I set up my computer?" is "Wherever you have room." Not surprisingly, however, there is (or, really, there should be) more to it than that. Specifically, you need to give some thought to setting up your work area to ensure that you're both comfortable and safe. Comfort's the easier of these to understand because the more comfortable you are, the more productive you'll be and the more pleasant your computing sessions will be. Safety, however, is a bit more opaque. What could be unsafe about using a computer? To be sure, computers *are* inherently safe devices, so outside of dropping your monitor or your laptop PC on your foot, your person is not at risk when you sit down in front of a PC. Rather, it's how you *use* your PC that raises a slight element of danger. Sitting at the computer, typing, and using the mouse for long periods can cause injuries, including repetitive stress injuries (RSI) such as carpal tunnel syndrome. Fortunately, you can take steps to prevent these injuries.

Location, Location, Etc.

The first order of business is deciding exactly where you want your new PC family member to stay. If you don't have just the right place picked out already (such as the den or a home office), here are a few factors to consider:

- **Clean**—Be sure to choose an area that's clean and uncluttered. Most computers keep their internal temperatures low by using fans to pull in outside air and direct it toward crucial system components such as the processor. If the PC's surrounding area has lots of dust and dirt, some of that will get sucked into the PC, which, as you can imagine, is not a good thing.

- **Dry**—Your PC is essentially an electrical device, so like almost all electrical devices, it simply does not like moisture because it can corrode components and cause electrical shorts. Therefore, the bathroom is obviously a poor choice for the PC, but so too is near an open window because precipitation might come through the window and hit the PC.

- **Not too hot, not too cold**—As I said before, your PC has internal fans that not only bring in outside air for cooling, but also remove the air that is naturally heated by the internal components. This airflow keeps most computers within a safe operating temperature, but that cooling system is all for naught if the PC resides in a hot room or has the sun shining on it for long periods. PCs also don't do well in the opposite environment where it's too cold. A bit of temperature variation won't hurt your PC, but your goal should be a temperate environment.

- **Lighting**—Unless you have a keyboard that lights up at night (they do exist), using a computer in the dark is pretty much impossible. Therefore, your location should have plenty of light—either natural daylight or artificial light that's eyeball-friendly (such as incandescent or LED). Also, try to situate your monitor or your lighting so that the room is lit from above or behind the monitor to prevent glare.

- **Electrical outlets**—All PCs need electrical power, some full-time (such as a desktop PC) and some part-time (such as laptops and tablets). Either way, you need an electrical outlet nearby to plug in your PC and possibly your monitor. If you have other devices that require power—such as a printer, external hard drive, Internet modem, or network access point—you need access to multiple wall outlets or to a power bar (also called a power strip; see Figure 3.1) that comes with multiple power sockets.

- **Traffic**—When you are positioning your PC, it's usually best to avoid high-traffic areas where people may bump into the computer case and possibly damage the system.

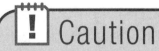

Caution

Protect Yourself Against Surges

Ideally, your power bar should have a built-in *surge protector*, which protects everything connected to the power bar from lightning strikes and other power surges. These surges *do* happen and they can wreck your PC, so a surge protector is a good investment.

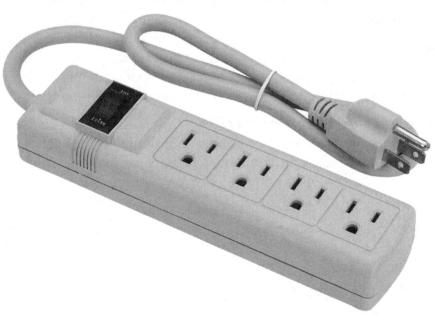

Figure 3.1 *A power bar is an easy way to get convenient access to multiple power sockets.*

Choosing Your Desk and Chair

The desk you use to hold your computer is an often-overlooked feature, with most people just using whatever old desk they have at hand. That's fine (desks are expensive, after all), but there are a few things you should consider before dragooning some ancient desk into a new role for which it might not be up to the task. For starters, the desk must be sturdy enough to hold all the new weight it's about to receive, particularly the system unit and monitor, and stable enough not to tilt (or even fall over) should it get bumped. Moreover, the desk should have a surface that's more than big enough to hold your PC-related stuff: the system unit, the monitor, the keyboard, the mouse, and whatever peripherals you're also connecting, such as a printer and external hard drive. Ideally, you should also have some extra room for your non-PC supplies, such as papers, pens, and, of course, this book!

Any old desk might be good enough, but you should never use just any old chair. Believe me (and I say this from hard-won experience), you will not enjoy sitting down in front of your PC for more than a few minutes if your chair is uncomfortable, unstable, or poorly designed. Do yourself a favor and get a chair that has a contoured seat, a generous back, a seat length that suits the length of your legs, and (this is crucial) good lower-back support. Another must-have: levers or similar mechanisms that enable you to adjust the seat height, the seat angle, and the back support angle.

Having a top-notch chair is a good start, but you also have to use it properly. This is where ergonomics comes in. *Ergonomics* is a set of principles and practices for setting up a computer work area to maximize comfort and safety. It sounds complex, but for our purposes, you have to take into account only four things:

- Use your chair's adjustment mechanisms to set the chair height so that when your hands are poised above the keyboard, your forearms are parallel to the floor. Also, your eyes should be level with the top of your monitor.

- Once you're in the chair, be sure to always sit up straight, square your shoulders, face the monitor directly, and have your feet flat on the floor.

- Avoid sitting at the computer for long periods of time. If you have lots to do, be sure to regularly—that is, every half hour or, at most, every hour—get out of your chair and do some stretching or go for a short walk.

- Feel free to use any of the myriad ergonomic accessories to ensure your comfort and safety. For example, if the top of your desk is too high to keep your arms parallel to the ground as you type, invest in an adjustable keyboard tray that attaches under the desk and ensures the keyboard (and possibly the mouse, too) is always at the correct height. You can also help keep your wrists straight by adding wrist rests below your keyboard and mouse. If you do tons of typing, consider using an ergonomic keyboard that angles the keys for more comfortable access. Finally, you can also use a footrest to ensure that your feet are flat.

Connecting the Components

With your work area chosen wisely and all set up, it's time to get your new PC set up by connecting all the components. The rest of this chapter takes you through the basic procedures for connecting just about any kind of device you might run into.

Unpacking the Components

When your new PC arrives, place the computer boxes on the floor and open them, preferably without using a knife. Remove each component and double-check with the packing list to ensure that you received everything that you ordered. Carefully remove any plastic bags that the computer and each component came in. There's a good chance your PC also came wrapped in a thin layer of plastic, which helps protect the finish during transit. Carefully remove this plastic layer to finally see your PC in all its glory.

 **Caution**

Easy Does it

Be sure to treat each component—particularly the system unit—reasonably gently. We're not talking fine china here, but you should take care not to drop anything or let any component slam heavily onto a surface.

Remember how I said earlier that your PC doesn't like temperature extremes? That tip also applies to the day your PC arrives. If it's very cold outside, your PC and all its parts will also be quite chilled when they arrive. So although you might be chomping at the bit to get your new machine up and running, you need to give the components an hour or two to warm up to room temperature.

Finally, even if your PC is the right temperature, don't plug anything into an electrical socket just yet. That's actually the *last* thing you'll do, so leave the power cord aside for the moment.

Positioning the System Unit

The nice thing about setting up a new PC is that you don't really have to make all that many decisions. As you'll see a bit later, most components can plug into only one place (or, at worst, a small number of identical places), so no decision-making brain cells are required. However, you *do* have to make a decision up front: where to put the system unit. Again, this decision is already made for you if you purchased a laptop, a tablet, or an all-in-one PC because these PCs sit on top of your desk. For the other styles of PC cases that we talked about in Chapter 1, "Getting to Know the PC," the decision isn't always so obvious:

- **Full-tower**—These PCs are tall, and although they tend to be a bit on the narrow side, they're still big items. Therefore, it's best to place the system unit for a full-tower PC on the floor, either beside the desk or under it, and close to some electrical outlets.

- **Mid-tower**—This type of case isn't as tall as a full-tower model, so as long as the unit isn't too deep and you have a big desk, you might be able to get away with

> **! Caution**
>
> **Keep Your PC Accessible For Now**
>
> Under the desk isn't a great place for a PC if you have pets because the pet hair tends to get inside the system unit. If you do decide to stick the system unit under the desk, remember that you still have to connect a bunch of components to the system unit's front and back ports. Therefore, leave the unit in a reasonably accessible place for now to make it easier to make those connections. After you finish attaching devices, you can then slide the unit into your preferred position.

placing it on the desk. Some people even lay the mid-tower case on its side so that they can put the monitor on top. (The only problem here might be using the built-in optical drive because the disc might fall out.) If the case is quite deep or you have a small desk, the floor is probably the best place for this system unit.

- **Micro-tower**—Most micro-tower system units are small enough to fit on even a medium-sized desk. If you're stuck with a teeny-tiny desk, then on the floor it goes.

- **Small form factor**—You shouldn't have any trouble fitting the system unit of a small form factor PC on your desk. Most people use it as a stand for the monitor.

Some Notes Before Making Any Connections

Finally, it's time to start making some connections. Before we get down to the specifics, it's worth noting that all modern PCs offer a couple of features that make it straightforward (and in some cases downright easy) to make connections:

- All the ports on your PC have a particular size and shape that's unique to each type of connection. Fortunately for you, the jack on the corresponding cable that plugs into each type of port has the same size and shape. For example, take a look at the port shown in Figure 3.2. This is called a Video Graphics Array (VGA) port, and it's often used to connect a monitor. That connection is handled by a VGA cable, one end of which looks like the plug shown in Figure 3.3. As you can see, both have a distinctive "D" shape, and the holes in the port align with the pins in the jack. All of this means that in almost all cases it's impossible to plug a jack into the wrong port or to plug a jack into the correct port the wrong way.

Figure 3.2 *A VGA port, which is available on most PCs and is used to connect a monitor.*

Figure 3.3 *The plug end of a VGA cable, which has a size, shape, and pin arrangement that's compatible with the VGA port shown in Figure 3.2.*

- Many of your PC's ports are color-coded to match the corresponding jacks on the cables that connect the devices. For example, a VGA port (see Figure 3.2) is blue and the plug on a VGA cable (see Figure 3.3) is also blue. So if you have any doubt about where to plug in a device, look for a part with the same color.

Connecting the Monitor

You connect your monitor to your PC using a monitor cable, where one end plugs into the monitor itself and the other end plugs into your PC. (I'm ignoring the monitor's other cable, which is the power cord. Leave that disconnected for now, and we'll get to it later in the "Connecting the Power Cords" section.) How this works depends on the type of connection, and most PCs these days offer three types, as pointed out in Figure 3.4.

Figure 3.4 *Most modern PCs come with the three types of monitor ports shown here.*

You saw in the preceding section that a VGA port requires a VGA cable, one end of which plugs into the VGA port on your PC and the other end of which plugs into a similar VGA port on your monitor.

You also have two other possibilities:

Note

If you don't see the port you want on the monitor (or any ports, for that matter), look underneath the monitor.

- **DVI**—A Digital Visual Interface connection requires a DVI cable that has on each end a jack similar to the one shown in Figure 3.5. You plug one of those jacks into the DVI port on your PC and the other end into a similar DVI port on your monitor.

- **HDMI**—A High-Definition Multimedia Interface connection requires an HDMI cable that has on each end a jack similar to the one shown in Figure 3.6. You plug one of those jacks into the HDMI port on your PC and the other end into a similar HDMI port on your monitor. You can also plug it into a high-definition TV that has an HDMI port.

Figure 3.5 *A DVI jack, which plugs into a DVI port on your PC.*

Figure 3.6 *An HDMI jack, which plugs into an HDMI port on your PC.*

So which one should you use? Your monitor might come with only one type of cable, so that's the one you'll have to use. If you have a choice, go with HDMI to get the best picture quality. If your choice is between DVI and VGA, go with DVI, which offers better quality and faster speeds than VGA.

Connecting USB Devices

With some exceptions (see, for example, "Sound System," later in this chapter), most of the devices you'll hook up to your PC use Universal Serial Bus (USB) connections:

- Keyboard

- Mouse

- Printer

- External hard drive

- External optical drive

- Document scanner

- Flash drive

- Digital camera or camcorder

- Media player (such as an iPod)

- Smartphone (such as an iPhone)

Tip

Adapting to the Situation

What happens if your monitor and PC don't have compatible monitor ports? For example, an older monitor might have only VGA, whereas a newer PC might have only DVI and/or HDMI. In this situation, you can purchase an adapter cable. For example, a VGA-to-DVI adapter cable has a VGA plug on one end and a DVI plug on the other. Similarly, you can also get adapters that enable you to connect a VGA cable to a DVI or HDMI cable.

That covers just about everything, which means you'll most likely be using USB connections quite a bit, so let's take a careful look at how USB works.

First, notice that your desktop PC is most likely brimming with USB ports. (Your laptop or tablet probably only has a few USB ports.) You likely have anywhere from four to eight USB ports on the back (see Figure 3.7), plus another two to four on the front (see Figure 3.8), depending on the size of your PC (generally, the smaller the PC, the fewer USB ports it offers).

Figure 3.7 *Your PC likely has a bunch of USB ports on the back.*

Figure 3.8 *Most PCs also come with a few USB ports on the front.*

Notice in Figures 3.7 and 3.8 that some of the ports are labeled USB 2.0 and some are labeled USB 3.0. What's the difference? The details are much too technical for our purposes, so suffice it to say that USB 3.0 is quite a bit faster than USB 2.0. However, you need devices that are compatible with USB 3.0 to take advantage of this speed. How can you tell the two types apart? Most PC manufacturers label each USB port using the logo for USB type. As you can see in Figure 3.9, the USB 2.0 logo is a trident, while the USB 3.0 logo is a similar trident with the letters "SS" (which stands for SuperSpeed) attached.

The PC side of the USB connection is relatively straightforward (the fine art of differentiating USB 3.0 and 2.0 ports notwithstanding), but things get a bit trickier on the device side of the connection. The reason is that there isn't a single way to connect a USB cable to a USB device. There are, in fact, four main types of USB plugs, and I've pointed them out in Figure 3.10.

Note

If you're running low on ports, you can connect a USB 2.0 device to a USB 3.0 port, and it will work just the same. It's also possible to connect a USB 3.0 device to a USB 2.0 port, but the device will run quite a bit slower.

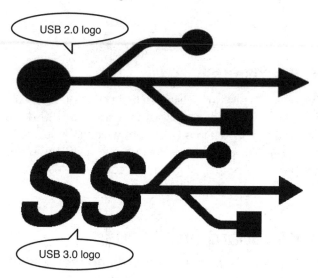

Figure 3.9 *You can identify USB 2.0 and 3.0 ports by their respective logos.*

As you can see, each type of plug has a unique shape and size, so you need to look for a port on the device that has a compatible shape and size. Finally, note that some manufacturers muddy the USB waters even further by using proprietary USB plugs. For example, most Apple devices (such as the iPhone and the older iPads) use a wide 30-pin plug, whereas newer models (such as the iPhone 5 and new iPad models) use a new Lightning plug. Again, just match the plug to the port on the device, and you'll be fine.

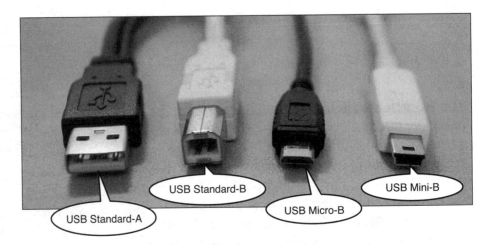

USB Standard-B

USB Mini-B

USB Micro-B

USB Standard-A

Figure 3.10 *The four standard USB plugs.*

Note

When You've Used Up Your USB

What happens if you've used up all your available USB ports, but you still have one or more USB devices to connect? One solution is to disconnect a USB device that you're not currently using. Alternatively, invest in a USB hub, which is a device that comes with several (usually four or more) USB ports. Plug the hub into a USB port and then plug your extra devices into the hub. Another alternative is to go wireless, which is a very common solution these days for the keyboard and mouse.

Connecting the Keyboard and Mouse

Chances are your PC comes with a keyboard and mouse that each use a USB connection. In this case, you plug each device into a free USB port, and you're done.

However, you have two other possibilities for connecting the keyboard and mouse:

- The keyboard and mouse use a wireless connection. This type of connection is quite common nowadays, and it means that the keyboard and mouse don't come with cables attached. Instead, they communicate with the PC using radio signals beamed from the device to a special component called a receiver that you plug into a USB port.

- The keyboard and mouse use connectors likes the ones shown in
  Figure 3.11. You can't tell in black-and-white, but the one on the left
  is the mouse connector, and it's green; and the one on the right is the
  keyboard connector, and it's purple. They connect to the corresponding
  green and purple ports on the back of the computer. Some PCs come
  with just a single keyboard/mouse port like the one shown in Figure
  3.12. Either way, you need to carefully line up the pins in the connector
  with the holes in the port.

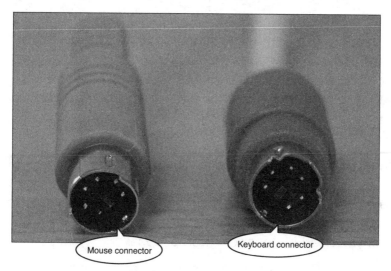

Figure 3.11   *Old-style keyboards and mice use these types of connectors.*

Figure 3.12   *Many newer PCs come with just a single keyboard/mouse port.*

Connecting Even More Devices

The monitor, keyboard, mouse, and USB components such as your printer and perhaps a wireless receiver are the standard devices on the vast majority of PCs. They are, however, not the only devices you can connect. There are, in fact, dozens of other device types, but over the next few sections I cover just a few of the more common ones.

Sound System

PCs are not quiet machines, not by a long shot. The Windows operating system makes all kinds of sounds that let you know when things are happening on the screen and within your PC. Similarly, programs such as music players and video players make plenty of noise. To get sound from your PC to your ears, you need some kind of sound output device, which means one of the following:

- **Speakers**—These speakers are much like the ones you use with your stereo system or TV. Many laptops and tablet PCs have built-in speakers (although the sound quality tends to be a bit low). Some monitors even come with speakers on the sides. For all other systems, however, you need to connect external speakers.

- **Headphones**—These are either standard headphones that fit over your ears or earbuds that fit inside your ears.

Although many headphones and even some speakers connect via USB, the more common connection is a stereo mini-jack like the one shown in Figure 3.13. For speakers and headphones, this jack is green, and the corresponding port on your PC is also green and is usually labeled Line Out, as shown in Figure 3.14.

Here are some other common sound system ports on your PC:

Note

Many desktop PCs also include a Line Out port on the front for easier access.

- **Mic In** or **Mic** (pink)—You use this port to connect a microphone.

- **Line In** (blue)—You use this port to connect an audio input device, such as a media player, CD player, or musical instrument.

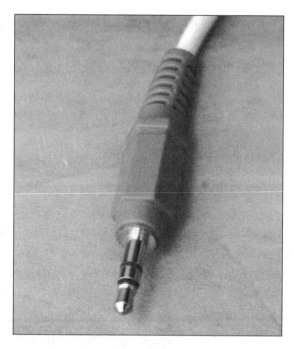

Figure 3.13 *A stereo mini-jack used for connecting most types of speakers or headphones.*

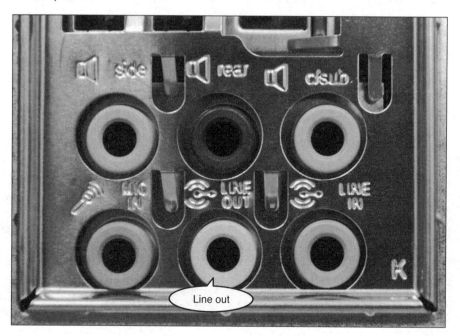

Figure 3.14 *Connect the jack shown in Figure 3.13 to the Line Out port on your PC.*

- **Rear** (black)—You use this port to connect the rear speakers in a surround sound system.

- **Side** (silver)—You use this port to connect the side speakers in a surround sound system.

- **Center/Sub** (orange)—You use this port to connect the center speakers and/or subwoofer in a surround sound system.

Memory Card

If your computer comes with a built-in memory card reader (or if you connected a card reader to the PC via USB), you can use it to access the contents of memory cards. Unfortunately, most card readers come with four or more slots, so how are you supposed to know which one to use? The answer is not straightforward, unfortunately, but there are a couple ways to get your bearings:

- On most card readers, each slot is accompanied by text that tells you which kinds of memory cards will fit. So, if you see MMC (or MultiMedia Card) on the card itself, look for the slot that includes "MMC" in the label.

- The slots are different shapes and sizes, which sounds like a bad thing, but it's not because any memory card will fit correctly into only a single slot. So if you're really not sure which one to use, try inserting the card (writing-side up) until you get a good fit.

Figure 3.15 shows a CompactFlash memory card inserted into a reader.

Figure 3.15 *A memory card inserted into a card reader.*

Wi-Fi Antenna

If your PC comes with built-in wireless fidelity (Wi-Fi), which is used for accessing a network over-the-air (see Chapter 10, "Getting Online," for more information), there's a good chance you'll have to connect the Wi-Fi antenna to your PC. (Note that this is not universal, by any means. Many desktop PCs don't require an antenna hookup, and no laptops, all-in-ones, or tablets require a visible antenna because theirs is built in.) On the back of the PC, look for a small, round, threaded piece of metal, which is the antenna connection (refer to Figure 1.11). The antenna itself is either an object tethered to a longish cable or a plastic cylinder with a hinge. Either way, screw the antenna to the Wi-Fi connection on the PC. If the antenna is a cylinder, screw it straight in to the connector, as shown in Figure 3.16; then, when the antenna is securely fastened, flip the hinge so that the antenna points straight up, as shown in Figure 3.17.

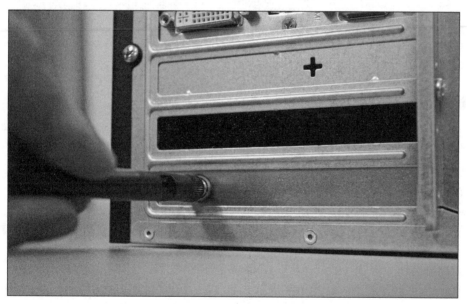

Figure 3.16 *Screw a cylinder-type antenna straight in to the PC.*

Figure 3.17 *When the antenna is secure, flip the hinge to point the antenna up.*

CD or DVD

Your PC comes with a built-in optical drive that you can use to insert a CD or DVD and access the files on the disc or install a program. There are two types of optical disc drives:

- **Tray drive**—For this type, a tray slides out for you to insert the disc. First, press the button on the front of the drive, which causes the disc tray to slide out. Now, remove the disc from its case or sleeve (be sure to touch only the edges of the disc) and then place the disc, writing-side up, in the drive's disc tray (see Figure 3.18). Now, close the disc tray—usually either by pressing the drive button again or by giving the tray a gentle push.

Figure 3.18 *For a tray-type drive, press the button to open the tray and then insert the disc into the tray.*

- **Slot drive**—For this type, you see a narrow slot in the front of the drive. Insert your disc into that slot until it catches and inserts itself the rest of the way. When you're done, press the drive button to eject the disc.

Connecting the Power Cords

At this stage of your PC setup, you should now have all your devices connected. This would be a good time to double-check your connections to make sure everything is properly inserted. With that done, go ahead and attach the power cords for every device that requires one. For most setups, that means just the PC and monitor, but other devices such as external hard drives also require a power source. As discussed previously, you should use a surge protector or power strip that has a built-in surge protector. Using this device ensures that a lightning strike won't damage the sensitive innards of your computer. You're now ready to start your PC for the first time, which I cover in the next chapter.

Chapter 4

Taking Your PC for a Spin

Now that you have your PC unpacked and positioned where you want it, and with the various parts and peripherals connected to the appropriate ports, your PC is ready for its first test drive. This chapter helps you do just that by showing you how to start your PC and how to negotiate the Windows 8 setup screens. From there, I take you on a tour of the Windows 8 Start screen and show you how to use your keyboard and mouse to get around. (For good measure, I also introduce you to a few touch gestures just in case you're using a tablet.) Finally, you also learn how to put your PC to sleep, restart your PC, and shut down your PC.

Starting Your PC

You start your PC in the same way that you start just about any device or appliance: by pressing the power button. That's the good news. The bad news is that it's often hard to locate a PC's power button! Here are some scenarios to consider:

- If you get lucky, you'll see a button or switch labeled "Power" or "On/Off," so no mystery there.

- Oftentimes the power button is labeled with either an icon, which is usually the one shown in Figure 4.1. Figure 4.2 shows a real example.

Figure 4.1 *This icon often appears near a PC's power button.*

Figure 4.2 *An example of a PC power button.*

- Occasionally, you'll see the cryptic characters "1|0" beside the power switch. For reasons far too technical to go into here, in computing circles a 1 stands for "On" and a 0 stands for "Off."

- On a notebook PC, the power switch often appears above the keyboard or in the upper-right or upper-left corner of the keyboard area. However, some notebooks place the power switch at the front or back of the machine.

- On a tablet PC, the power switch appears on one of the edges, usually the top edge.

- If you have a tower PC and you don't see a power button (or any buttons at all), the button is likely hidden behind a panel. Check the front of the tower for a panel that swings out to reveal the power button.

Note

If Your PC Won't Start

If your PC doesn't start when you push the power button, double-check that it's plugged firmly into an electrical outlet. If it's plugged into a power strip, make sure the strip itself is plugged in and turned on.

Push (or flick or flip) the power button to get things started. Make sure you also press the power button on your monitor and any other devices that are plugged into an electrical outlet.

Setting Up Windows 8

The first time you start your PC, it runs through a few initialization chores that enable you to set up your PC. These are one-time-only tasks, so you don't have to go through all of this every time you start your PC. Note, too, that these tasks apply only to new PCs, so if you've inherited an older PC, you don't have to bother with this.

At first, you might see a screen or two added by the PC manufacturer, but eventually you get to the Windows 8 portion of the show. The first screen you see is called Personalize, and it's shown in Figure 4.3.

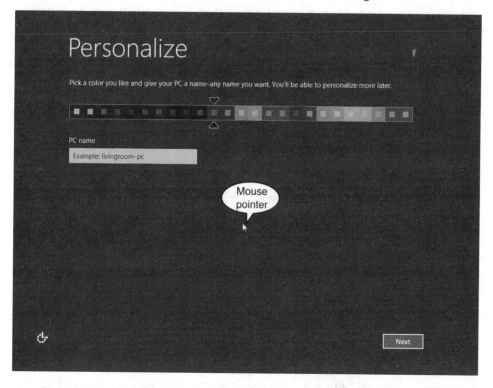

Figure 4.3   *This is the first of Windows 8's setup screens that you have to trudge through when you first start your PC.*

A Digression: Learning How to "Click" Things

To successfully navigate these setup screens (and, indeed, all of Windows 8), you need to know how to use a mouse, trackpad, or touchscreen to make things happen. We get into navigation in more detail later in this chapter, but for now you need to know how to "click" things to make things happen on the screen. If you've used a mouse, trackpad, or touchscreen before, feel free to skip to the next section.

Here are the basics:

- **Mouse**—First, locate the mouse pointer (see Figure 4.3). As you move the mouse, the mouse pointer moves along the screen in the same direction. So the basic idea is to move the mouse pointer over the object you want to click and then press and release the left mouse button.

- **Trackpad**—Most notebook PCs come with a trackpad, a rectangular, flat surface just below the keyboard. Place a finger on the touchscreen and then as you move your finger along the trackpad, notice that the mouse pointer (see Figure 4.3) moves along with it. Move the mouse pointer over the object you want to click; then tap and release the trackpad surface. In some cases you might have to press the trackpad surface fairly hard to make it "click," whereas other trackpads have separate buttons that you need to press and release (if you see two buttons, press and release the left button).

- **Touchscreen**—If you have a tablet, you "click" by using your finger (or perhaps a digital stylus that came with the tablet) to briefly tap the screen. Note that you often don't see a mouse pointer because you can just tap things directly on the screen.

Back to the Tour

Okay, now you can continue the Windows 8 setup. Here's what happens:

1. On the Personalize screen, click the color you want to use. You can change this color later if you change your mind.

2. Click inside the **PC Name** box and then type a name for your PC. Don't use any spaces in the name.

3. Click **Next**. The Settings screen appears.

4. This one's easy: Click **Use Express Settings**. The Sign In to Your PC screen appears.

5. This screen asks for your email address, but it's simpler to avoid all that for now, so click **Sign In Without a Microsoft Account** and then click **Local Account**. This takes you to the screen shown in Figure 4.4 (which I've shown here already filled in).

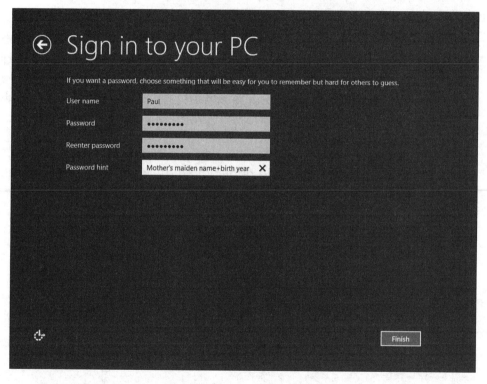

Figure 4.4 *Use this screen to set up your Windows 8 user account.*

6. Click inside the **User Name** box and type the name you want to use (such as your first name).

7. Click inside the **Password** box and then type a password. (Note that the password appears as a series of dots, for security.)

8. Click inside the **Reenter Password** box and then re-type your password.

9. Click inside the **Password Hint** box and then type something that will help you remember your password.

10. Click **Finish**. Windows 8 records your settings and then plays an animation that shows you how to use Windows 8. After a few more minutes, Windows 8 completes its setup chores and loads the Start screen.

Starting Windows 8 Next Time

The next time you start your PC (and, indeed, every time you start your PC from now on), you have to follow these steps to get to the Start screen:

1. After you start your PC, you eventually end up at the Lock screen, which you'll recognize because it shows the current date and time on a colorful background image (see Figure 4.5). Click the **Lock** screen. (If you have a touchscreen, place your finger on the screen and then move it up quickly to dismiss the Lock screen.) Windows 8 prompts you for your password.

2. Type your password.

3. Press **Enter** or click **Submit** (the right-pointing arrow). The Start screen appears a few moments later.

Figure 4.5 *After you start your PC, you see the Lock screen.*

Getting to Know the Mouse

Unless you're using Windows 8 on a tablet PC, you'll mostly use your mouse (or your notebook PC's trackpad) to get around in Windows 8 and make things happen. You already know how to click something (see "A Digression: Learning How to 'Click' Things"), but there are a few other mouse moves you need to know:

- **Point**—This means that you move the mouse pointer so it's positioned over some particular object on the screen. For example, if I tell you to "point at the Weather tile," this instruction means that you move the mouse pointer over the Start screen's Weather tile.

- **Double-click**—This means that you press and release the left mouse button *twice,* one press immediately after the other with little or no delay between each press.

- **Right-click**—This means that you press and immediately release the *right* mouse button.

- **Click and drag**—This means that you point at some object, press and *hold down* the left mouse button, move the mouse, and then release the button. You almost always use this technique to move an object from one place to another.

- **Scroll**—This means that you turn the little wheel that's nestled between the left and right mouse buttons, which usually scrolls something up and down (or left and right) on the screen.

Getting Comfy with the Keyboard

I mentioned in the previous section that you'll mostly use your mouse to make Windows 8 do your bidding, but your keyboard certainly won't go to waste. In fact, Windows 8 comes with quite a few keyboard shortcuts and techniques that can actually make your Windows 8 life easier. First, let's take a quick look at a few important keys on your keyboard:

- **Windows key**—This key has the Windows logo on it, and on most keyboards it appears in the bottom row on the left side, between the Ctrl and Alt keys. (Some larger keyboards come with a second Windows key on the right side of the bottom row.) Pressing the

Windows key by itself returns you to the Start screen if you're using an app. You can also use the Windows key in combination with other keys. For example, if you hold down the Windows key, tap L, and then release Windows (a key combo that I abbreviate as Windows Logo+L), you jump immediately to the Lock screen. (If you try this out, remember that you can return to Windows 8 by pressing any key, typing your password, and then pressing Enter.)

- **Ctrl and Alt keys**—You don't use Ctrl (control) or Alt (alt as in *alternate*) by themselves, but as part of key combinations. For example, the keyboard method for copying something is Ctrl+C. That is, you hold down Ctrl, press C, and then release Ctrl.

- **Esc key**—You usually use the Esc (short for *escape*) key to cancel the current operation and return to a previous screen.

- **Numeric keypad**—On a standard keyboard layout, the numeric keypad is a separate collection of numbered keys on the right. The numeric keypad usually serves two functions, and you toggle between these functions by pressing the Num Lock key. (Most keyboards have a Num Lock indicator light that tells you when Num Lock is on.) When Num Lock is on, you can use the numeric keypad to type numbers. When Num Lock is off, the other symbols on the keys become active. For example, the up-pointing arrow on the 8 key becomes active, which means you can use it to move up within a program. Some keyboards (called *extended keyboards*) have a separate keypad for the insertion-point movement keys, and you can keep Num Lock on all the time on these keyboards.

Using Gestures on a Tablet

How do you make Windows 8 do anything if you have a tablet PC but you don't have a mouse or keyboard? For such situations, Windows 8 was built with *touch* in mind. That is, instead of using a mouse or keyboard to manipulate Windows 8, you use your fingers to touch the screen in specific ways called *gestures*. (Some tablet PCs also come with a small pen-like device called a *stylus,* and you can use the stylus instead of your finger to perform some actions.)

What are these specific ways? There are tons of them, but here's just a short list to get you started (I talk about the rest as we go through the book):

- **Tap**—Use your finger (or the stylus) to touch the screen and then immediately release it. This is the touch equivalent of a mouse click.

- **Double-tap**—Tap and release the screen *twice,* one tap right after the other. This is the touch equivalent of a mouse double-click.

- **Tap and hold**—Tap the screen and leave your finger (or the stylus) resting on the screen until the shortcut menu appears. This is the touch equivalent of a mouse right-click, and it works most often in desktop apps, not Windows 8 apps.

- **Slide**—Place your finger on the screen, move your finger, and then release. This is the touch equivalent of a mouse click and drag, so you usually use this technique to move an object from one place to another or for scrolling the screen.

- **Swipe**—Quickly and briefly run your finger along the screen. This usually causes the screen to scroll in the direction of the swipe; it's roughly equivalent to scrolling with the mouse wheel.

- **Pinch**—Place two fingers apart on the screen and bring them closer together. This gesture zooms out on whatever is displayed on the screen, such as a photo.

- **Spread**—Place two fingers close together on the screen and move them farther apart. This gesture zooms in on whatever is displayed on the screen, such as a photo.

- **Turn**—Place two fingers on the screen and turn them clockwise or counterclockwise. This gesture rotates whatever is displayed on the screen, such as a photo.

You can also use touch to enter text by using the onscreen touch keyboard, shown in Figure 4.6. To display the keyboard in a Windows 8 app, tap inside whatever box you'll be using to type the text; in a Desktop app, tap the Keyboard icon that appears in the taskbar.

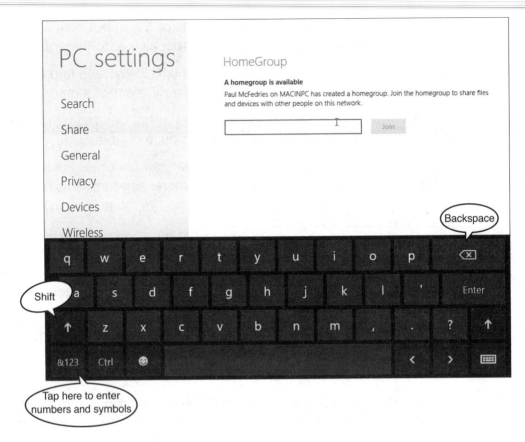

Figure 4.6 *To type on a tablet PC, use the touch keyboard.*

Taking a Tour of the Windows 8 Interface

After you start your PC and enter your account password, you end up at the Start screen, which will look something like (but probably not exactly like) the screen shown in Figure 4.7.

To help you get your bearings, note that the default Start screen has these main features:

- **Tiles**—The rectangles you see each represent an *app*, which is a program designed to help you perform a particular task. For example, you use the Calendar app to monitor your appointments, the Photos app to view your digital photos, and the Weather app to get the latest forecast. To launch an app, you click its tile.

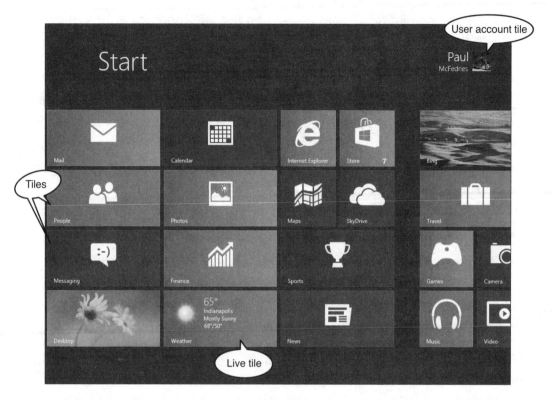

Figure 4.7   *The Windows 8 Start screen.*

- **Live tiles**—Many of the Start screen tiles are "live" in the sense that they display often-updated information instead of the app icon. For example, the Weather tile shows the current weather for your default location; the Mail tile displays recent email messages; and the Calendar tile shows your upcoming events.

- **User account tile**—Clicking this tile gives you access to several account-related tasks, such as locking your PC and signing out of your account.

When you move your mouse, you see the Start screen scrollbar at the bottom of the screen, and it works like a traditional horizontal scrollbar. That is, to scroll the Start screen right or left, you use any of the following techniques:

- Drag the white scroll box right and left.

- Click the scroll arrows that appear on the left and right edges of the scrollbar.

- Click between the scroll box and the scroll arrows.

Note that all Windows 8 apps are also oriented horizontally and come with their own horizontal scrollbars, so you can use these same techniques to navigate any Windows 8 app.

For my money, however, the scrollbar is a really inefficient way to navigate the Start screen or a Windows 8 app. A much faster and more elegant method is to use your mouse's scroll wheel (if it has one):

- Turn the wheel forward to scroll the screen to the right.

- Turn the wheel backward to scroll the screen to the left.

The App Bar

You can hunt around all you like, but you won't find menu bars, toolbars, or taskbars anywhere in Windows 8's new interface. The only "bar" you'll (eventually) see is a new interface element called the *app bar* (or sometimes *application bar*), which contains app-related commands, features, controls, and settings. In any new Windows 8 screen—the Start screen, the Apps screen, a Windows 8 app screen, and so on—you display the app bar by using one of the following techniques:

- Right-click the screen.

- Press **Windows Logo+Z**.

- If you're using a touchscreen, swipe up from the bottom edge of the screen (or swipe down from the top edge).

For example, if you right-click a Start screen tile (or swipe down on a tile if you're using a touchscreen), the app bar that appears contains commands related to that tile, as shown in Figure 4.8.

Closing the App Bar

To dismiss the app bar without doing anything, right-click the same object, press either **Esc** or **Windows Logo+Z**, or repeat the swipe gesture that you used to display the app bar.

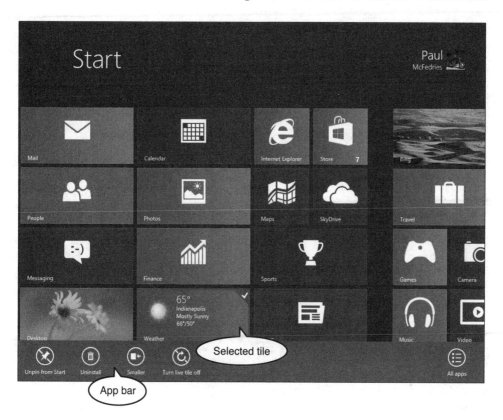

Figure 4.8 *The app bar for a Start screen tile.*

The Charms Menu

The other piece of the Start screen that you need to know about is the Charms menu, which you display by using one of the following techniques:

- Point the mouse at the top-right (or bottom-right) corner of the screen, and then when the Charms icons appear, move the pointer straight down (or up) to display the full Charms menu.

- Press **Windows Logo+C**.

- If you're using a touchscreen, swipe left from the right edge of the screen.

Figure 4.9 shows the Charms menu. Note, too, that Windows also displays a box showing the current date and time, the Network icon, and the Power icon.

Figure 4.9 *The Windows 8 Charms menu.*

The Charms menu offers the following items (yes, they're called charms; I don't know why):

- **Search**—Select this charm to search your PC.

- **Share**—Select this charm to use a Windows 8 app (such as Mail) to send a file or some data to a friend.

- **Start**—Select this charm to return to the Start screen.

- **Devices**—Select this charm to open a screen that shows you all the major devices and hardware doodads attached to your computer.

- **Settings**—Select this charm to configure various Windows 8 options and settings.

Navigating the Start Screen

If the simplicity of the Start screen makes it hard to figure out what to do with Windows 8, it also makes it hard to figure out how to navigate

Windows 8. With no traditional navigational aids such as scrollbars and tabs in sight, how do you get around the Start screen? The next three sections provide the answers to that question.

Putting Your PC to Sleep

If you won't be using your PC for a little while, it's a good idea to put it into *sleep mode*, which turns off components such as the monitor and hard drive to save energy. Here's how you go about that:

1. Display the **Charms** menu, as described earlier in this chapter.

2. Select **Settings**. The **Settings** pane appears on the right side of the screen.

3. Select the **Power** button. Windows 8 displays a menu of commands, as shown in Figure 4.10.

Figure 4.10 *Open the Settings pane and then select Power to see the commands shown here.*

4. Select **Sleep**. Windows 8 puts your PC into sleep mode.

Restarting Your PC

If you find that your PC is acting strangely, you can often solve the problem by restarting the PC. Note, too, that many programs ask you to restart your PC after they've installed new updates, so this is a task that will come in handy fairly often. Here's how it works:

1. Display the **Charms** menu, as described earlier in this chapter.

2. Select **Settings**. The Settings pane appears on the right side of the screen.

3. Select the **Power** button. Windows 8 displays the menu of commands shown earlier in Figure 4.10.

4. Select **Restart**. Windows 8 shuts down your PC and then restarts it.

Shutting Down Your PC

If you won't be using your PC for a long time, you should turn off the power. However, you should never just flick off the PC's power button because you could damage the data on your PC and cause problems. Instead, follow these steps to shut down your PC properly:

1. Display the Charms menu, as described earlier in this chapter.

2. Select **Settings**. The Settings pane appears on the right side of the screen.

3. Select the **Power** button. Windows 8 displays the commands shown earlier in Figure 4.10.

4. Select **Shut Down**. Windows 8 turns off your PC.

Chapter 5

Learning Windows Basics

At the most basic level, all PCs operate using a combination of input and output. *Input* refers to information provided to the PC, which could be characters you type on your keyboard, mouse actions such as clicks and right-clicks, and touchscreen gestures such as taps and swipes. *Output* refers to data generated by the PC that appears on your monitor (or perhaps on your printer). And you know from Chapter 1, "Getting to Know the PC," that inside your PC the CPU is processing data, the hard drive is storing data, the memory is enabling data to be worked with, and so on. In other words, there's a lot going on both inside and outside your PC, so who or what is making sure it all happens smoothly and accurately?

The answer is a special program called the *operating system*, which has the unenviable task of processing your input, sending data out to the right place, and coordinating the activities of hardware such as the CPU, hard drive, and memory. On your PC, the operating system is called Windows, and in this book I'm assuming you have the latest version, which is called Windows 8.

Fortunately for you, the vast majority of the tasks Windows performs occur behind the scenes, as it were, so you never have to think twice (or even once, for that matter) about them. Instead, you get the much more pleasant task of learning the various programs—called *apps*—that Windows 8 makes available. This chapter gets you off to a good start with your app learning by showing you a few general principles for working with apps and then showing you some specific app tasks, such as working with appointments, contacts, and maps.

I should mention right off the bat that many of the apps you learn about in this chapter require not only an Internet connection but also a Microsoft account. So before you dive too deeply into this chapter, you might want to pay a visit to Chapter 10, "Getting Online," to learn how to set up your Internet connection and create a Microsoft account, if you haven't done so already.

Working with Apps

When you start up your PC and enter your account password, you wind up at the Start screen, which as you've seen is populated with nearly 20 tiles, each of which represents an app that you can use to perform a specific task (or sometimes two or three related tasks). For example, you use the Calendar app to track upcoming events, you use the Maps app to get directions to a location, and you use the Internet Explorer app to visit websites.

Here's a summary of the default Start screen tiles:

- **Mail**—You use this app to send and receive email messages, as you learn in Chapter 12, "Exchanging Email."

- **Calendar**—You use this app to schedule appointments, meetings, and other events. See "Tracking Your Appointments," later in this chapter.

- **Internet Explorer**—You use this app to weave your way around the Web, as I explain in Chapter 11, "Surfing the Web."

- **Store**—This tile represents the Windows Store, which you can use to purchase software right from the comfort of your home, as shown in the "Installing New Apps" section, later in this chapter.

- **Bing**—This tile opens the Bing search engine, which you can use to search for information on the Web.

- **People**—This app connects you with the people in your life by letting you store contact info (see "Managing Your Contacts," later in this chapter) and connect with your Facebook and Twitter accounts.

- **Photos**—This app lets you peruse the photos and other pictures that you have on your computer. The details can be found in Chapter 7, "Dealing with Digital Photos."

- **Maps**—This app lets you get there from here by showing you locations on a map and providing directions. Check out "Getting Directions to a Location," later in this chapter.

- **SkyDrive**—You can use this app to send files to your SkyDrive, which is an online storage area associated with your Microsoft account.

- **Travel**—This app enables you to research destinations, plan trips, and book flights and hotel rooms. See "Planning a Trip," later in this chapter.

- **Messaging**—This app lets you send text messages to your friends and family.

- **Finance**—You can use this app to track stocks, get financial news, and more. See "Monitoring a Stock," later in this chapter.

- **Sports**—You can use this app to get the latest sports schedules and scores, follow your favorite teams, view standings and statistics, and more. See "Following Your Favorite Team," later in this chapter.

- **Games**—This app lets you download games that you can play either on your PC or on your Xbox gaming console.

- **Camera**—This app connects with your computer's built-in or attached camera to take a picture or video. I show you how it works in Chapter 7.

- **Desktop**—This app represents the Windows 8 desktop.

- **Weather**—You can fire up this app to get the latest weather and forecast for one or more cities.

- **News**—You can use this app to read the latest news in categories such as politics, technology, and entertainment. See "Tracking a News Topic," later in this chapter.

- **Music**—This app lets you play the music files that you have stored on your PC. You can also use it to search for new artists, preview their music, and then purchase songs or albums that tickle your fancy. See Chapter 8, "Working with Digital Music," to find out more.

- **Video**—This app lets you watch the videos and movies that reside on your computer. You can also use it to search for new movies, watch trailers, and then buy or rent any movie that catches your eye. Chapter 9, "Working with Digital Video," gives you the details.

Starting an App

Getting any of the Start screen apps up and running couldn't be easier:

- **Mouse**—Click the tile of the app you want to start.

- **Keyboard**—Press **Tab** until you see the Mail tile selected (that is, the tile is surrounded by a white border), use the arrow keys to select the tile of the app you want to start, and then press **Enter**.

- **Touch**—Tap the tile of the app you want to start.

There's actually another screen you can use to start apps, and it contains quite a few more tiles. This screen is called, appropriately enough, Apps, and you display it by right-clicking an empty section of the Start screen and then clicking **All Apps** in the app bar that appears. (If you're using a touchscreen, swipe up from the bottom edge of the screen and then tap **All Apps**.) Figure 5.1 shows the Apps screen, which includes smaller versions of the tiles from the Start screen as well as tiles for just about every other app installed on your PC. You use the same techniques to start an app from this screen as you do from the Start screen.

Figure 5.1 *You can also use the Apps screen to start any of the apps on your PC.*

Returning to the Start Screen

When you start a Windows 8 app, the program takes up the entire screen, and you no longer see the Start screen. If you later want to start a different program, how are you supposed to do that if the Start screen is nowhere in sight? You can use any of the following techniques to return to the Start screen:

- **Mouse**—Move the mouse pointer to the bottom-left corner of the screen, and when you see the miniature version of the **Start** screen appear, click the mouse.

- **Keyboard**—Press the **Windows Logo** key.

- **Touch**—Swipe left from the right edge of the screen to display the **Charms** menu and then tap **Start**.

Switching Between Apps

Windows is capable of *multitasking*, which means running two or more apps at the same time. That might sound like an odd feature, but it's often handy to have multiple apps on the go. For example, you could be perusing the News app and decide to research a news item on the Internet, which requires the Internet Explorer app. If you then want to send your findings to a friend or colleague via email, that requires the Mail app.

That's all well and good, but you have to switch from one app to another for all this to work. Whenever you have multiple Windows 8 apps going, Windows 8 gives you two ways to switch between them using a mouse:

- Position the mouse pointer in the top-left corner of the screen. Windows responds by showing you a thumbnail version of the next running app (see Figure 5.2); click to switch to that app. If you want to cycle through the apps, leave the mouse pointer in the top-left corner and keep clicking.

- Move the mouse pointer into the top-left corner of the screen, and when the thumbnail of the next app appears, slide the mouse pointer straight down. When you get below the next app, Windows 8 displays a list of all running Windows 8 apps, as shown in Figure 5.3. Click the app you want to use.

Figure 5.2 *Move the mouse pointer to the top-left corner of the screen to see a thumbnail of the next running app.*

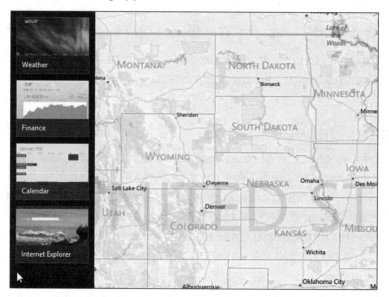

Figure 5.3 *Move the mouse pointer to the top-left corner of the screen and then slide it down to see a list of your up-and-running Windows 8 apps.*

Here are the techniques to use to switch between Windows 8 apps using a touchscreen:

- To switch to the next running app, slide to the right from the left edge of the screen. Your finger drags in a thumbnail of the next app, and when you release your finger from the screen, the app fills up the screen.

- To see the list of running Windows 8 apps, slide in from the left edge again, but this time when you see the next app appear under your finger, reverse course and slide your finger back to the left edge of the screen. As soon as your finger hits the ledge, the app disappears and you see the list of running apps. You can then tap the one you want.

Shutting Down an App

Generally speaking, you don't have to worry about shutting down Windows 8 apps because they take up very few system resources when you're not using them. However, if you're having trouble with a Windows 8 app or if you just want to make it easier to switch between the other running apps, you need to know how to shut down the current Windows 8 app:

- **Mouse**—Move the mouse pointer to the top of the screen, where it changes to a hand, and then click and drag the hand down. As you drag, the Windows 8 app window shrinks down to a thumbnail window. Keep dragging the window all the way to the bottom of the screen and then release the mouse button.

- **Keyboard**—Press **Alt+F4**.

- **Touchscreen**—Place your finger at the top edge of the screen and then slide down until the Windows 8 app window shrinks down to a thumbnail window. Keep dragging your finger to the bottom of the screen and then release your finger.

Tip

App Switching Via the Keyboard

You can also switch to another Windows 8 app using the keyboard. For example, you can quickly switch between the current Windows 8 app and the Start screen by pressing the **Windows Logo** key. You can also hold down the **Windows** key and then tap **Tab**. When you do this, Windows 8 displays the list of running Windows 8 apps. With the Windows key held down, keep pressing **Tab** until the app you want is highlighted and then release the Windows key.

Installing New Apps

Windows 8 ships with a decent collection of apps, but there are a few glaring gaps in that collection. For example, there are no apps for editing photos, reading e-books, learning recipes, writing notes, or playing games. Fortunately, you can fill in any or all of these holes by using the Windows Store, which enables you to add new apps with just a few clicks of the mouse or taps of the screen. Some of the apps cost a few dollars, but many are free for the taking.

The main Store screen is divided into a number of app categories, including Spotlight, Games, Social, Entertainment, Photo, Lifestyle, and Tools. In each category, you have four choices:

- Select an app tile to see that app's details.

- Select **New Releases** to see a list of the latest apps added to the category.

- Select **Top Free** to see a list of the most popular free apps in the category.

- Select the category name to see a complete list of the apps in the category. From there, you can filter the apps by price (for example, Free or Paid), and you can sort the apps (for example, by highest rating or by newest).

Selecting an app displays the app's details (see Figure 5.4), including its user rating, price, description and features, and user reviews.

Figure 5.4 *Select an app to see its details.*

Here are the steps to follow to install an app from the Windows Store:

1. On the Start screen, click **Store**. The Windows Store appears.

2. Open the app that you want to install.

3. If it's a paid app, tap **Buy** and then tap **Confirm**; for a free app, tap **Install**.

4. If you're installing a paid app, you need to enter your Microsoft account password and then provide your payment info.

Tip

To search for an app, open Windows Store, display the **Charms** menu, select **Search**, type a word or two that describes what you're looking for, and then press **Enter** or tap the magnifying glass.

Uninstalling Windows 8 Apps

If you have an app that you no longer use, you can free up some disk space and reduce clutter on the Start screen by uninstalling that app. Here's how it works:

1. Use the **Start** screen or the **Apps** screen to locate the Windows 8 app that you want to uninstall.

2. Right-click or swipe down on the app tile. Windows 8 displays the app bar.

3. Click **Uninstall**. Windows 8 asks you to confirm.

4. Click **Uninstall**. Windows 8 removes the app.

Tracking Your Appointments

If you're used to keeping track of your upcoming appointments, get-togethers, and meetings using a paper calendar or day timer, you might be wondering why you'd want to start using a PC to track these events instead. There are actually quite a few good reasons to switch to the electronic method, but here are my three favorites:

• Your PC can display a reminder before an appointment so you don't forget.

• If you have an appointment that repeats at a regular interval (say, once a week or once a month), you need only enter one of these appointments, and your PC can automatically fill in all the future appointments.

- If you have a Microsoft account (again, see Chapter 10), you need only enter an appointment on your PC, and Windows 8 will automatically add that same appointment to any other Windows 8 device you use (such as a tablet or smartphone).

You use the Calendar app to track your appointments. Follow these steps to use Calendar to add an appointment:

1. On the **Start** screen, open the **Calendar** app, which displays an onscreen calendar that shows the current month.

2. Navigate to the month when your appointment occurs:

    ### Tip

    Changing the View

    Instead of viewing an entire month at a time, you can see just a week's worth or a day's worth of the calendar. Right-click the screen (or swipe up from the bottom edge on a tablet) and then select either **Week** or **Day**. You can also select **Month** to return to the Month view.

   - **Mouse**—Move the mouse and then click the right-pointing arrow near the top right of the screen to see the next month; move the mouse and then click the left-pointing arrow near the top left of the screen to see the previous month.

   - **Keyboard**—Press **Page Down** to move to the next month; press **Page Up** to move to the previous month.

   - **Touchscreen**—Swipe left to navigate to the next month; swipe right to navigate to the previous month.

3. Click the date when the appointment occurs. Calendar displays a new screen that you use to enter the specifics of the appointment.

4. Type a title for the appointment.

5. Use the **Start** list to select the time the appointment begins.

6. Use the **How Long** list to select the length of the appointment. If the appointment is one that has no set time (such as a birthday or a full-day meeting), choose **All Day** in the list.

7. Use the **Where** text box to type the location of the appointment.

8. Select **Show More** to see more options.

9. If the appointment repeats, use the **How Often** list to select the repeat interval.

10. Use the **Reminder** list to select the amount of time before the appointment that you want to be reminded about it.

11. Click **Add a Message** and write down anything that you might want to remember about the appointment: notes, questions, the location's address, and so on. Figure 5.5 shows a completed appointment ready to be added to the calendar.

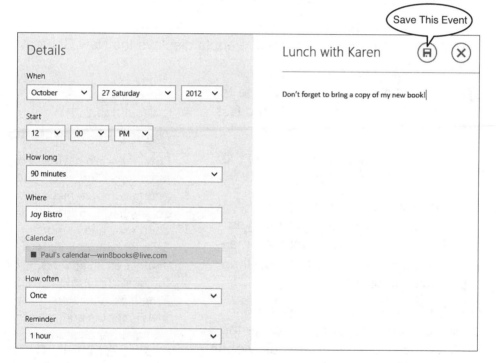

Figure 5.5   *An appointment filled out and ready to add to the Calendar app.*

12. Select **Save This Event** (pointed out in Figure 5.5). The Calendar app returns you to the calendar and displays the appointment on the day you chose.

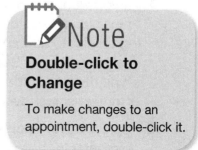

Note

Double-click to Change

To make changes to an appointment, double-click it.

Managing Your Contacts

Windows 8's People app is your electronic equivalent of an address book because it enables you to store data about your friends, family members, work colleagues, clients, and so on. For each person, you can store data such as first and last name, company name, email address, one or more phone numbers, street address, job title, and more.

Here are the steps to use the People app to add a contact's info:

1. On the **Start** screen, select **People** to load the app.

2. Right-click the screen (or swipe up from the bottom edge on a touchscreen) and then select **New**. People displays the New Contact screen.

3. Use the **First Name** and **Last Name** text boxes to type the person's first and last names.

4. Use the **Company** text box to type the person's company name.

5. Use the **Email** text box to type the person's email address. Note that you can also change the label for the email address by clicking **Personal** and then clicking **Work** or **Other**.

6. Use the **Phone** text box to type the person's phone number. To change the label for the phone number, click **Mobile** and then click a new label.

7. If you want to add other info, select the plus sign (+) beside the type of data. For example, to add another phone number, select **+ Phone**. Select the type of field you want to use and then type the info in the new field that appears. Figure 5.6 shows the New Contact screen with the **Job Title** field added.

8. Select **Save**. People saves your work and adds the person to your list of contacts.

> **Note**
>
> **Adding Multiple Items**
>
> Lots of people have two or more email addresses and phone numbers these days, so feel free to add multiple addresses and numbers for your contacts. To add another email address, click the circled plus sign beside **Email**, click a category, and then enter the address. To add another phone number, click the circled plus sign beside **Phone**, click a category, and then enter the number.

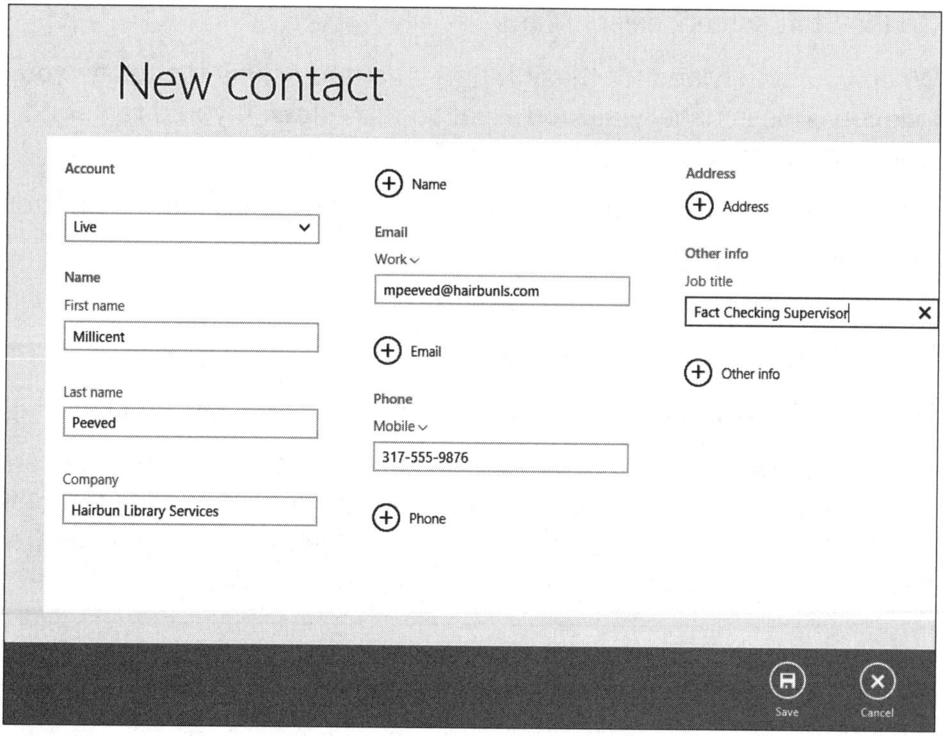

Figure 5.6 *Use the New Contact screen to fill in the details about your contact.*

Getting Directions to a Location

One of the most useful innovations of recent years is the digital map, which is an electronic version of the paper road maps that you're used to. Digital maps offer many advantages over their paper predecessors. For example, you can use a digital map to pinpoint your current location, which is very handy if you're in a new city or an unfamiliar part of town and you want to get your bearings. You can also use digital maps to search for locations based on the address or the name of a building or an organization. Digital maps can even show traffic conditions in some cities!

But perhaps the most useful function of a digital map is to give you specific directions on how to get from one location to another. You can do this (as well as all the other functions I just mentioned) with Windows 8's Maps app by following these steps:

1. On the Start screen, select **Maps**.

2. When you start Maps for the first time, the app asks if it can use your location. This is usually a good idea, so tap **Allow**. If you'd rather not give away your current location, tap **Block** instead.

3. Right-click the screen (or, on a touchscreen, swipe up from the bottom of the screen) to display the app bar.

4. Select **Directions**. Maps displays the Directions pane.

5. Use the **From** box to enter the address of your starting point.

6. Use the **To** box to enter the address or name of your destination.

7. Press **Enter** or select the arrow to the right of the **To** box. As you can see in Figure 5.7, Maps displays the route on the map. At the top of the screen, Maps also tells you the distance and approximate time of the trip and displays the first couple of instructions for the trip.

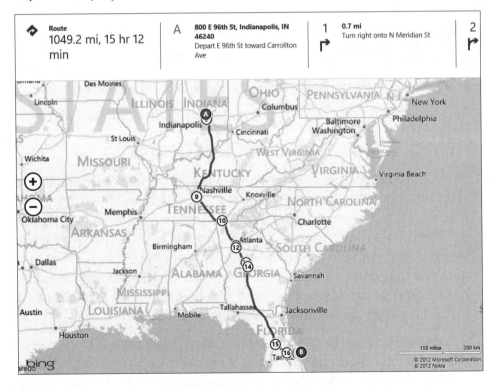

Figure 5.7 *Getting from here to there using the Maps app.*

8. In the list of directions, select **A**. Maps zooms in on the map to show the start of the journey.

9. Begin your journey, and when you near 1 on the map, select **1** in the list of instructions to see what you do next.

10. As you complete each leg of the trip, select the next leg (2, 3, and so on) to see further instructions until you arrive at your destination.

Tracking a News Topic

Keeping up with current events is a sign of an engaged citizen and a curious person. Not all that long ago, getting your news fix meant reading a daily newspaper and perhaps perusing a weekly newsmagazine. That was fine for its time, but a daily paper gives you only a single (and very local) view of events, while the "news" in a typical magazine is more than a week old by the time it gets to you.

The News app solves both problems. For one, it gives you access to news from a wide variety of sources—more than two dozen in all—including *The New York Times, The Washington Post, USA Today,* CNN, Fox News, and the BBC. For another, the stories provided by the News app are usually no more than a few hours old, and some have been posted for only a few minutes.

When you start the News app, the initial screen shows the top story as selected by the editors. As you scroll to the right (by dragging the scrollbar box right, pressing the right-arrow key, or swiping to the left on a touchscreen), you see the latest articles in various categories, such as World, Technology, Entertainment, Politics, and Sports. You can see more stories in a particular category by selecting the category name.

If you're particularly interested in a specific topic, you can also customize the News app to show you stories related to that topic. Follow these steps to set up News to track a specific topic:

1. If you haven't done so already, use the Start screen to select **News**.

2. Right-click the screen (or swipe down from the top edge on a touchscreen) to display the app bar.

3. Select **My News**. The News app opens the My News screen.

4. Select + under the **Add a Section** heading. The Add a Section panel appears.

5. Type a word or two that identifies the topic you want to track. As you type, News displays a list of suggested topics, as shown in Figure 5.8.

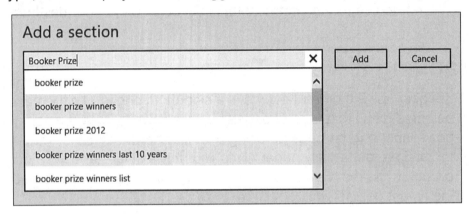

Add a section

| Booker Prize | × | | Add | | Cancel |

booker prize

booker prize winners

booker prize 2012

booker prize winners last 10 years

booker prize winners list

Figure 5.8   *News displays a list of topics that match what you've typed.*

6. When you see the topic you want to add, select it. If you don't see your topic in the list, complete your typing and then select **Add**. News returns you to the My News screen and displays articles related to your topic.

 **Tip**

The Sources List

To see a complete list of the sources used by the News app, right-click the screen (or swipe down from the top edge on a touchscreen) to display the app bar and then select **Sources**.

Monitoring a Stock

Given the economic woes of the past few years, keeping up with business news and the stock market is as important as ever. Fortunately, Windows 8 can help you do just that by offering the Finance app. This app's opening screen shows the top business story as selected by the editors. As you scroll to the right (by dragging the scrollbar box right, pressing the right-arrow key, or swiping to the left on a touchscreen), you see recent market numbers for the Dow and the NASDAQ exchanges (among others), more business news stories, a "watchlist" of stock prices, a list of stocks with the highest percentage gains and losses on the day as well as the most actively traded stocks; recent values for various currencies, bonds, commodities, and exchange-traded funds; recent rates for mortgages, savings accounts, and credit card accounts; and lists of top-performing mutual funds in various categories.

There's a lot to digest, but the Watchlist screen is particularly useful because it enables you to track any stock that interests you. Here are the steps to add a stock to the watchlist:

1. If you haven't done so already, use the Start screen to select **Finance**.

2. Scroll to the Watchlist screen. You can also right-click the screen (or swipe down from the top edge on a touchscreen) to display the app bar and then select **Watchlist**.

3. Select **+**. The Add to Watchlist panel appears.

4. Type the name of the company or the company's stock symbol. As you type, Finance displays a list of suggested stocks, as shown in Figure 5.9.

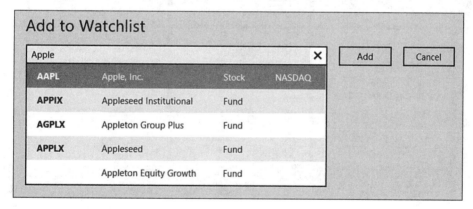

Figure 5.9 *Finance shows a list of stocks that match what you've typed.*

5. When you see the stock you want to track, select it. Finance returns you to the Watchlist screen and displays data for your stock.

Following Your Favorite Team

If you're a sports fan, you'll likely spend an inordinate amount of time using the Sports app, which offers sports scores, schedules, and stories. The

Sports app's opening screen shows the top sports story as selected by the editors. As you scroll to the right (by dragging the scrollbar box right, pressing the right-arrow key, or swiping to the left on a touchscreen), you see more sports-related stories, a schedule of the day's games, and a selection of magazine articles. If you have a favorite team that you just can't get enough of, you can add it to the Favorite Teams screen to get extra information related to that team, including news (see Figure 5.10), schedules, results, individual stats, team stats, and the team roster.

Figure 5.10 *Add your favorite team to the Sports app to see team news as well as schedules, results, and stats.*

Follow these steps to add a favorite team:

1. If you haven't done so already, use the Start screen to select **Sports**.

2. Right-click the screen (or swipe down from the top edge on a touchscreen) to display the app bar.

3. Select **Favorite Teams**. Sports displays the Favorite Teams screen.

4. Select **+**. The Add to Favorite Teams panel appears.

5. Type the name of the team. As you type, Sports displays a list of suggested teams.

6. When you see the team you want to follow, select it. Sports returns you to the Favorite Teams screen, which now includes your team.

Planning a Trip

Before you go on a vacation or trip, you need to do some research, including deciding where to go and what to do when you get there. Windows 8's Travel app can be a big help here because it has lots of resources that enable you to research destinations. The main Travel screen begins with the top travel destination of the day. As you scroll to the right (by dragging the scrollbar box right, pressing the right-arrow key, or swiping to the left on a touchscreen), you see the Featured Destinations screen, which offers several tiles displaying travel destinations chosen by the editors of Bing Travel (you can also click **More** to see an additional list of destinations); the Panoramas screen, which displays 360-degree images from various locations; and the Articles screen, which has news articles about locations and traveling.

When you select a destination, Travel displays a screen devoted to that location (see Figure 5.11), which includes an overview, maps, weather, the recent currency exchange rate, photos and panoramas, lists of attractions, hotels, restaurants, and travel guides.

You can also see more destination and travel stories by right-clicking the screen and then clicking **Destinations** or **Best of Web**.

When you know where you're going, you can then use Travel to book your flight and hotel. Here's how it works:

1. If you haven't done so already, use the Start screen to select **Travel**.

2. Right-click the screen (or swipe down from the top edge on a touchscreen) to display the app bar.

3. Click **Flights**. The Flights screen appears.

4. Use the **From** box to select your departure city.

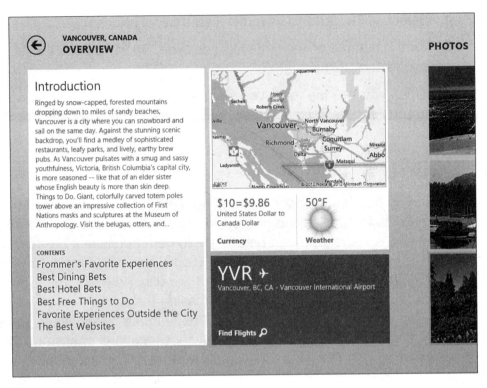

Figure 5.11 *Each destination screen offers lots of information of interest to potential travelers.*

5. Use the **To** box to select your destination city.

6. Fill in your departure and return dates using the **Depart** and **Return** calendars.

7. Use the **Cabin** list to select a cabin type.

8. Use the **Passengers** list to specify the number of passengers.

9. Select **Search Flights**. Travel displays a list of matching flights.

10. Select the flight you want, select **Book**, and then select the booking partner. Travel then transfers you to Internet Explorer so that you can book your flight with the partner company.

11. Return to the Travel app and right-click the screen (or swipe down from the top edge on a touchscreen) to display the app bar.

12. Click **Hotels**. The Hotels screen appears.

13. Use the **City** box to select your destination city.

14. Use the **Check-in** and **Check-out** calendars to fill in your check-in and check-out dates.

15. Use the **Rooms** list to specify the number of rooms you need.

16. Use the **Guests** list to specify the number of guests.

17. Select **Search Hotels**. Travel displays a list of matching hotels.

18. Select the hotel you want, select **Book,** and then click a booking partner. Travel then transfers you to Internet Explorer so that you can book your hotel room with the partner.

Chapter 6

More Windows Techniques You Should Know

I introduced you to many of the Windows 8 apps in Chapter 5, "Learning Windows Basics," but your tour of Windows 8 isn't over, not by a long shot. This chapter continues your Windows 8 education by showing you a few useful and practical tools and techniques that will help you get more out of your PC investment. For example, I show you a few ways to customize Windows 8 to suit your own personal style. You also learn how to search for things in Windows 8 and how to work with files and folders. Later in the chapter, you learn a few highly useful techniques for overcoming visual, hearing, and physical limitations. This chapter is a veritable Windows smorgasbord!

Personalizing Windows 8

You may be surprised to learn that what you see when you start Windows 8 isn't set in stone. There are actually a number of ways that you can customize Windows 8 to end up with a look that's more to your taste. You can change your account picture, change the Start screen background and colors, add more tiles to the Start screen, move the tiles around, and more. The next few sections provide the details.

Changing Your Account Picture

When you install Windows 8, the setup program takes you through several tasks, including choosing a username and password. However, it doesn't ask you to select a picture to go along with your user account. Instead, Windows 8 just supplies your account with a generic illustration. This picture appears in various places within Windows 8, so rather than using the default illustration, you might prefer to use a photo or other artwork. In that case, you can configure your user account to use another picture, which can be either an existing image or a new shot taken with your PC's camera.

First, let's go through the steps to use an existing photo as your account picture:

1. On the Start screen, click your user account tile (top right) and then select **Change Account Picture**. Windows 8 opens the PC Settings app.

2. Select **Browse**. A file chooser screen appears.

3. Select **Files** and then select the folder that contains the image you want to use.

4. Select the image.

5. Select **Choose Image**. Windows 8 applies the new picture to your user account.

Alternatively, if your computer comes with a webcam or you have a similar camera attached to your PC, you can use the camera to take your account picture. Follow these steps:

1. On the Start screen, click your user account tile (top right) and then select **Change Account Picture**. Windows 8 opens the PC Settings app.

2. Select **Camera** to open the Camera app.

3. Compose your shot and then click the screen to take the picture.

4. Click and drag the account picture box to set the image area and then click **OK**. (Alternatively, if you're not happy with the result, click **Retake** to try again.)

If you prefer to use a short video (up to 5 seconds) instead, follow steps 1 and 2 and then select the **Video Mode** button to switch to video mode. Click the screen to begin recording and then click the screen again when the recording is complete. Click **OK** to set the video as your account picture.

Customizing the Start Screen

During the Windows 8 setup procedure, you were asked to choose a color scheme. If you regret your initial choice or if you're just hankering for something different, you can change to a different color scheme with just a few clicks (or taps). While you're at it, you can also change the Start screen background, which is the image that appears "behind" the Start screen tiles. Here are the steps to follow:

1. Press **Windows Logo+I** (or, on a touchscreen, swipe left from the right edge and then tap **Settings**). The Settings pane appears.

2. Select **Change PC Settings**. Windows 8 opens the PC Settings app.

3. Select **Personalize**.

4. Select the **Start Screen** tab to display the screen shown in Figure 6.1.

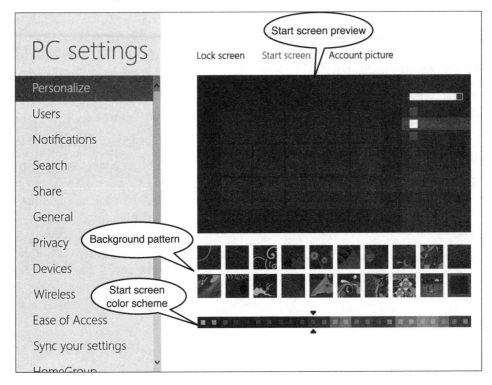

Figure 6.1 *Use the Start Screen tab to customize the background pattern and color scheme.*

5. Click the background pattern you want to use (see Figure 6.1). Windows 8 applies the new pattern.

6. Click the color scheme you want to use. Windows 8 applies the new colors.

Customizing the Lock Screen

If you use the Lock screen frequently, you might prefer to view a background image that's different from the default image. To choose a different Lock screen background, follow these steps:

1. Press **Windows Logo+I** (or, on a touchscreen, swipe left from the right edge and then tap **Settings**). The Settings pane appears.

2. Select **Change PC Settings**. Windows 8 opens the PC Settings app.

3. Click **Personalize**.

4. Click **Lock Screen**. The PC Settings app displays the Lock Screen tab, as shown in Figure 6.2.

5. If you want to use one of the predefined images (pointed out in Figure 6.2), select the image and then skip the rest of these steps. Otherwise, select **Browse**.

6. Select **Files** and then select the folder that contains the image you want to use.

7. Select the image.

8. Select **Choose Picture**. Windows 8 applies the new picture to your Lock screen.

Note

Using the Photos App

Another way to apply one of your own images as the Lock screen background is to launch the Photos app, display the image you want to use, right-click the screen, and then select **Set As, Lock Screen**.

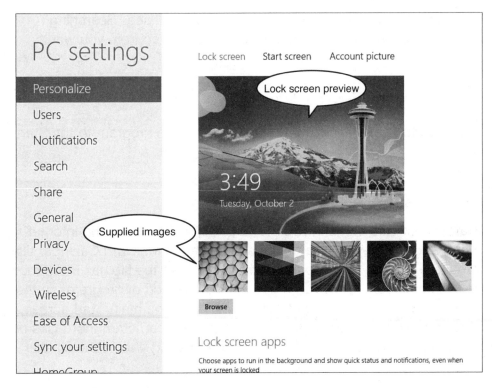

Figure 6.2 *Use the Lock Screen tab to customize the background image displayed on the Lock screen.*

Pinning a Program to the Start Screen

One of the significant conveniences of the Start screen is that the apps you see can all be opened with just a single click or tap. Contrast this with the relatively laborious process required to launch just about any other program on your PC: Right-click the **Start** screen (or swipe up from the bottom edge on a tablet), click **All Apps**, scroll through the Apps screen to find the program you want to run, and then click it.

This seems like a lot of effort to launch a program, and it's that much worse for a program you use often. You can avoid all that extra work and make a frequently used program easier to launch by pinning that program to the Start screen:

1. Use the Apps screen or the Apps search screen (see "Searching Windows 8," later in this chapter) to locate the program you want to pin.

2. Right-click the program tile (or, on a tablet PC, swipe down on the tile) to display the app bar.

3. Click **Pin to Start**. Windows 8 adds a tile for the program to the Start screen.

Resizing a Tile

The Start screen tiles come in two sizes: small, as seen with the Internet Explorer and Store tiles, and large, as seen with the Mail and Calendar tiles. The large size is useful for tiles that are live because the tile has more room to display information. However, if you pinned a bunch of programs to the Start screen, some of them might not be visible on the main Start screen, requiring you to scroll to the right to see them. You can cram more tiles on the main Start screen by resizing some of the existing tiles to the smaller size.

Whatever the scenario, you can resize a tile by right-clicking it (or swiping down on it if you're using a tablet PC) to display the app bar and then clicking **Smaller** (if the tile is currently large; see Figure 6.3) or **Larger** (if the tile is currently small).

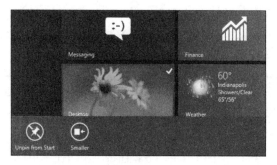

Figure 6.3 *Right-click (or swipe down on) a tile and then click Smaller or Larger.*

Moving a Tile

One of the problems many new users have with the Windows 8 Start screen is the slight delay that occurs when they try to find the app they want to launch. This is particularly true when you have many live tiles showing information, because you no longer see the app name in each tile, just the app icon. If this is the case with just the default Start screen tiles displayed, it's only going to get worse when you start adding more tiles (see "Pinning a Program to the Start Screen," earlier in this chapter).

One way to reduce this problem is to rearrange the Start screen in such a way that it helps you locate the apps you use most often. For example, you could place your favorite apps on the left side of the screen, or you could arrange similar apps together (for example, all the media-related apps).

Here are the techniques to use to move an app tile:

- **Regular PC**—Use your mouse to click and drag the tile and then drop it on the new location.

- **Tablet PC**—Use your finger (or a stylus) to tap and drag the tile and then drop it on the new location.

Searching Windows 8

If you use your PC regularly, there's an excellent chance that its hard drive is crammed with thousands, perhaps even tens of thousands, of files that take up hundreds, perhaps even thousands, of gigabytes. That's a lot of data, but it leads to a huge and growing problem: finding things. Of course, we all want to have the proverbial information at our fingertips. These days, though, our fingertips tend to fumble around more often than not while we're trying to locate not only documents and other data we've created ourselves, but also apps, Windows settings, and that wealth of information that exists "out there" on the Web, in databases, and so on.

Windows 8 attempts to solve this problem by combining *all* search operations into a single element called the Search pane. When you use this deceptively simple pane with its single text box, Windows 8 enables you to search for apps by name, for Windows 8 settings and features, for documents, for program data, and more.

To get to the Search pane, display the Charms menu and select **Search**. (There are also shortcut methods you can use, which I discuss shortly.) Figure 6.4 shows the Search pane that appears.

Figure 6.4 *The Windows 8 Search pane.*

The Search pane consists of a text box followed by a collection of icons. Here's what they do:

- **Apps**—Select this icon to search for an app by name. Note, too, that app searching is the default in Windows 8, so you can initiate an app search from the Start screen just by typing your search text.

- **Settings**—Select this icon to search for a setting that enables you to modify Windows 8 in some way. To display the Search pane with the Settings icon preselected, press **Windows Logo+W**.

- **Files**—Click this icon to search through your user account libraries. To display the Search pane with the Files icon preselected, press **Windows Logo+F**.

- **Within apps**—The rest of the Search pane icons represent individual apps that implement a search feature. When you select one of these icons, you're doing a search within the app. For example, click **Internet Explorer** to search the Web; click **Maps** to search for a location; or click **Music** to search for bands, songs, or albums.

As you type, Search displays the results that match your search text, as shown in Figure 6.5. When you see the item you want, select it.

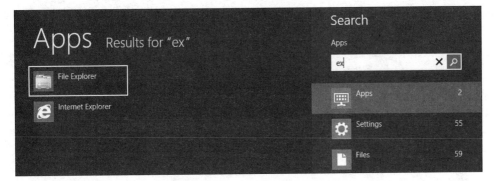

Figure 6.5 *The Search pane displays as-you-type results.*

Working with Files and Folders

When you add a bit of data to your PC—for example, a photo from your digital camera or a document that you create with a program—it's stored on your PC's hard drive as a *file* and the specific storage location is called a *folder*. If you ever need to work with your files by, for example, moving them to a different location, renaming them, or deleting them, you use a program called File Explorer. You start this program using either of the following techniques:

- In the Windows 8 Start screen, type **explorer** and then select the **File Explorer** tile in the search results that appear.

- Select the Start screen's **Desktop** tile and then select the **File Explorer** icon in the taskbar, pointed out in Figure 6.6.

When you first start File Explorer, it shows the contents of a folder called Libraries, which contains icons for the following storage locations:

- **Documents**—This folder stores all the documents that don't fit into more specific folders such as Music and Pictures.

- **Music**—This folder stores your music and sound files.

- **Pictures**—This folder stores your digital images and photos.

- **Videos**—This folder stores your digital videos and movies.

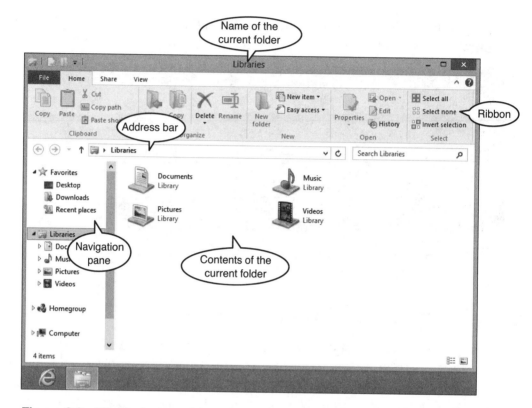

Figure 6.6 *File Explorer enables you to view and work with your PC's files and folders.*

To open a folder, either double-click it or, if it's shown in the navigation pane on the left side of the window, click it. File Explorer now displays the contents of that folder. For example, Figure 6.7 shows what happens when I open my Music folder. In this case, you can see that I have quite a few more folders (which are called *subfolders*). You can keep double-clicking folders until you get to the file you want to work with. You can use the **Back** and **Forward** buttons (see Figure 6.7) to go up and down the folder levels, or you can use the **Address** bar to click a folder name and jump directly to that folder.

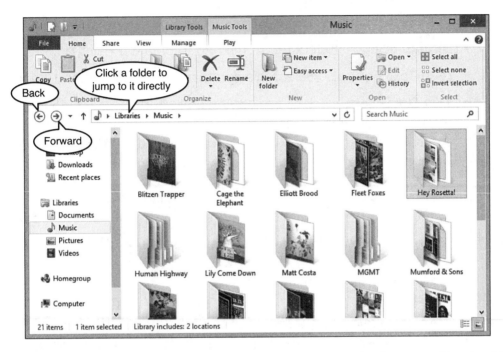

Figure 6.7 *Navigating File Explorer often means navigating several levels of folders.*

Creating a New File or Folder

Windows 8 comes with a few programs that enable you to create files. For example, you can use WordPad (on the Start screen, type **wordpad** and then select the WordPad tile) to create text documents, and you can use Paint (on the Start screen, type **paint** and then select the Paint tile) to create drawings. When you start these programs, they automatically create a new file for you. You then select **File** and then the **Save** command to save the file to your hard disk.

However, you can also create a new file or even a new folder within File Explorer itself by following these steps:

1. Open the folder in which you want to create the file. If you're not sure which folder to use, open the **Documents** folder.

2. In the ribbon (pointed out earlier in Figure 6.6), select the **Home** tab and then select **New Item**. A menu opens with several options, the most important of which for our purposes are the following:

- **Folder**—Select this command to create a new subfolder.

- **Bitmap Image**—Select this command to create a Paint file.

- **Rich Text Format**—Select this command to create a WordPad file.

- **Text Document**—Select this command to create a document that uses only plain text (as opposed to a rich text document, which can use fonts and colors). You work with text documents using the Notepad program.

3. Select the type of file you want. Windows 8 creates the new file and displays a generic name—such as New Text Document—in a text box.

4. Type the name you want to use and then press **Enter**.

Selecting Files and Folders

To work with files or folders, you first need to select them. Let's begin with the simplest case: selecting a single file or folder. This is a two-step procedure:

1. Open the folder that contains the file or subfolder you want to work with.

2. In the folder contents list, click or tap the file's icon.

If you need to select multiple files or folders, you can use the following methods:

- **Selecting consecutive items**—If the files or folders you want to select are listed consecutively, select the first item, hold down the **Shift** key, select the last item, and then release Shift. Windows 8 automatically selects all the items in between.

- **Selecting nonconsecutive items**—If the files or folders you want to select are in various places within the current folder, select the first item, hold down the **Ctrl** key, click each of the other items, and then release Ctrl.

- **Selecting all items**—If you want to select everything inside a folder, select the ribbon's **Home** tab and then the **Select All** command, or press **Ctrl+A**.

Copying and Moving a File or Folder

A copy of a file or folder is an exact replica of the original that you store on another part of your hard disk or on a removable disk (such as a flash drive or memory card). Copies are useful for making backups or if you want to transport a file or folder to another computer. Alternatively, you can also move a file or folder from its current location to a new location.

Either way, here are the steps to follow:

1. Select the files or folders you want to copy or move.

2. Select the **Home** tab.

3. Select one of the following commands:

   • **Copy**—Select this command if you're copying files or folders.

   • **Cut**—Select this command if you're moving files or folders.

4. Navigate to the destination folder or disk drive.

5. Select the **Home** tab and then select **Paste**.

Only Move Your Own Files

Move only a file or folder that you created yourself or that you added to your PC's hard drive yourself. Moving any other file or folder could cause problems with your PC.

Renaming a File or Folder

If you don't like the current name given to one of your files or folders, you can rename it by following these steps:

1. Select the file or folder you want to rename. (You can work with only one item at a time for this procedure.)

2. Select the Home tab's **Rename** command, or press **F2**. Windows 8 creates a text box around the name.

Only Rename Your Own Files

As with moving items, you should rename only a file or folder that you created yourself or that you added to your PC's hard drive yourself.

3. Edit the name. Note that the name can be up to 255 characters long and can include all keyboard characters (including spaces) except for the following: * | \ : " < > ? /.

4. When you're done, press **Enter**.

Deleting a File or Folder

If you have a file or folder that you no longer require, you should delete it to reclaim the disk space and avoid cluttering your folders. Here are the steps to follow:

1. Select the files or folders you want to delete.

2. Select the **Home** tab.

3. Select the top half of the **Delete** button (you can also just press **Delete**). Windows 8 removes the files or folders.

Overcoming Visual Challenges

If your eyesight isn't what it used to be, Windows 8 offers a few tools that can help you see what's on the screen.

Making Screen Items Appear Bigger

If everything on your screen looks tiny and hard to decipher, Windows 8 can scale everything up to a larger size. Here's how it works:

Tip

Restoring a Deleted File

If you delete a file accidentally, immediately press **Ctrl+Z** to get it back. If that doesn't work, double-click the desktop's **Recycle Bin** icon to open a folder that contains a list of all the files and folders you've deleted recently. Select the files or folders you want to recover, select the **Manage** tab, and then select **Restore the Selected Items**.

Note

If You Can't Make Everything Bigger

If you can't change the **Make Everything on Your Screen Bigger** setting, it means your PC doesn't support this feature. The usual culprit here is that your PC's graphics card—the internal component that generates what you see on your monitor—isn't powerful enough. You might want to book an appointment with a local PC technician to see if you can upgrade your graphics card to one that supports a higher resolution.

1. Press **Windows Logo+I** (or, on a touchscreen, swipe left from the right edge and then tap **Settings**). The Settings pane appears.

2. Select **Change PC Settings**. Windows 8 opens the PC Settings app.

3. Select **Ease of Access**.

4. Click or tap the **Make Everything on Your Screen Bigger** switch to the **On** position. Windows 8 immediately scales up the text and other screen items to make them appear larger.

Magnifying the Screen

Windows 8 comes with a feature called Magnifier that can zoom in on specific areas of the screen, which is useful if you come across an icon or some text that's too small to make out. Follow these steps to use Magnifier:

1. On the Start screen, type **magnifier** and then select the **Magnifier** icon.

2. Select **Views** and then select **Lens**. Magnifier displays a rectangle that magnifies whatever area of the screen it's over.

3. Select **Zoom In** (the + icon) or **Zoom Out** (the – icon) until you get the magnification you want.

4. Move the mouse pointer over the area you want to magnify (the lens moves along with the mouse pointer). Figure 6.8 shows the Magnifier lens zoomed in on a portion of the File Explorer ribbon.

Magnifier also offers the following keyboard shortcuts:

Press	To
Ctrl+Alt+F	Turn off the lens and see the full screen
Ctrl+Alt+L	Display the lens
Windows Logo+Plus sign (+)	Increase the magnification
Windows Logo+Minus sign (–)	Decrease the magnification

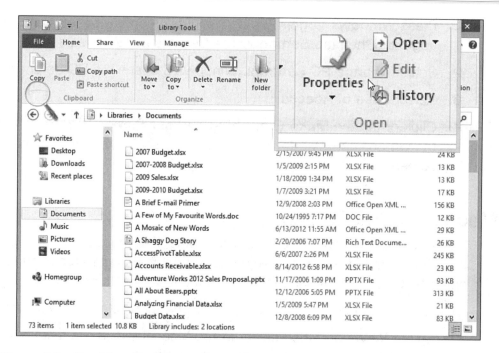

Figure 6.8 *Use Magnifier's lens tool to enlarge parts of the screen.*

Switching to a High-Contrast Screen

If you're having trouble making out text because it seems to blend in with the other colors on the screen, you can configure your PC to display a high-contrast screen that shows white text on a black background and other vivid color combinations.

Follow these steps to apply a high-contrast theme:

1. Press **Windows Logo+I** (or, on a touchscreen, swipe left from the right edge and then tap **Settings**). The Settings pane appears.

2. Select **Change PC Settings**. Windows 8 opens the PC Settings app.

3. Select **Ease of Access**.

4. Click or tap the **High Contrast** switch to the **On** position. Figure 6.9 shows the **Ease of Access** screen with high contrast turned on.

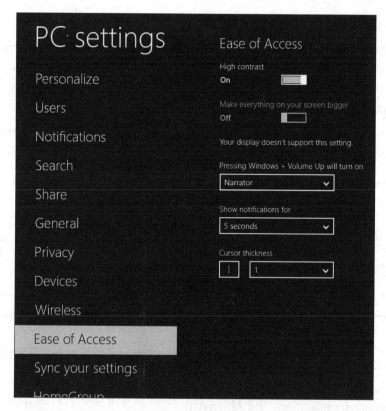

Figure 6.9   *The Ease of Access screen with the High Contrast switch in the On position.*

Making the Cursor Easier to See

When you select a text box, Windows adds a vertical line—called the *cursor*—inside the box, and that line tells you where the next character will appear. The line blinks on and off (so that you don't confuse it with, say, the letter *I* or the number *1*), but it's quite thin and therefore hard to see. You can make it easier to see by following these steps to widen the blinking cursor:

1. Press **Windows Logo+I** (or, on a touchscreen, swipe left from the right edge and then tap **Settings**). The Settings pane appears.

2. Select **Change PC Settings**. Windows 8 opens the PC Settings app.

3. Select **Ease of Access**.

4. Use the **Cursor Thickness** list to select the size you want to use. (The preview box on the left shows you an example.)

Hearing What's on the Screen

If you find that you're really having trouble making out what's on the screen, Windows comes with an assistive technology called Narrator that can help. Narrator's job is to read aloud whatever text appears in the current window or dialog box. Narrator also does many other things, including the following:

- Tells you the name of the current window or dialog box and lists the contents of that window or dialog box.

- Tells you the name of the dialog box control that currently has the focus, the type of control (for example, a check box), and the control's current state (for example, checked).

- Echoes your most recent keystroke. For example, if you press Tab to move to the next dialog box control, Narrator says "Tab."

- Tells you the text of the selected link in Internet Explorer.

To turn on this feature, display the Start screen, type **narrator**, and then select the **Narrator** tile. To turn off Narrator later on, click the **Desktop** tile, click the **Narrator** button in the taskbar, click **Exit**, and then click **Yes** when it asks you to confirm.

Tip

An Easier Narrator Start

If your PC has a Volume Up key or button, you can also start Narrator by pressing **Windows Logo+Volume Up**.

Adjusting the Volume

If your hearing has deteriorated over the years, or if you have a hearing impairment in one or both ears, detecting system sounds and enjoying music and movies can be a challenge. Fortunately, help is at hand, because Windows 8 has a few tools that you can configure to help or work around your hearing issues.

The *system volume* is the volume that Windows uses for all things audio on your computer: the sounds that Windows itself makes (warning beeps, the logon and logoff tones, and so on) and the sounds that waft from your applications (such as music from Media Player and the new-mail notification from Windows Live Mail).

Windows 8 offers two methods for controlling the system volume:

- If you're hanging out in the Start screen, press **Windows Logo+I** to open the Settings pane, click the **Speaker** icon, and then drag the slider up or down to set the volume.

- If you're on the desktop, click the **Volume** icon in the taskbar's notification area to open the Volume Control, shown in Figure 6.10. Use your mouse to drag the slider to the volume level you prefer, or click **Mute Speakers** to get the sounds of silence.

The Mute button

The Volume icon

Figure 6.10   *Click the Volume icon and then drag the slider to set the system volume.*

Note

Speakers or Headphones?

If your hearing loss is severe, consider using headphones instead of speakers. Headphone sounds take a shorter and more direct path to your ear, which can make the sounds sharper and easier to discern. If you use an in-the-ear (ITE) hearing aid, look for ear-pad headphones (also called on-ear headphones), which rest on your ears; if you use a behind-the-ear (BTE) hearing aid, you'll need to move up to full-size headphones (also called full-cup, ear-cup, or over-the-ear headphones), which are large enough to cover not only your ear but also your hearing aid microphone.

If your hearing aid comes with a telecoil mode (which enables the hearing aid to process sounds sent electromagnetically), be sure to get telecoil-compatible headphones (which broadcast sounds electromagnetically).

Overcoming Physical Limitations

If you find that your PC is hard to use because of some physical limitations, Windows 8 offers a few tools that can help, as you see in the next couple of sections.

Showing Notifications for a Longer Time

When something happens on your PC, such as an incoming email or instant message, Windows 8 displays a notification, which is a banner that appears in the upper-right corner of the screen. You can then click the banner to see the message or perform some other task. Unfortunately, the banner appears for only about five seconds, so you might not be able to react in time to click the notification. If that happens once too often, fight back by following these steps to select a longer time to display notifications:

1. Press **Windows Logo+I** (or, on a touchscreen, swipe left from the right edge and then tap **Settings**). The Settings pane appears.

2. Select **Change PC Settings**. Windows 8 opens the PC Settings app.

3. Select **Ease of Access**.

4. Use the **Show Notifications For** list to select the amount of time you want Windows 8 to display the notification banners.

Controlling Your PC with Speech Recognition

If due to injury or age you find that using a mouse and keyboard is too time-consuming, too difficult, or too frustrating, you might think you're out of luck—because how else are you supposed to control your computer? Fortunately, there *is* another way: voice commands. Using the Speech Recognition feature, you can speak commands into a microphone, and Windows will do your bidding.

 Tip

Speech Recognition By the Numbers

One of Speech Recognition's handiest tricks is for you to say "Show numbers," which then overlays a number on everything in the current window that can be clicked. You can then say the number of the item you want and say "OK," and Speech Recognition will "click" that item for you *and* tell you the correct command name.

Does it really work? Actually, most of the time, yes—it really does. Windows 8 has very good voice-recognition technology, and as long as you're in a relatively quiet room and speak clearly, Windows will recognize actions such as *click, double-click,* and *select;* commands such as *Save, Copy,* and *Close;* keystrokes such as *Backspace, Delete,* and *Enter;* and screen features such as *Minimize, Scroll,* and *Back.*

To start, you need to attach a microphone to your computer. A microphone that's part of a headset is easiest to use, but you can also use a standalone microphone that sits on your desk.

With your microphone attached to your computer, your next task is to configure the Speech Recognition feature:

1. In the Start screen, type **speech** and then click **Windows Speech Recognition**. The Setup Speech Recognition wizard appears.

2. Click **Next**. The wizard asks what type of microphone you have.

3. Make your selection (such as **Headset Microphone** or **Desktop Microphone**); then click **Next**. The wizard displays a screen that tells you about the proper placement of your microphone.

4. After you've read the text and made the necessary adjustments, click **Next**. The wizard now displays some text for you to read aloud.

5. Read the text in your normal voice; then click **Next**. The wizard lets you know that your microphone is set up and ready for use.

6. Click **Next**. Now, the wizard asks whether it can examine your documents to look for words that it should learn.

7. This is a good idea, so select **Enable Document Review** and click **Next**. Now, the wizard wants to know how you want to activate speech recognition.

8. The easiest route here is to select **Use Voice Activation Mode**, which means you can start Speech Recognition by saying "Start listening" and stop Speech Recognition by saying "Stop listening." (If you choose **Use Manual Activation Mode** instead, you must manually activate Speech Recognition each time by pressing **Windows Logo+Ctrl** or by clicking the microphone icon in the Speech Recognition window.) Click **Next**. The wizard suggests that you print the Speech Reference Card, which contains a list of useful commands.

9. If you want to print the card, click **View Reference Card** and then click the **Print** button in the Help window that appears.

10. Return to the Set Up Speech Recognition wizard (if you printed the card in the previous step); then click **Next**. The wizard wonders whether you want to start Speech Recognition automatically each time you start your computer.

11. This is a good way to go, so leave the **Run Speech Recognition at Startup** check box activated and click **Next**. The wizard now offers to take you through a Speech Recognition tutorial, which enables you to practice the voice commands.

12. The tutorial is definitely worthwhile, so click **Start Tutorial**.

13. When you're done, click **Finish**.

With all that out of the way, you can start using Speech Recognition, which appears as a small window at the top of the desktop. You speak your commands, and Speech Recognition either carries them out or says "What was that?" if it doesn't recognize what you said.

Chapter 7

Dealing with Digital Photos

A *digital photo* is a photographic image that, instead of residing on film (which those of us of a certain age still remember) or as a print, resides on your PC's hard drive or on a memory card. The "digital" part just means that the photo consists of the same electronic bits and pieces as anything else that's stored on your PC—files, documents, apps, and so on. Having your photos in digital form makes it easy to organize and view your photos, run a slideshow, and manipulate your photos (for example, by removing bits of the photo you don't want).

Windows 8 isn't a digital photo powerhouse by any stretch of the imagination, but it does come with some tools that help you perform these and a few other photo-related tasks. This chapter provides you with the details.

Getting Photos onto Your PC

You can't do much of anything with Windows 8's photo tools until you get some honest-to-goodness photos on your PC. Fortunately, Windows 8 can help here by offering a wealth of ways to get digital photos from out there to in here. In all, there are four methods you can use, and the next four sections take you through the necessary steps.

Transferring Photos from a Digital Camera

The most common scenario these days is to take a bunch of photos using a digital camera, which might be either a dedicated camera or a smartphone that comes with a camera feature. Either way, your next chore is to transfer some or all of those photos from the camera to your PC.

Begin by connecting your digital camera to your PC. How you proceed from here depends on whether this is the first time you're connecting your camera. Here are the various possibilities:

- **Connecting your digital camera for the first time**—In this case, after a few seconds you see a notification similar to the one shown in Figure 7.1. Select the notification to see a list of actions you can perform with the camera and then select **Import Photos and Videos**. Windows displays a list of the photos on the digital camera.

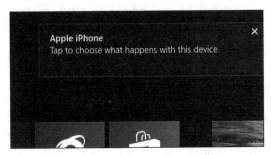

Figure 7.1 *You see a notification similar to the one shown here the first time you connect your digital camera.*

- **Connecting your digital camera after the first time**—Since you've already told Windows what action you want to take when you connect your digital camera, Windows just goes ahead and performs that action automatically. In this case, Windows displays a list of the photos on the digital camera.

- **Connecting your digital camera does nothing or you miss the notification**—If nothing happens when you connect your digital camera, or if the notification disappears before you have a chance to select it, you're not out of luck. On the Windows 8 Start screen, select the **Photos** tile to launch the Photos app. Right-click the screen (or swipe up from the bottom edge of a touchscreen) and then select **Import**. In the **Choose a Device to Import From** dialog box (see Figure 7.2), select your digital camera. Windows displays a list of the photos on the digital camera.

Figure 7.2 *Open the Photos app, display the app bar, select Import, and then select your camera.*

Whichever scenario you're in, you end up seeing a list of the photos on the digital camera. Follow these steps to proceed from here:

1. Select **Clear Selection**.

2. Select each photo you want to import. The Photos app adds a check mark to the upper-right corner of each selected photo, as shown in Figure 7.3.

3. Use the text box at the bottom of the screen to type a name for the folder that Windows 8 will use to store the photos.

4. Select **Import**. Windows 8 imports the photos to your PC.

When the import is complete, you can either select **Open Folder** to display the photo files or press **Windows Logo** to return to the Start screen.

Figure 7.3 *Photos selected for import have a check mark in the upper-right corner.*

Transferring Photos from a Memory Card

If your photos are located on a memory card, the import process is similar:

1. Insert the memory card.

2. As with a digital camera, the next step you take depends on whether you've inserted a memory card previously:

   - If this is the first time you've inserted the memory card, you see a notification like the one shown in Figure 7.4. Select the notification that appears and then select **Import Photos and Videos**.

   - If you've inserted the memory card before, Windows 8 should take you straight to the list of photos on the card, so you don't need to do anything at this stage.

- If Windows 8 does nothing when you insert the memory card, open the **Photos** app, right-click the screen (or swipe up from the bottom edge), select **Import**, and then select your memory card.

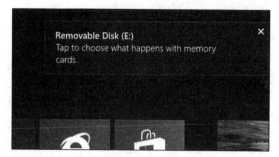

Figure 7.4 *You see a notification similar to the one shown here the first time you insert a memory card.*

3. When Windows displays a list of the photos on the memory card, select **Clear Selection**.

4. Select each photo you want to import.

5. Use the text box at the bottom of the screen to type a name for the folder that Windows 8 will use to store the photos.

6. Select **Import**. Windows 8 imports the photos to your PC.

Scanning a Photo

If you have a document scanner or a multifunction printer that includes a scanning feature, you can use it to turn a hard-copy photo into a digital photo on your PC. Windows 8 comes with a Scanner and Camera Wizard to give you a step-by-step method for scanning photos. First, place the photo on the scanner glass. Then launch the **Scanner and Camera Wizard** using either of the following methods:

- If your printer has some kind of scan button, press that button.

- On the Start screen, press **Windows Logo+W**, type **devices**, select **Devices and Printers**, select your printer, and then select **Start Scan**.

Whichever method you choose, you see the New Scan dialog box. You can select the **Preview** button to see what your image will look like before fiddling with any of the options or committing yourself to the scan. A preview of your scan appears as shown in Figure 7.5.

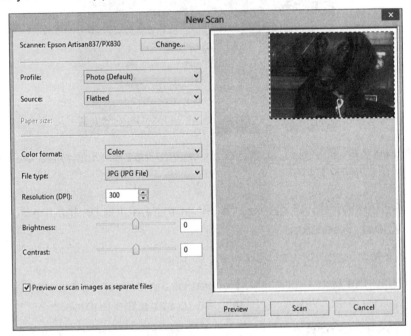

Figure 7.5 *You use the New Scan dialog box to scan a photo from a multifunction printer.*

If the dotted rectangle in the preview area isn't the same size as the image, click and drag the bottom-right corner of the rectangle to make it the same size (as I've done in Figure 7.5).

When you're ready to scan, select **Scan**. After Windows 8 scans the image, the Importing Pictures and Videos dialog box appears. Select the **Import All New Items Now** option, type a name for the image in the text box, and then select **Import**.

Note

Adjusting the Resolution

Before scanning, you might want to adjust the Resolution value. The *resolution* determines the overall quality of the scanned photo: The higher the resolution, the higher the quality but the bigger the resulting file. Resolution is measured in dots per inch (DPI).

Taking a Photo with the PC's Camera

If your PC has either a built-in camera or an external camera connected to a USB port, you can use the Windows Camera app to take a picture. This feature is great for self-portraits, but you can also take shots of your surroundings, particularly if you're using a tablet PC that has a rear camera.

Follow these steps to take a picture using the Camera app:

1. On the Start screen, select the **Camera** tile to open the Camera app. The first time you do this, Windows 8 asks if the Camera app can use your camera (which Windows 8 called a *webcam*) and microphone.

2. Select **Allow**. The Camera app loads and you see a live shot of yourself (or something near you, depending on where your PC's camera is pointing).

3. Aim your camera as needed.

4. If you'd like the Camera app to delay slightly before taking the shot, select **Timer**. (Note: This button is "on" when it has a white background.)

5. If you want to take a video instead of a photo, select the **Video Mode** button. (Again, this button is "on" when it has a white background.)

6. Click or tap the screen. If you turned on Timer mode, there's a three-second delay before you hear a shutter noise and the Camera app snaps a photo. If you're recording a video, the app beeps and then begins the recording.

7. If you're recording a video, click or tap the screen when you're done.

The Camera app saves your photo or video into a new album called Webcam that it adds to your Pictures library (see the next section to learn more about this library).

Viewing Photos

Now that you've loaded up your PC with a few photos, you're ready to start viewing them, either by scrolling through them manually or by playing a slideshow. Windows keeps your photos in a special storage location called the Pictures library, which usually consists of several folders that Windows created when you imported photos from a digital camera or memory card. There's also a folder called Webcam that contains photos you've taken with the Camera app.

Looking Through Your Photos

To get started, select the Start screen's **Photos** tile to open the Photos app and then select the **Pictures Library**. This opens the Pictures Library, which includes a tile for each folder within your Pictures library as well as for any individual photos that aren't part of any album (see Figure 7.6).

> ### Note
>
> **Facebook, SkyDrive, and Flickr Photos**
>
> When you first load the Photos app, you might notice the three other tiles there: Facebook, SkyDrive photos, and Flickr photos. They are Internet-based photo services, and to use them, you need a Microsoft account (see Chapter 10, "Getting Online").

Figure 7.6   *The Photos app displays a tile for each folder in the Pictures library.*

Select the folder you want to view and then double-click a photo to open it up full screen. From here, you navigate the photos like so:

- **View the next photo**—Move the mouse pointer over the current photo and then click the right arrow or press the **right-arrow** key on the keyboard; on a tablet, slide the current photo off to the left.

- **View the previous photo**—Move the mouse pointer over the current photo and then click the left arrow or press the **left-arrow** key on the keyboard; on a tablet, slide the current photo off to the right.

- **Jump to any photo**—Press **Esc** to return to the album, use the scrollbar to locate the photo (or swipe your touchscreen), and then double-click the photo.

Watching a Photo Slideshow

Viewing photos one at a time by hand gives you control over what you view and how long you view it, but it's a bit of work. If you feel like making your PC do some of the work for a change, follow these steps to see a slideshow of the photos in a Pictures library folder:

1. Run the Photos app and open the **Pictures** library.

2. Open the folder you want to view.

3. (Optional) To start the slideshow with a particular photo, double-click that photo to open it.

 Tip

Using a Photo as the Lock Screen Background

You can use one of your own photos as the background image for the Windows 8 Lock screen. To set this up, use the Photos app to open the folder that contains the photo you want to use and then open the photo itself. Right-click the screen (or swipe up from the bottom edge), select **Set As**, and then select **Lock Screen**.

 Tip

Deleting a Photo

To delete a photo you no longer want to keep, use the Photos app to open the folder that contains the photo you want to delete and then open the photo itself. Right-click the screen (or swipe up from the bottom edge) and then select **Delete**. When Photos asks you to confirm, select **Delete**.

4. Right-click the screen (or swipe up from the bottom edge of your touchscreen) and then select **Slide Show**. Photos begins running through the photos, with each photo displayed onscreen for about three seconds.

5. When you're done, press **Esc** to stop the slide show. Press **Esc** again to exit the current image.

Fixing Your Photos

No matter how good your photography skills, mistakes happen. Your photo might be rotated the wrong way, or the image includes some extra, unwanted material (such as a thumb). The Photos app can help here, but only just: The app comes with just two tools for fixing your photos—one for rotating photos and another for cropping out unwanted elements. The next two sections provide you with the details.

Note

Not All Tools Are Available For All Photos

The Photos app's scant editing tools are even more limited in that they're not available for all types of photos. If you follow the techniques that I outline in the next two sections and find that you don't see the tools that I describe, it means that they're not available for that particular type of image.

Rotating a Photo

All digital cameras enable you to rotate the camera to pictures that are either wider than they are tall (this is called *landscape* orientation because the typical shot would be a wide landscape) or taller than they are wide (this is called *portrait* orientation because the typical shot would be a picture of a person). If you find that you have a photo that isn't being displayed with the correct orientation, you can use the Photos app to rotate the photo into the correct position. Here are the steps to follow:

1. Run the Photos app and open the **Pictures** library.

2. Open the folder that contains the photo you want to rotate.

3. Double-click the photo to open it.

4. Right-click the screen (or swipe up from the bottom edge of your touchscreen) and then select **Rotate**. The Photos app rotates the photo 90 degrees clockwise.

5. Repeat step 4 until the photo is in the correct orientation.

Cropping Out Unwanted Elements

Despite your best efforts, you might end up with a photo that includes some unwanted element near the edge of the photo. It might be a tree branch that you didn't notice, a person who walked into the frame at the last second, or a bit of a finger that accidentally covered part of the lens.

Fortunately, you can get rid of these eyesores by cutting them out of the photo using a process known as *cropping*. With this technique, you specify a rectangular area of the photo that you want to keep. Anything outside that rectangle is removed from the photo. Here's how it works:

1. Run the Photos app and open the **Pictures** library.

2. Open the folder that contains the photo you want to crop.

3. Double-click the photo.

4. Right-click the screen (or swipe up from the bottom edge of your touchscreen) and then select **Crop**. The Photos app displays the cropping rectangle on your photo, as shown in Figure 7.7.

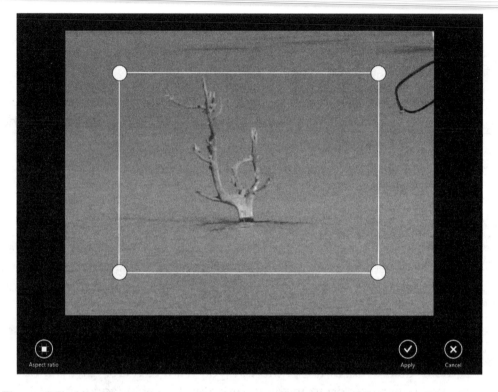

Figure 7.7 *Use the cropping rectangle to specify the area of the photo that you want to retain.*

5. Drag the corners of the rectangle to set the area of the photo that you want to preserve.

6. Select **Apply**. The Photos app crops the photo.

Chapter 8

Working with Digital Music

You might be used to dealing with music that comes in a physical format, such as an audio CD, a cassette, or even a vinyl album. I hate to be the bearer of sad tidings, but these physical music formats are now—or really, have been for a number of years—at the very least old-fashioned, but are more accurately described as obsolete. What's taken their place? *Digital* music, which refers to songs and albums that are made from the same electronic stuff as the rest of the files on your PC. Digital music's main advantages are that it's much easier to buy, and it enables you to find and play music quickly. Some audiophiles think digital music doesn't sound as good as analog (physical) music, but most people can't tell the difference.

This chapter introduces you to Windows 8's two main music tools: the Music app and the Media Player program.

Easy Listening with the Music App

At this point you might be wondering just how you're supposed to get some of this newfangled digital music onto your PC. There are actually many ways to go about this, but the two most common are to purchase songs or albums and to copy tracks from an audio CD to your PC. In Windows 8, the easiest way to purchase new music is to use the Music app, which you learn about in the following section. You use Media Player to copy tracks from an audio CD, so I cover that a bit later in this chapter (see "Copying Music from a Music CD").

Navigating the Music App

You use the Music app to play the music that's on your PC or to purchase new songs or albums. Go ahead and click or tap the Start screen's **Music** tile to load the app. The main Music screen is divided into four sections, which are arranged side by side, so you navigate them by using the scrollbar or by flicking the touchscreen left and right. Here's a summary of the four sections, from left to right:

- **My Music**—This section displays tiles for several of your albums, plus an extra tile that includes a **Play All Music** button. See "Playing Music" to learn more about this section.

- **Now Playing**—This section offers previews of upcoming music. Click a tile and then click **Play Top Songs** to hear snippets from the album. This section also includes a large **Now Playing** tile that tells you what's currently playing in the app.

- **All Music**—This section offers several tiles for newly released albums. You can also click **All Music** to see a complete list of new music organized by genre.

- **Top Music**—This section offers several tiles for the most popular albums. You can also click **Top Music** to see a complete list of popular music organized by genre.

Buying Music

When you're ready to buy music, select an album to open it (see Figure 8.1) and then click **Play** to get a taste. If you like what you hear, select **Buy Album**. Alternatively, if you want only a particular song, select it, right-click the screen (or swipe up from the bottom edge of a tablet) and then select **Buy Song**.

Note

Microsoft Account Required

To purchase music, you need to configure your Windows 8 user account to use a Microsoft account. See "Creating a Microsoft Account" in Chapter 10, "Getting Online."

Figure 8.1 *When you open an album, you can either buy the entire album or just a song.*

Either way, you then follow these steps to complete your purchase:

1. If you haven't yet specified a payment method or if you don't want to use the displayed payment method, select **Change Payment Option**. Either select a different payment option and select **Next**; or select **Add a New Credit Card**, enter your card details, and then select **Save**.

2. Select **Confirm**. The Music app finalizes the purchase.

3. Select **Done**. The Music app returns you to the album info screen and begins downloading the album or song.

4. When the download is complete, select **Play** to launch the music.

Note

Credit Card Safety

As I explain in more detail in Chapter 14, "Maximizing Internet Security and Privacy," you should always exercise caution when giving out your credit card number online. However, the Music store is run by Microsoft, one of the most trusted companies in the world, so you're safe giving out your credit card number here.

Searching for Music

If you can't find what you want in the Music app (and you probably can't), use the Search feature to find what you're looking for:

1. While you have the Music app onscreen, display the Charms menu by pressing **Windows Logo+C** or swiping in from the right edge.

2. Select **Search** to open the Search pane for the Music app.

3. Type the name of the band, album, or song you're looking for.

4. In the search results, select the band, album, or song to open it within the Music app.

Playing Music

When you have some music on your PC, the Music app's My Music section displays tiles for several of your albums, plus an extra tile that includes a Play All Music button. To see all your music, select **My Music**. To listen to an album, select it and then select **Play Album**. When you have an album open, you can also select a song and then select **Play** (see Figure 8.2) to hear just that song. Click **Add to My Music** to show the current music in the main screen's **My Music** tile.

Right-click the screen to display the playback controls. You can then click the **Pause** button to stop playback (and **Play** to resume it); **Next** to skip to the next track; **Previous** to return to the previous track; **Shuffle** to play the songs randomly; or **Repeat** to play the album continuously.

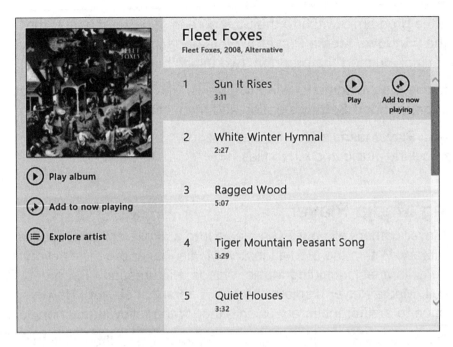

Figure 8.2 *In the Music app, select My Music, select an album to open it, and then select either Play Album or select the song you want to play.*

Making Beautiful Music with Media Player

The Music app is great if all you want to do is buy and play albums and songs. However, if you want to go beyond that—specifically, if you want to copy tracks from a music CD to your PC and to create your own custom audio CDs—you need to look elsewhere. That is, you need to give a program called Windows Media Player a try. Media Player is a kind of one-stop media shop, with support for playing not only digital music and music CDs, but also digital videos, Internet radio, and recorded TV shows. And, for our purposes in much of what follows, Media Player is also the Windows 8 program of choice for copying tracks from music CDs and making your own audio CDs.

To start the program, switch to the Start screen, type **media**, and then select the **Windows Media Player** tile that appears in the search results. The first time you start the program, two things happen:

- You see the Welcome to Windows Media Player dialog box. Select the **Recommended Settings** option and then select **Finish**.

- Media Player takes a few minutes to scour your PC for media, particularly music and video files.

Navigating Media Player

Media Player gathers all your PC's media into a single collection called the Media Library. Within the Media Library, Media Player organizes everything into several libraries, including Music, Videos, Pictures, and Recorded TV. By default, Media Player displays the Music library at startup. However, you can change to a different library using either of the following techniques:

- Click the **Library** list (pointed out in Figure 8.3) and then click the library you want.

- Use the navigation pane (also pointed out in Figure 8.3) to select the library you want.

The information near the top of the window tells you the name of the current library as well as the current view, which is a way of organizing the media. For example, in the Music library, you can organize the tunes by artist, album, or genre.

Playing Music

To play some music in Media Player, first locate the album or song you want to play. Note that if you switch to a different view, you usually need to double-click an icon to see an item in that view. For example, if you switch to **Artist** view, you need to double-click the icon for an artist to see a list of that artist's albums and songs. After you've located what you want to play, double-click it to start the music.

Figure 8.3 *You navigate to a different library using either the Library list or the navigation pane.*

To control the playback, you can use the following buttons at the bottom of the Media Player program (see Figure 8.4):

- **Turn shuffle on/off**—Toggles shuffle mode on and off. Shuffle mode means that the songs in the current album play in random order.

- **Turn repeat on/off**—Toggles repeat mode on and off. When repeat mode is on, Media Player plays the current album file over and over.

- **Stop**—Stops the music and returns to the beginning of the file (or to the beginning of the current music CD track).

- **Previous**—Plays the previous song.

- **Play/Pause**—Starts the song or pauses the song when it's playing.

- **Next**—Plays the next song.

- **Mute**—Turns off the sound.

- **Volume**—Controls the playback volume. Drag the slider to the left to reduce the volume or to the right to increase the volume.

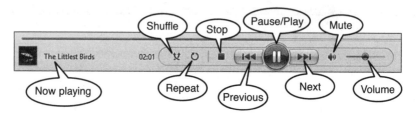

Figure 8.4 *Use the buttons at the bottom of the Media Player window to control the music playback.*

Playing a Music CD

Later in this chapter, I show you how to copy tracks from a music CD to your PC. However, you can also just listen to tunes directly from a music CD. When you insert a music CD into your PC's optical drive, Windows 8 wakes up and displays a notification asking what you want to do with music CDs each time you insert them, as shown in Figure 8.5. Click the notification to see a list of choices similar to the one shown in Figure 8.6 and then select **Play Audio CD**.

Figure 8.5 *You see this notification the first time you insert a music CD.*

> ### ✔ Tip
>
> Many of today's keyboards are media-enhanced, which means they come with extra keys that perform digital media functions such as playing, pausing, and stopping media; adjusting the volume; and changing the track. In addition, here are a few Windows Media Player shortcut keys that you might find useful while playing media files:
>
> Ctrl+P Play or pause the current song
>
> Ctrl+S Stop the playback
>
> Ctrl+B Go to the previous song
>
> Ctrl+F Go to the next track
>
> Ctrl+H Toggle shuffle mode
>
> Ctrl+T Toggle repeat mode
>
> F7   Mute sound
>
> F8   Decrease volume
>
> F9   Increase volume

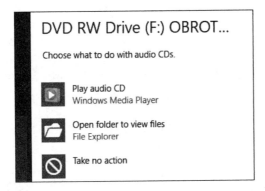

Figure 8.6 *Click the notification and then click Play Audio CD.*

If you don't currently have Media Player running, you see a smaller version of the program called the Now Playing window, shown in Figure 8.7. When you move the mouse pointer over the Now Playing window, you see the playback buttons as shown in Figure 8.7. You can control the playback from there, or you can select the **Switch to Library** icon to return to the full Media Player window.

Figure 8.7 *Move the mouse pointer over the Now Playing window to see the playback controls.*

Copying Music from a Music CD

Windows Media Player comes with the welcome capability to copy (*rip* in the vernacular) tracks from a music CD to your PC's hard disk. This feature enables you to play the album on your PC without having to insert the disc, which is much more convenient.

Here are the steps to follow:

1. Insert the audio CD.

2. If the notification appears, click it and then click **Take No Action**.

3. If the Now Playing window appears, select **Switch to Library**.

4. In the navigation pane, select the name of the music CD. Media Player displays a list of the tracks on the CD.

5. Deselect the check boxes beside any tracks you don't want to copy.

6. Select **Rip CD**. Media Player begins copying the tracks to your PC and uses the **Rip Status** column to show the progress (see Figure 8.8): You see **Ripped to Library** for completed tracks; **Ripping** for the track currently being copied; and **Pending** for tracks not yet copied.

Note

Ejecting the CD

When the copying is complete, you can eject the CD by right-clicking it in the navigation pane, and then selecting **Eject**.

Figure 8.8 *The Rip Status column tells you which tracks have been copied and which track is currently being copied.*

Copying Music to a Recordable CD

Windows Media Player can also perform the opposite task: copying media files from your computer to a recordable CD or portable device.

Creating a Playlist

Most people find recording is easiest if it's done from a *playlist*, a customized collection of music files. Here's how to create a new playlist:

1. Select the **Playlists** library.

2. Select **Create Playlist**. Media Player adds the new playlist.

3. Type a name for the playlist and press **Enter**.

4. For each song you want to include in the new playlist, right-click the song, select **Add To**, and then select the name of the playlist. You can also use your mouse to click and drag a song and then drop it on the name of the playlist in the navigation pane.

After your playlist has been created, you can edit the list by selecting it in the navigation pane. Use your mouse to drag the songs up or down to set the order you prefer them to play. To remove a song, right-click it and then select **Remove from List**.

Recording to a CD

Here are the steps to follow to record (or *burn*) music files to a recordable CD:

1. Insert a recordable CD. Windows 8 displays a notification asking what you want to do with blank CDs.

2. Click the notification and then click **Burn an Audio CD**. Windows 8 opens Media Player and displays the Burn tab on the right.

3. For each playlist or song you want to burn, drag it from the library to the Burn tab. Media Player adds each track to the Burn List, as shown in Figure 8.9.

Note

Watch Your Minutes

The Burn tab tells you the number of minutes of music you have added (see Figure 8.9). An audio CD can hold a maximum of about 70 minutes of music, so be sure to add close to that amount to the Burn List.

4. Click **Start Burn**. Media Player begins copying the tracks to the recordable CD.

Figure 8.9 *To create a custom audio CD, first add tracks to the Burn tab's Burn List.*

Chapter **9**

Working with Digital Video

Digital video refers to any video content that can be played directly on your PC. It could be home movies that you record yourself using a smartphone, camcorder, or digital camera or commercial releases such as motion pictures and TV show episodes. Windows 8 doesn't offer many video-related tools, but it does enable you to import videos from your smartphone, camcorder, or digital camera, and it does let you rent or purchase movies and TV show episodes. You can then use the Video app to watch your video right on your monitor.

This chapter shows you how to import videos, buy or rent videos, and play videos on your PC.

Importing Video to Your PC

If you enjoy recording videos of family affairs, vacations, and other life events, you probably don't want to watch them on your camera's teensy playback screen. A much better option is to import those videos to your PC where you can then use the Video app to watch them on the relatively spacious expanse of your monitor. The next two sections show you how to import videos using a smartphone, camcorder, digital camera, and a memory card.

Importing Video from a Smartphone, Camcorder, or Digital Camera

Follow these steps to import one or more videos from a smartphone, camcorder, or digital camera to your PC:

1. Connect your smartphone, camcorder, or digital camera to your PC. After a few seconds, you see a notification similar to the one shown in Figure 9.1.

Figure 9.1 *You see a notification similar to the one shown here the first time you connect a smartphone, camcorder, or digital camera.*

2. Select the notification. Windows 8 displays a list of actions, as shown in Figure 9.2.

Figure 9.2 *Click the notification to see this list of actions.*

3. Select **Import Photos and Videos**. Windows displays a list of the photos and videos on the camcorder or digital camera.

4. Select **Clear Selection**.

5. Select each video you want to import. Videos have a right-pointing arrow with a circle around it, as you can see in Figure 9.3.

Figure 9.3 *In the list of files on the smartphone, camcorder, or digital camera, the videos are shown with a right-pointing arrow.*

6. Use the text box at the bottom of the screen to type a name for the folder that Windows 8 will use to store the videos.

7. Select **Import**. Windows 8 imports the videos to your PC.

When the import is complete, you can either select **Open Folder** to display the video files or press **Windows Logo** to return to the Start screen.

Importing Video from a Memory Card

If your videos are located on a memory card, the import process is similar:

1. Insert the memory card. After a few seconds, you see a notification like the one shown in Figure 9.4.

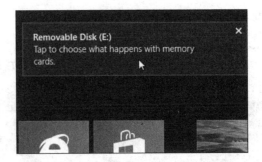

Figure 9.4 *When you insert the memory card, you see a notification similar to the one shown here.*

2. Select the notification. Windows 8 displays a list of actions.

3. Select **Import Photos and Videos**. Windows displays a list of the photos and videos on the memory card.

4. Select **Clear Selection**.

5. Select each video you want to import.

6. Use the text box at the bottom of the screen to type a name for the folder that Windows 8 will use to store the videos.

7. Select **Import**. Windows 8 imports the videos to your PC.

Navigating the Video App

You use Windows 8's Video app to play the digital videos that are on your PC, to purchase or rent movies, or to purchase TV show episodes. The main Video screen is divided into four sections, which are arranged side by side, so you navigate them by using the scrollbar or by flicking the touchscreen left and right. Here's a summary of the four sections, from left to right:

• **My Videos**—This section displays tiles for several of your videos.

• **Spotlight**—This section offers previews of upcoming movies and TV shows. This section also includes a Now Playing tile that shows you what's currently playing in the app.

- **Movies Store**—This section offers several tiles for newly released movies. You can also click **Movies Store** to see a complete list of movies organized by various categories (Featured, New Releases, Top Selling, Genres, and Studios).

- **Television Store**—This section offers several tiles for new TV shows. You can also click **Television Store** to see a complete list of TV shows organized by various categories (Featured, Last Night's Shows, Free TV, Top Selling, Genres, and Networks).

Renting or Buying Videos

As I mentioned earlier, besides importing your own videos into your PC, the other main way to load up your computer with video content is to throw some money at the problem. Using the Video app, you can rent movies, purchase movies, and purchase TV show episodes. The next few sections provide the details.

Renting a Movie

With the exception of some recently released films, the movies you see on the Video app are available for rent. You have 14 days to begin watching the movie and then 24 hours to complete the movie after you start watching it. Here are the steps to follow to rent a movie:

1. Start the **Video** app, if you haven't done so already.

2. Select **Movies Store**.

3. Select a Movies Store category: **New Releases**, **Featured**, **Top Selling**, **Genres**, or **Studios**.

4. Select a subcategory. For example, if you selected the **Genres** category, select a subcategory such as **Action/Adventure** or **Comedy**.

> ### Note
>
> **Microsoft Account Required**
>
> To buy or rent a movie or purchase a TV show episode, you need to configure your Windows 8 user account to use a Microsoft account. See "Creating a Microsoft Account" in Chapter 10, "Getting Online."

5. Use the **Arrange By** list to sort the movies based on one of the following: **Top Rented**, **Top Selling**, or **Release Date**.

6. Select the movie you want to rent. The Video app displays the movie details, as shown in Figure 9.5.

Note

Searching for Movies

If you can't find the movie you want, see "Searching for Movies and TV Shows," later in this chapter.

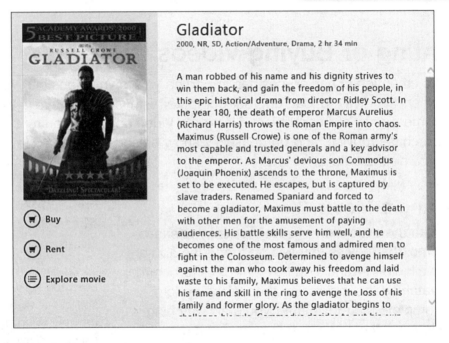

Gladiator

2000, NR, SD, Action/Adventure, Drama, 2 hr 34 min

A man robbed of his name and his dignity strives to win them back, and gain the freedom of his people, in this epic historical drama from director Ridley Scott. In the year 180, the death of emperor Marcus Aurelius (Richard Harris) throws the Roman Empire into chaos. Maximus (Russell Crowe) is one of the Roman army's most capable and trusted generals and a key advisor to the emperor. As Marcus' devious son Commodus (Joaquin Phoenix) ascends to the throne, Maximus is set to be executed. He escapes, but is captured by slave traders. Renamed Spaniard and forced to become a gladiator, Maximus must battle to the death with other men for the amusement of paying audiences. His battle skills serve him well, and he becomes one of the most famous and admired men to fight in the Colosseum. Determined to avenge himself against the man who took away his freedom and laid waste to his family, Maximus believes that he can use his fame and skill in the ring to avenge the loss of his family and former glory. As the gladiator begins to

Buy

Rent

Explore movie

Figure 9.5 *Select a movie to open it.*

7. Select **Rent** and then enter your Microsoft account password. The Viewing Options screen appears.

8. Select how you want to rent the movie:

   • **Download**—Choose this option to wait until the entire movie is on your PC before watching it, which means you don't need to be connected to the Internet to watch the movie. In some cases you also have a choice between standard definition (SD) or high definition (HD). The latter is higher quality but more expensive.

- **Stream**—Choose this option to begin watching the movie right away, although you need to remain connected to the Internet while the movie is playing. Again, some movies offer both SD and HD streams.

9. Select **Next**.

10. If you haven't yet specified a payment method or if you don't want to use the displayed payment method, select **Change Payment Option**, select **Add a New Credit Card**, enter your card details, and then select **Save**.

11. Select **Confirm**. The Video app finalizes the rental.

12. Select **Done**. The Video app returns you to the movie info screen.

13. If you elected to download the movie, select **Download**.

14. If you elected to stream the movie, or if the download is complete, and you're ready to start watching the show, return to the main Video app screen, display the **My Videos** section, and then select your movie.

Buying a Movie

Here are the steps to follow to purchase a movie:

1. Start the **Video** app.

2. Select **Movies Store**.

3. Select a Movies Store category: **New Releases**, **Featured**, **Top Selling**, **Genres**, or **Studios**.

4. Select a subcategory. For example, if you selected the **Genres** category, select a subcategory such as **Action/Adventure** or **Comedy**.

5. Use the **Arrange By** list to sort the movies based on one of the following: **Top Rented**, **Top Selling**, or **Release Date**.

6. Select the movie you want to purchase.

7. Select **Buy** and then enter your Microsoft account password. For most movies, the Viewing Options screen appears.

8. Select either **HD** (if available) or **SD** and then click **Next**.

9. Select **Confirm**. The Video app finalizes the purchase.

10. Select **Done**. The Video app returns you to the movie info screen and begins downloading the movie.

11. Return to the main Video app screen, display the **My Videos** section, and then select your movie.

Buying a TV Show Season or Episode

Here are the steps to follow to purchase a season or an episode of a TV show:

1. Start the **Video** app.

2. Select **Television Store**.

3. Select a Television Store category: **New Releases**, **Featured**, **Last Night's Shows**, **Top Selling**, **Genres**, or **Networks**.

4. Select a subcategory. For example, if you selected the **Genres** category, select a subcategory such as **Drama** or **News**.

Note

Searching for TV Shows

If you can't find the show you want, see "Searching for Movies and TV Shows," later in this chapter.

5. Use the **Arrange By** list to sort the shows based on one of the following: **Top Selling** or **Release Date**.

6. Select the show you want to purchase.

7. Select **View Seasons**. The Video app displays a list of the show's seasons.

8. Select the season you want. The Video app displays information about the show, as well as a list of the season's episodes (see Figure 9.6).

9. To purchase the entire season, select **Buy Season** and then enter your Microsoft account password. To purchase a single episode, instead, select the episode and then select **Buy Episode**. For most shows, the Viewing Options screen appears.

10. Select either **HD** (if available) or **SD** and then click **Next**.

11. Select **Confirm**. The Video app finalizes the purchase.

12. Select **Done**. The Video app returns you to the TV show info screen and begins downloading the show.

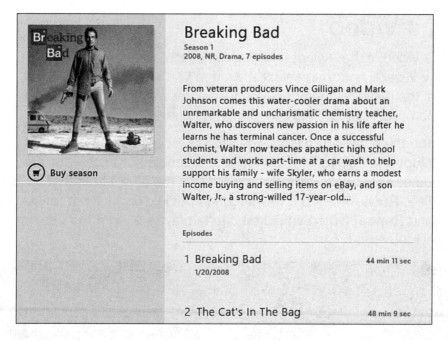

Buy season

Breaking Bad

Season 1
2008, NR, Drama, 7 episodes

From veteran producers Vince Gilligan and Mark
Johnson comes this water-cooler drama about an
unremarkable and uncharismatic chemistry teacher,
Walter, who discovers new passion in his life after he
learns he has terminal cancer. Once a successful
chemist, Walter now teaches apathetic high school
students and works part-time at a car wash to help
support his family - wife Skyler, who earns a modest
income buying and selling items on eBay, and son
Walter, Jr., a strong-willed 17-year-old...

Episodes

1 Breaking Bad   44 min 11 sec
  1/20/2008

2 The Cat's In The Bag   48 min 9 sec

Figure 9.6 *Select a season to see a description of the TV show and a list of the
season's episodes.*

13. Return to the main Video app screen, display the **My Videos** section,
and then select your show.

Searching for Movies and TV Shows

The Video app offers access to a large collection of movies and TV shows,
but chances are you're having trouble finding specific movies or shows.
To work around this problem, use the **Search** feature to find what you're
looking for:

1. While you have the Video app onscreen, display the **Charms** menu by
pressing **Windows Logo+C** or swiping in from the right edge.

2. Select **Search** to open the Search pane for the Video app.

3. Type the name of the movie, TV show, actor, or director you're looking for.

4. In the search results, select the movie or show to open it within the
Video app.

Playing a Video

To view a video, either select it in the Video app's **My Videos** section, or select **My Videos** and then select the video you want to watch. For a digital video file, the playback begins immediately; for a commercial movie or TV show, you need to select **Play** to get things started.

Click or tap the screen to display the playback controls (see Figure 9.7), which include the **Pause/Play** button and a scrubber to scroll through the video. You can also right-click the screen to a set of controls that include **Pause/Play**, **Previous** (skip a few seconds back), **Next** (skip a few seconds ahead), and **Repeat** (when activated, starts playback from the beginning after the video ends).

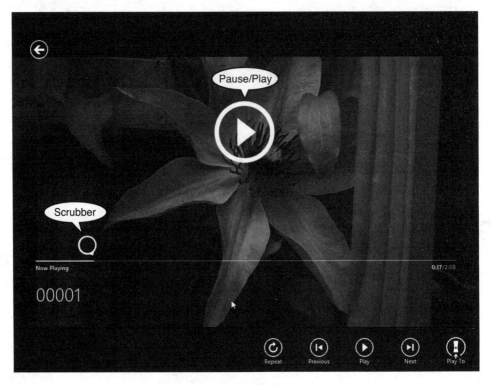

Figure 9.7 *Click or tap the screen to see the controls.*

Playing Video on Your TV

There are many ways to configure your PC as an entertainment hub, but the simplest and most common is to connect the PC to a TV, which enables you to "watch" what's on the PC using the TV instead of a regular computer monitor. In particular, it means that whatever you do with the Video app—watch a digital video file, movie, or TV show—appears on the TV.

How you connect your computer to the TV depends on the configuration of both, but you need to know two basic concepts:

- You attach one end of a cable to a video output port on your PC and the other end to an input port in back of your TV.

- The PC port and the TV port either must be the same type, or you can get an adapter (such as a DVI-to-HDMI adapter).

For example, if you have a newer HDTV and PC, you most likely need an HDMI cable. If your equipment is a bit older, you most likely need component cables or an S-Video cable instead. Even older than that, and you'll most likely be using a cable with RCA connectors, which are the red, white, and yellow jacks that were commonly used with audiovisual equipment.

Chapter **10**

Getting Online

As you've seen so far, you can do plenty of things with your PC right out of the box, including managing your photos, listening to music, and watching videos. However, if you want to get the most out of your PC investment, you need to think outside the PC box and get yourself connected to the Internet.

This chapter helps you do just that by showing you how to set up a *broadband* Internet connection, which is a high-speed connection provided by your local cable company, a phone company (which usually calls the connection a Digital Subscriber Line), or via satellite. I'm going to assume that you already have an account and that the broadband provider has given you a device called a *broadband modem* that handles the connection.

In this chapter, you learn about two ways to set up the connection:

- If you're the only person who will be using the Internet and don't need to access the connection from different places in your home, I show you how to connect the modem directly to your computer.

- If you want to share that connection with other people in your home or if you want to be able to access that connection from anywhere in your home, I show you how to set up a wireless connection to the broadband modem.

Getting Online Using a Broadband Modem Connected Directly to Your PC

A *broadband modem* is a high-speed modem used for *Digital Subscriber Line (DSL)*, cable, or satellite Internet access. In almost all cases, the *Internet service provider (ISP)* provides you with a broadband modem that's compatible with its service. Getting the broadband modem connected is the first step in putting your network together.

Of the two connection types I mentioned in the introduction to this chapter, by far the most common is the wireless connection. I show you how that works a bit later, but note that such a setup is not required for many situations. For example, if you have only one computer and don't need to access the connection from different places in your home, there's no need to set up wireless access to the Internet, so you should connect the broadband modem directly to your PC. Similarly, even if you have multiple computers, for safety reasons you might prefer that only one of them access the Internet (for example, you might not want small children having direct access to the Internet).

Begin by connecting and plugging in the modem's power adapter. Make sure the modem is turned off. If the modem doesn't come with a power switch, unplug the power adapter for now.

Attaching the Internet Connection Cable

The next step is to attach the cable that provides the ISP's Internet connection:

- **DSL broadband modem**—Run a phone line from the nearest wall jack to the appropriate port on the back of the modem, which is usually labeled DSL, as shown in Figure 10.1.

Note

Installing Phone Filters

Many DSL providers require that you install a phone filter device to protect your telephones. Each phone filter comes with two phone jacks, usually labeled Line and Phone. Run a phone cable from the wall jack to the Line port on the phone filter, and run a second phone cable from the Phone port on the filter to your telephone. You need to do this for each telephone in your home or office.

Figure 10.1 *For a DSL broadband modem, plug a phone cable into the DSL port on the back of the modem.*

- **Cable broadband modem**—Run a TV cable line from the nearest wall jack to the cable connector on the back of the modem, which is usually labeled Cable, as shown in Figure 10.2.

Figure 10.2 *For a cable broadband modem, plug a TV cable into the Cable connector on the back of the modem.*

Connecting the Modem to Your PC

Now you need to connect your broadband modem to your PC. Most broadband modems give you two ways to do this (see Figure 10.3):

- **Ethernet**—All broadband modems have a network port on the back that's labeled Ethernet, LAN, or 10BASE-T. Run a network cable from this port to a network port on your PC.

- **USB**—Most newer broadband modems also come with a USB port on the back. If you're working with a PC that doesn't yet have a network port, or if the network port already has a cable attached, you can use USB instead. Run a USB cable from the USB port on the modem to a free USB port on your PC. You also need to install the broadband modem's USB device driver, which should be on a CD that your ISP provided.

> **! Caution**
>
> **Network *or* USB, Not Both**
>
> On the broadband modem, use either the network port or the USB port, but not both. Connecting both ports to your PC can damage the modem.

Figure 10.3 *Almost all newer broadband modems come with both a network port (labeled Ethernet here) and a USB port.*

Turn on the broadband modem and wait until it makes a connection with the line. All broadband modems have an LED on the front that lights up to indicate a good connection. Look for an LED labeled Online, DSL, or something similar, and wait until you see a solid (that is, not blinking) light on that LED.

Registering the Modem

How you proceed from here depends on the ISP. Nowadays, many ISPs insist that you register the broadband modem by accessing a page on the ISP's website and sometimes entering a code or the serial number of the modem. Read the instructions that came with your ISP's Internet kit to determine whether you must first register your broadband modem online.

Creating a Windows 8 Broadband Internet Connection

If you have a broadband account with your Internet service provider, and you have connected your broadband modem directly to your PC as described in the previous sections, you can configure Windows 8 to use a broadband Internet connection. This type of connection works with the PPPoE (this stands for Point-to-Point Protocol over Ethernet) connection type, so first make sure your ISP supports that type. To create the connection, you also need to know the username and password that Windows 8 must enter to authorize the connection.

Here are the steps to follow:

1. On the Start screen, press **Windows Logo+W** to open the Settings search pane.

2. Type **broadband** and then click the **Set Up a Broadband Connection** item that appears in the search results. Windows 8 opens the Create a Broadband Connection dialog box.

3. Type the username of your broadband Internet account.

4. Type your account password.

5. To avoid having to type the password when you connect in the future, select the **Remember This Password** check box.

6. Edit the connection name, if desired. Figure 10.4 shows a filled-in version of the Create a Broadband Connection dialog box.

7. Click **Create**. Windows 8 sets up the connection.

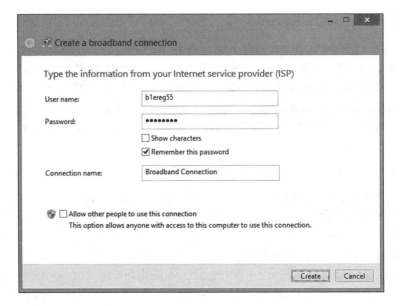

Figure 10.4 *Fill in the Create a Broadband Connection dialog box.*

Making the Connection

With your broadband connection ready to go, follow these steps to get online:

1. On the Start screen, press **Windows Logo+I** to display the Start settings pane.

2. Select **Network**. The Networks pane appears.

3. Select the broadband connection you created in the previous section.

4. Select **Connect**. Windows 8 connects to your ISP through the broadband modem.

Note

Disconnecting

If you don't want other people to use your computer to access the Internet while your computer is unattended, it is best to disconnect. To do this, press **Windows Logo+I** to open the **Start** settings pane, select **Network**, select the broadband connection, and then select **Disconnect**.

Getting Online Using a Wireless Broadband Connection

Connecting a broadband modem directly to a PC is the simplest way to get online, but it's not always the most convenient. For example, if other people in your house want to use the Internet, they must do so through the same PC that's connected to the modem. Similarly, if you have a notebook or other portable PC, you may be able to take the PC to different places in your house, but you can't take the Internet connection with you.

The solution to both problems is to create a *wireless* broadband connection that enables other PCs to share the same connection and enables you to access the connection from different parts of your house.

What Is Wireless Networking?

Wireless devices transmit data and communicate with other devices using *radio frequency* (RF) signals that are beamed from one device to another. Although these radio signals are similar to those used in commercial radio broadcasts, they operate on a different frequency. For example, if you use a wireless keyboard and mouse, you have an RF receiver device plugged into, usually, a USB port on your computer. The keyboard and mouse have built-in RF transmitters. When you press a key or move or click the mouse, the transmitter sends the appropriate RF signal, that signal is picked up by the receiver, and the corresponding keystroke or mouse action is passed along to Windows, just as though the original device had been connected to the computer directly.

A *radio transceiver* is a device that can act as both a transmitter and a receiver of radio signals. All wireless devices that require two-way communications use a transceiver. In wireless networking (also called a *wireless local area network* [WLAN]), your PC uses a special network adapter that comes with a built-in transceiver that enables the adapter to send and receive RF signals. (For more information, see "Understanding Wireless Network Adapters," next.)

The resulting beam takes the place of the network cable. The wireless network adapter communicates with a nearby *wireless access point*, a device that contains a transceiver that enables the device to pass along network signals. (For more details, see "Understanding Wireless Routers," later in this chapter.)

The most common wireless networking technology is *wireless fidelity*, which is almost always shortened to *Wi-Fi* (which rhymes with *hi-fi*).

Understanding Wireless Network Adapters

As I mentioned in the preceding section, wireless networking requires that your PC have a wireless network adapter, which is a transceiver that can both transmit data to the network and receive signals from the network.

There are two main types of wireless network adapters:

- **Internal**—This type is an internal card that inserts into a free slot inside your computer. This is the most common type, and almost all PCs come with an internal wireless network adapter preinstalled. The back of the adapter usually includes a small post onto which you screw the antenna, either directly or via a longish wire that enables you to position the antenna to avoid interference. Figure 10.5 shows both types.

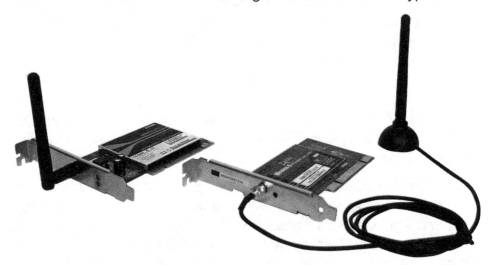

Figure 10.5 *Examples of internal wireless network adapters.*

- **External**—If you don't feel comfortable installing an internal circuit board (and there's no one hardware savvy nearby to do it for you), you can still go wireless by attaching an external wireless network adapter to an open

USB port. USB wireless network adapters either attach directly to the USB port, or they come with a USB cable, as shown in Figure 10.6.

Figure 10.6   *Examples of external wireless network adapters.*

Understanding Wireless Routers

A *wireless router* (Figure 10.7 shows a couple of examples) is a device that receives and transmits signals from wireless computers to form a wireless network, as shown in Figure 10.8.

Figure 10.7   *Examples of wireless routers.*

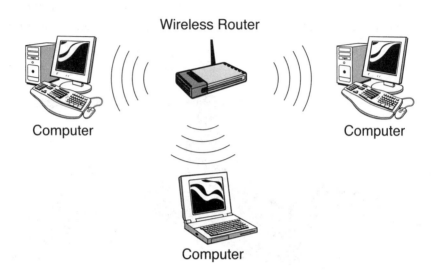

Figure 10.8   *Add a wireless router to create a wireless network.*

Gaining wireless access to other computers on your network and being able to share files are worthy goals, but what we're really after here is wireless Internet access, not only for your PC but also for the other PCs on your network. Fortunately, wireless routers have the capability of connecting to your ISP via your broadband modem. When the wireless router has that connection going, your PC and all your network PCs can share it and access the Internet wirelessly.

The secret is to connect the wireless router and the broadband modem, as shown in Figure 10.9. Before getting to that, however, you have to configure the wireless router to connect to your ISP, which is the subject of the next section.

Configuring the Wireless Router to Connect to Your ISP

The main point of adding a wireless router to your network is to share a broadband Internet connection with the network computers, which means users don't have to worry about either setting up a connection or logging on to the Internet. With the broadband modem connected to the wireless router, the latter takes over the duties of initiating and managing the Internet connection. Before it can do that, however, you need to configure the router with the Internet connection settings that your broadband provider provided to you.

Figure 10.9 *With a combination wireless router and modem, you can give wireless network users access to the Internet.*

Your broadband connection will almost certainly fall under one of the following types:

- **Dynamic (DHCP)**—With this connection type, your ISP provides the router with its external IP address automatically. Some ISPs require that you configure the router with a specific name and also that you specify a hostname (also called a system name or an account name) and a domain name. This is the most common type of broadband connection, particularly with cable providers.

- **Static**—With this type of connection, your ISP gives you an IP address that never changes, and you must configure the router to use this as its external IP address. Your ISP will in most cases also provide you with a subnet mask, gateway IP address, and one or more *domain name server* (DNS) addresses. This type of broadband connection is rare these days.

- **PPPoE**—With this connection type, your ISP provides you with a username and password that you use to log on. Some ISPs also require that you configure the router with a specific name, and also that you specify a hostname and domain name. This type of broadband connection is most commonly used with DSL providers.

- **PPTP**—With this type of connection, your ISP usually provides you with a static IP address, subnet mask, gateway IP address, username, and password. This broadband connection type is mostly used by DSL providers in European countries.

- **Telstra BigPond**—With this connection type, your ISP provides you with a username and password. This broadband connection type is used by Australian DSL providers.

The Internet kit provided by your ISP tells you which of these connection types it requires. How you set this up varies depending on the wireless router, but here are the general steps to follow:

1. Make sure the Internet connection cable is attached to the broadband modem (see "Attaching the Internet Connection Cable," earlier).

2. Connect the broadband modem to your PC (see "Connecting the Modem to Your PC," earlier).

3. On your PC, select **Internet Explorer**.

4. Type the wireless router address and press **Enter**.

5. If you see a message telling you that private network access is off for this site, select **Turn On Access**.

6. If required, type the wireless router's username and password. The wireless router's setup page appears. Note that the layout of the setup page varies depending on the device.

 Tip

For most wireless routers, an easier way to access the router is to switch to the Start screen, type **network**, and then select the **Network** icon in the search results. In the Network window, look in the **Network Infrastructure** section for an icon that represents your wireless router. Double-click the icon. Internet Explorer appears and accesses the wireless router.

7. Select the type of broadband connection your ISP uses.

8. Type the connection's username and password. Figure 10.10 shows a sample router page for setting up a PPPoE connection.

9. Save your changes.

Note

If you're not sure of the wireless router's address, username, or password, see the manual that came with the wireless router.

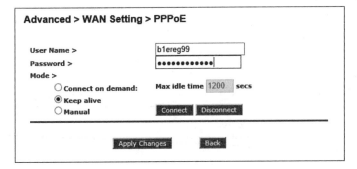

Figure 10.10 *A typical wireless router setup page for a PPPoE broadband Internet connection.*

Configuring Your Wireless Network Settings

While you have your wireless router's setup pages open, you should also take a few minutes to configure a couple of settings for your wireless network. Look for a "WiFi" or "Wireless network" section (see Figure 10.11 for an example) and then configure the following three settings:

• **Network name**—This is the name of your wireless network, which is often called the *service set identifier*, or *SSID*. All routers come with a default SSID, usually some variation on the manufacturer's name, such as linksys or belkin54g. Changing the SSID to something memorable will help you to identify your network in the Windows list of available wireless networks, and it will prevent confusion with other nearby wireless networks that still use the default name.

• **Authentication**—This is the type of security your network uses. Security is crucial if you don't want total strangers accessing your network (and, believe me, you don't), so choose the WPA2 (or WPA2PSK) option.

- **Password**—This is the password that you and others will use to access your wireless network. This is sometimes called the *security key* or the *preshared key*. You should assign a strong password here to prevent others from accessing your network. See Chapter 13, "Getting More Out of the Web," to learn how to create a strong password.

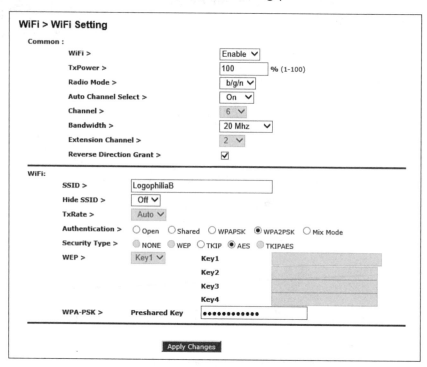

Figure 10.11 *A typical wireless router setup page for wireless network settings.*

Registering the Modem

If your ISP insists that you register the broadband modem by accessing a page on the ISP's website and sometimes entering a code or the serial number of the modem, this is the time to do that. Read the instructions that came with your ISP's Internet kit to determine whether you must first register your broadband modem online.

Connecting the Broadband Modem to the Wireless Router

You're now ready to set up your broadband modem so that its Internet connection can be shared with each computer and device on your network. You do that by connecting the broadband modem to your router. First, however, make sure that you turn off the modem and disconnect the network or USB cable that is connecting the router and your PC.

Examine the back of your wireless router and locate the port that it uses for the Internet connection. Some access points label this port WAN (see Figure 10.12), whereas others use Internet (see Figure 10.13). Some routers don't label the Internet port at all, but instead place the port off to the side so that it's clearly separate from the router's network ports.

Figure 10.12   *Some wireless routers use the label WAN to indicate the port used for the Internet connection.*

Figure 10.13   *On other routers the Internet connection port is labeled Internet.*

With the broadband modem and router turned off, run a network cable from the broadband modem's network port to the WAN port on the router. Figure 10.14 shows a sample setup (using DSL).

Tip

On my network, I keep the broadband modem and the wireless router side by side on a desk so that I can easily see the LEDs on the front of both devices (particularly the LED on the broadband modem that indicates a good Internet connection). If you do this, purchase a 1-foot Ethernet cable to connect to the two devices.

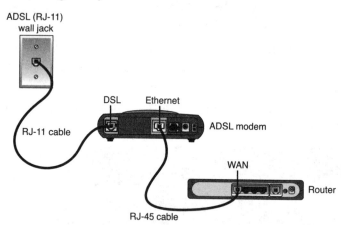

Figure 10.14 *Connect the broadband modem's network port to the router's WAN or Internet port.*

You're now ready to turn on your devices. Begin by turning on the broadband modem and waiting until it has a solid connection with the line. Then turn on your router.

Connecting to Your Wireless Network

At long last, you're ready to connect to your wireless network. This gives you online access through your wireless router's Internet connection. Here are the steps to follow:

1. Press **Windows Logo+I** to open the Settings pane.

2. Select the **Network** icon. Windows 8 displays a list of nearby wireless networks.

3. Select your wireless network.

4. To have Windows 8 connect to your network automatically in the future, select the **Connect Automatically** check box.

Note

To disconnect from the network, press **Windows Logo+I**, select the **Network** icon, select your network, and then select **Disconnect**.

5. Select **Connect**. Windows 8 asks you to enter your network security key (that is, your password).

6. Type the security key.

7. Select **Next**. Windows 8 connects to the network.

Creating a Microsoft Account

Now that you're online, you're free to surf the Web, exchange email, and much more, all of which I cover in the next few chapters. Before we get to all that, however, let's take a second to create a Microsoft account. Why? Simply because you can get more—*much* more—out of Windows 8 by using a Microsoft account with your Windows 8 user account.

When you connect a Microsoft account to your Windows 8 user account, many previously inaccessible Windows 8 features become immediately available. For example, you can use the Mail app to access your email and the Messages app to exchange text messages with other Microsoft account users. You can also download apps from the Windows Store; purchase music, movies, and TV shows; access your photos and documents anywhere online; and even sync your settings with other PCs where you use the same account.

Here are the steps to follow to get started creating a Microsoft account:

1. Press **Windows Logo+I** to open the Settings pane.

2. Select **Change PC Settings** to open the PC Settings app.

3. Select the **Users** tab.

4. Select **Switch to a Microsoft Account**. Windows 8 asks you to verify your current account password.

5. Type your password and then select **Next**. Windows 8 asks you to enter your email address.

6. Type your email address. You have three ways to proceed here:

   • **Use an existing Live.com or Hotmail.com address**—If you already have a Microsoft email address that ends with @live.com or @hotmail.com, type that address, select **Next**, type the account password, and then select **Next**.

- **Create a new Live.com or Hotmail.com address**—If you want to create a new address that ends with @live.com or @hotmail.com, type the username you prefer to use, followed by either **live.com** or **hotmail.com**, and then select **Next**. Assuming the username has not been taken, Windows 8 will recognize that this is a new address and create the new account automatically. From here, type your password in both text boxes, type your first and last name, choose your country, type your ZIP code, and then select **Next**.

- **Use a non-Microsoft email address**—Windows 8 doesn't require that you use a Live.com or Hotmail.com email address from Microsoft. If you have an email address that you use regularly, you are free to use that same address with your Windows 8 account. Type the address and then select **Next**.

Another advantage you get with using a Microsoft account with Windows 8 is that it can also help you if you forget your account password and cannot log in. You can provide Microsoft with your mobile phone number, so that if you ever forget your password, Microsoft sends you a text message to help you reset your password. You can also give Microsoft an alternative email address, or you can provide the answer to a secret question.

To provide this data, you use the **Add Security Verification Info** screen, shown in Figure 10.15. Note that Windows 8 requires you to choose at least two of these three methods before it lets you complete your account.

If you're creating a new account, Windows 8 asks for some extra information, as shown in Figure 10.16. Fill in your birth date, gender, and the text you see in the box. Select **Next** and then select **Finish** to complete your account setup.

Windows 8 connects the Microsoft account to your user account, so the next time you start Windows 8, use your Microsoft account email address and password to log in.

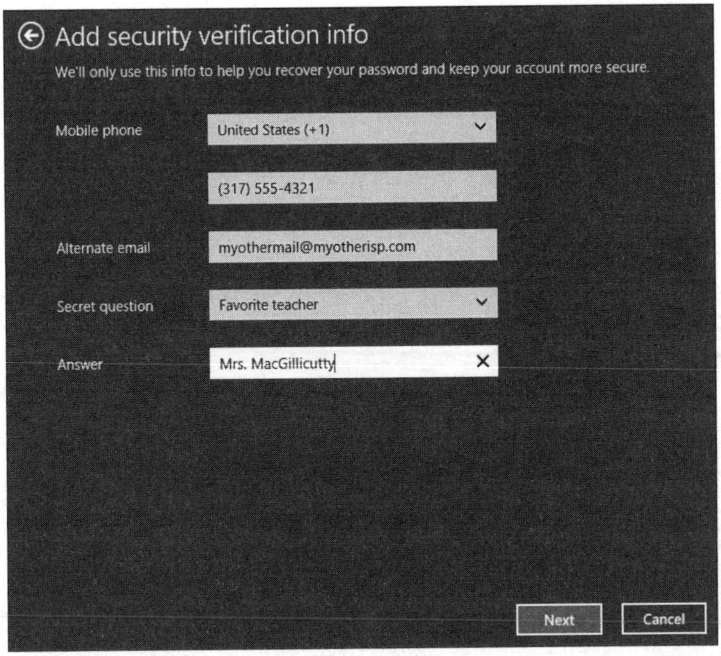

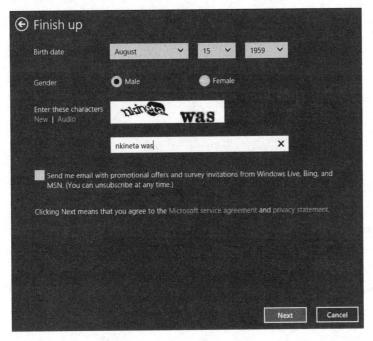

Figure 10.15 *The information you provide here can help you recover your Windows 8 password if you forget it later.*

Figure 10.16 *Complete your new Microsoft account by filling in this screen.*

Chapter 11

Surfing the Web

After all your hard work getting yourself online in the preceding chapter, it's time to reap the harvest and enjoy the bounty that is otherwise known as the Internet. In this chapter, I introduce you to the biggest online bounty of them all: the World Wide Web—or simply the Web, as everyone calls it nowadays. Actually, it would almost be better to shorten its name to the "World" because in some very meaningful ways the Web is a kind of online mirror of the world around us.

For example, the Web is an online repository for information about, well, pretty much everything. If you can think of a topic, chances are someone somewhere on the Web has put up some information about it. You'll also find lots of people on the Web, and online socializing has become one of the world's most popular pastimes. You can also shop on the Web, sell things, share photos, read news, perform research, view maps, and much more.

You learn about most of these activities in Chapter 13, "Getting More Out of the Web." For now, this chapter serves as an introduction to the Web and how to navigate it using Windows 8.

Understanding the Web

Before getting down to the specifics of navigating the Web, let's take a few moments to understand a bit more about it. Here's a list of a few key concepts you need to know:

- **Web browser**—This is a program on your PC that you use to navigate the Web. In Windows 8, the default web browser is called Internet Explorer.

- **Web page**—Almost everything you see on the Web is presented to you in the form of a web page, which you display on your PC using a web browser. Each web page can combine text with images, sounds, music, and even videos to present you with information on a particular subject. The Web consists of billions of pages covering almost every imaginable topic.

- **Website**—This term refers to a collection of web pages associated with a particular person, business, government, school, or organization. Some websites deal with only a single topic, but most sites contain pages on a variety of topics.

- **Web server**—Websites are stored on a web server, which is a special computer that makes web pages available for people to browse. A web server is usually a powerful computer capable of handling thousands of site visitors at a time. The largest websites are run by *server farms*, which are networks that may contain hundreds or even thousands of servers.

- **Link**—This is a kind of cross-reference to another web page. A link can appear as text that is usually underlined and in a different color from the regular text on the page. A link can also appear as an image. When you click the link, the other page loads into your web browser automatically. The link can take you to another page on the same site, or to a page on another website.

- **Web address**—Every website and web page has its own web address that uniquely identifies the site or page. This address is the uniform resource locator, or URL (pronounced *yoo-ar-ell* or *erl*). If you know the address of a page, you can type that address into your web browser to view the page.

- **URL**—The URL of a website or page usually takes the following form:

  http://*host.domain/directory/file.name*

host.domain	The domain name of the host computer where the page resides.
directory	The host computer directory that contains the page.
file.name	The page's filename. Note that most web pages use the extensions `.html` or `.htm`.

  Most web domains use the www prefix and the com suffix (for example, www.mcfedries.com). Other popular suffixes are edu (educational sites), gov (government sites), net (networking companies), and org (not-for-profit sites). Note, too, that most servers don't require the www prefix (for example, mcfedries.com).

Surfing the Web with Internet Explorer

As I mentioned earlier, your vehicle for your Web surfing safaris is the Internet Explorer browser, which you can load by selecting the Start screen's **Internet Explorer** tile. Figure 11.1 shows the Internet Explorer app.

What you see when you open Internet Explorer will be quite a bit different from what I've shown in Figure 11.1, but the following are universal features of Internet Explorer and whatever page you see:

- **Lots of links**—Most web pages contain quite a few links to other pages. These links sometimes appear underlined or in a different color, but most of the time they appear just as regular text.

- **The "pointing finger" mouse pointer**—If a link appears as regular text, how do you know what's a link and what isn't? The only surefire way to tell is to position the mouse pointer over the text. If the regular mouse pointer changes to a hand with a pointing finger, as shown in Figure 11.1, you know you're dealing with a link.

- **The link address banner**—When you point to a link, Internet Explorer also shows you the address of whatever page the link takes you to. This address appears in a banner that pops up near the bottom-left corner of the screen, as pointed out in Figure 11.1.

Figure 11.1 *A typical web page shown in the Internet Explorer app.*

- **The Address box**—This text box appears in the Internet Explorer app bar at the bottom of the screen and shows the address of the current page.

The first page you see when you launch Internet Explorer might have lots of interesting things to read, but you'll eventually want to explore more of the Web. The easiest way to go about that is to select a link to open the page associated with that link. You can then click another link on that page, another link on the page that follows, and so on. This is called *surfing* the Web, and it's a classic technique for exploring the online world (and, yes, using up quite a bit of time!).

Entering a Web Page Address

Alternatively, if you know the address of the page you want to visit, click or tap inside the **Address** box. (If you don't see the Address box onscreen, press **Alt+D**; you can also right-click the screen or swipe up from the bottom edge and then click or tap inside the Address box.) Internet Explorer hides the rest of the app bar and displays just the Address box. As you can see in Figure 11.2, Internet Explorer also displays the *Frequent list,* which includes tiles for the web pages you've visited most often so far. If you see the page you want in that list, select its tile. Otherwise, type the page address and then either press **Enter** or select the **Go** button (pointed out in Figure 11.2).

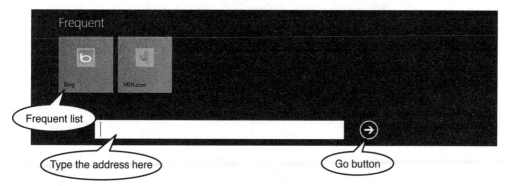

Figure 11.2 *Click or tap inside the Address box to type the address of the page you want to visit.*

 Tip

Easier Addressing

Here are a few tips to bear in mind when entering web page addresses using the Address box:

- Internet Explorer monitors the address as you type. If any previously entered addresses match your typing, they appear in a Results list shown above the Address box. If you see the page you want, select it from that list.

- Internet Explorer assumes that any address you enter is for a website. Therefore, you don't need to type the http:// prefix because Internet Explorer adds it for you automatically.

- Internet Explorer also assumes that most web addresses are in the form http:// www.*something*.com. Therefore, if you type just the *something* part and press **Ctrl+Enter**, Internet Explorer automatically adds the http://www. prefix and the .com suffix. For example, you can get to the Microsoft home page (http://www. microsoft.com) by typing **microsoft** and pressing **Ctrl+Enter**.

Navigating the Pages You've Visited

To return to a page you visited previously in this session, either select Internet Explorer's **Back** button (see Figure 11.3) or press **Alt+Left arrow**. After you go back to a page, you move ahead through the visited pages by selecting the **Forward** button (again, see Figure 11.3) or pressing **Alt+Right arrow**.

Figure 11.3 *You can use the Back and Forward buttons to revisit pages you've surfed in the current session.*

Opening Multiple Pages with Tabs

Surfing from link to link and address to address is a great way to discover new things and get acquainted with the Web's myriad resources and sites. However, what if you come across a useful or entertaining page that you know you'll want to refer to again? If you surf to another page or two, you can use the **Back** button to return to that page, but that's not always convenient. Wouldn't it be nice if there was a way to keep a page open while you surf to other pages?

Happily, I can tell you that Internet Explorer offers a feature called *tabbed browsing* that gives you a way to do this. When you create a new tab in Internet Explorer, you're essentially opening up a second copy of the browser. Your current page remains open in the original version of Internet Explorer and you can then open a completely different page in the second version of the app.

You can even open more tabs if you need to reference multiple pages, and Internet Explorer makes it relatively easy to switch from one open tab to the other. The next couple of sections give you more details on using tabbed browsing with the Internet Explorer app.

Opening a Page in a New Tab

Tabs are only as useful as they are easy to use, and Internet Explorer does a decent job of smoothing the transition to tabbed browsing. One way that it does this is by giving you a satisfyingly wide variety of methods to use for opening a page in a new tab. There are four in all:

- **Hold down Ctrl and click a link in a web page.** This technique creates a new tab and loads the linked page in the background.

- **Right-click a link and then click Open Link In New Tab.** This technique creates a new tab and loads the linked page in the background.

- **Type the page URL in the Address box and then press Alt+Enter.** This technique creates a new tab and loads the page in the foreground.

- **Right-click (or swipe down from the top edge) and then select the New Tab (+) button (see Figure 11.4; you can also press Ctrl+T) to display a blank tab.** Type the page URL in the Address box and then press **Enter** or select **Go**. This loads the page in the foreground.

Figure 11.4 shows Internet Explorer with several tabs open.

Figure 11.4 *Internet Explorer supports tabbed browsing to enable you to keep multiple pages open at once.*

Navigating Tabs

When you have two or more tabs open, navigating them is straightforward:

- Right-click the screen (or swipe down from the top edge) and then select the tab of the page you want to use.

- With your keyboard, press **Ctrl+Tab** to navigate the tabs from left to right (and from the last tab to the first tab); press **Ctrl+Shift+Tab** to navigate the tabs from right to left (and from the first tab to the last tab).

To close a tab, right-click the screen (or swipe down from the top edge) and then select the tab's **Close Tab** button (see Figure 11.4).

Searching the Web

Veteran surfers, having seen a wide range of what the Web has to offer, usually prefer to tackle it using a targeted approach that enables them to find information quickly and do research. This means using one or more of the Web's many search engines (such as Bing.com or Google.com). It's usually best to deal with a search engine site directly, but Windows 8 offers two easier Web searching options:

- **Internet Explorer**—With the Internet Explorer app onscreen, press **Windows Logo+C** or swipe left from the right edge to display the **Charms** menu and then select **Search**. Enter your search term (or terms) in the Search box and then press **Enter** or select **Search** (the magnifying glass).

- **Bing**—On the **Start** screen, select the **Bing** tile to open the Bing app. Use the large text box to type your search terms and then press **Enter** or select **Search**.

Bing displays tiles showing the search results. Select the tile you want, and Windows 8 switches to Internet Explorer to load the page.

Refining Your Search Results

Depending on the search term you use, your search will likely return thousands or even millions of results. If the information you seek doesn't appear in the first couple of pages of results, you need to refine your search. Try entering two or more words that define what you're looking for. To match an exact phrase, surround it with quotation marks. You can also separate two terms with **OR** to return pages that match one term or the other (or both).

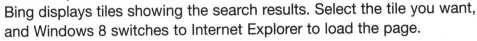

Saving Your Favorite Pages

The sad truth is that much of what you'll see on the Web is utterly forgettable and not worth a second look. However, there are all kinds of gems waiting to be uncovered—sites you'll want to visit regularly. Instead of memorizing the appropriate addresses or jotting them down on sticky notes, you can keep track of your choice sites using Internet Explorer, which offers a couple of methods.

Adding a Page to the Internet Explorer Favorites List

Internet Explorer maintains a list called Favorites that enables you to return to a page with just a few clicks or taps. To add a page to the Favorites list, follow these steps:

1. Navigate to the page you want to save.

2. Select the **Pin Site** icon, which is the pushpin (pointed out in Figure 11.5) that appears to the right of the Address box. Internet Explorer displays the menu shown in Figure 11.5.

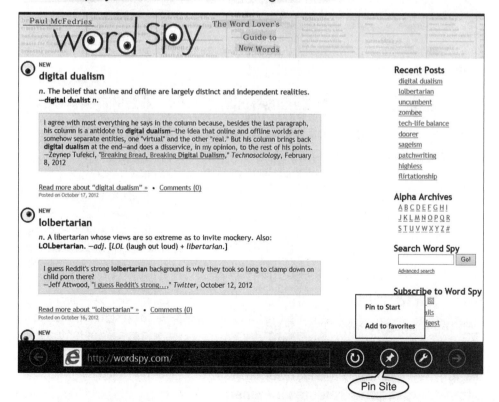

Figure 11.5 *Surf to the web page and then click the Pin Site icon to see this menu.*

3. Select **Add to Favorites**. Internet Explorer adds the page to the **Favorites** list.

To return to a favorite page, click or tap in the **Address** box. Internet Explorer displays the Frequent list, but to its right it also displays the Favorites list. Scroll right until you see the page you want to visit and then select its tile.

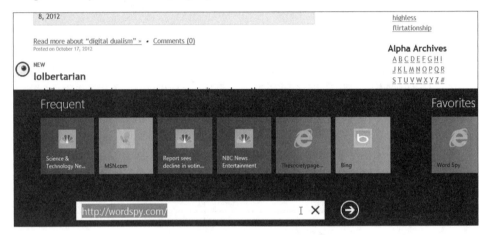

Figure 11.6   *Click or tap in the Address box to see the Favorites list.*

Pinning a Page to the Start Screen

If you have a web page that you visit often, you can use the Internet Explorer app to pin the page to the Start screen. This means that you can surf to that site simply by clicking its **Start** screen tile.

Follow these steps:

1. Navigate to the website you want to pin.

2. Select the **Pin Site** icon (see Figure 11.5).

3. Select **Pin to Start**.

4. Edit the website name, if needed.

5. Select **Pin to Start**. Windows 8 adds a tile for the website to the Start screen. Internet Explorer also creates a *Pinned list,* which you can display by clicking or tapping in the **Address** box.

Note

Removing a Pinned Page

To remove a tile from the Start screen, right-click it (or, on a tablet PC, swipe down on the tile) and then click **Unpin from Start**. Windows 8 removes the tile from the Start screen. To remove a page from the Favorites or Pinned list, right-click the page in the list (or tap and hold the page) and then select **Remove**.

Chapter 12

Exchanging Email

The Web with its splashy graphics and seemingly endless supply of information and entertainment gets the lion's share of press and punditry. By contrast, you hardly hear anyone talk about email, which is all the more surprising because, with the exception of a few texting-only teens, *everyone* uses email. This lack of attention is probably due to a simple fact: Email just isn't glamorous or exciting. However, what email lacks in excitement, it more than makes up for in usefulness. Using the Mail app in Windows 8, you can send a message to just about anyone whose address you know. That person will then receive your message within a few seconds or, at most, a few minutes, whether that person resides across town, across the country, or across the ocean. It's much faster than postal mail and less interruptive than a phone call, so it's pretty much the ideal communications medium.

My goal in this chapter is to give you a taste of what the Mail app can do. I take you through subjects such as setting up accounts, handling incoming messages, managing your Inbox, and sending messages.

Setting Up a Mail Account

The good news about setting up your email account in the Mail app is that if you've already configured your Windows 8 user account to use a Microsoft account with an address that ends with either live.com or hotmail.com, everything is done for you automatically. That is, the Mail app has already configured itself to use your Microsoft account, so you don't need to do anything. In that case, feel free to skip this section.

On the other hand, if you're using a Microsoft account that doesn't have either a live.com or hotmail.com address, you need to set up the account yourself.

First, note that the Mail app doesn't support the Post Office Protocol (POP) accounts that are typically offered by an Internet service provider. However, Mail does support Internet Message Access Protocol (IMAP) accounts that are typically offered by Web-based email services. Check with your email service provider to see which type of account you have.

To set up an IMAP account, you usually need only your email address and password because Mail understands how to configure many of these accounts (such as Gmail accounts, for example). However, it doesn't understand all of them, so it might ask you for the following extra bits of information:

- **Incoming email server**—This is the Internet name of the computer that the provider uses to process email messages that are sent to you. The address usually looks something like imap.*provider*.com, where *provider* is the name of your email provider.

- **Incoming email server port**—This is a two- or three-digit number that defines the channel through which the Mail app communicates with the incoming mail server to look for and download messages sent to you.

- **Whether the incoming email server requires Secure Sockets Layer (SSL)**—SSL is an extra security layer that some email providers require to protect incoming messages.

- **Outgoing email server**—This is the Internet name of the computer that the provider uses to process email messages that you send. The address usually looks something like smtp.*provider*.com, where *provider* is the name of your email provider.

- **Outgoing email server port**—This is a two- or three-digit number that defines the channel through which the Mail app communicates with the outgoing mail server to send your messages.

- **Whether the outgoing email server requires SSL**—SSL is an extra security layer that some email providers require to protect outgoing messages.

- **Whether the outgoing email server requires authentication**— Authentication is an extra step (that's invisible to you, fortunately) that the Mail app has to go through before it can send your messages. Basically, it requires the Mail app to confirm with the outgoing server that you are who you say you are.

- **The username and password to use if the outgoing email server requires authentication**—In almost all cases, these are the same as your email account username and password. If not, you need to know your outgoing email username and password.

This discussion probably sounds like so much gobbledygook at the moment, but rest assured that you don't need to memorize any of this to exchange email messages with your kids and grandkids. The kit provided by your email service should have all this info. If you don't have such a kit, you might need to contact the service or go to the website's customer service or technical support section to look for it.

Here, finally, are the steps to follow to set up an IMAP account in the Mail app:

1. On the Start screen, select the **Mail** tile to launch the Mail app. The first time you do this, you see the Add Your Email Account screen.

2. Select the **IMAP** option and then select **Connect**.

3. Type your account password and then click **Connect**. Mail attempts to connect to your email service. If it is successful, you can skip the rest of these steps; otherwise, you see an expanded list of options. The following steps show you how to fill in these new settings.

4. Type your account username (which is often the same as your email address).

5. In the **Incoming (IMAP) Email Server** text box, type the name of the incoming mail server, and in the **Port** text box beside it, type the server's port.

6. Select the **Incoming Server Requires SSL** check box if your incoming server needs to use SSL.

7. In the **Outgoing (SMTP) Email Server** text box, type the name of the outgoing mail server, and in the **Port** text box beside it, type the server's port.

8. Select the **Outgoing Server Requires SSL** check box if your outgoing server needs to use SSL.

9. Select the **Outgoing Server Requires Authentication** check box if your outgoing server uses authentication.

10. Select the **Use the Same Username and Password to Send and Receive Email** check box if the outgoing server requires your account username and password for authentication. If it requires a different set of credentials, deselect this check box, and then in the **Username** and **Password** text boxes, enter the new credentials.

11. Click **Connect**. Mail sets up your account.

Handling Incoming Messages

Each time you run Mail, it automatically checks for new incoming messages. Even better, as soon as any new message is sent to you, Mail automatically downloads the message to your PC. If you think that the automatic download might not be working, you can perform a manual check by right-clicking the screen (or swiping up from the bottom of the touchscreen) and then selecting **Sync**. Mail checks for new messages and displays Syncing in the upper-right corner of the screen, as shown in Figure 12.1.

 **Tip**

Seeing More Mail

By default, Mail displays only the last two weeks' worth of messages you've received. To see more, display the Charms menu by pressing **Ctrl+C** or swiping left from the right edge of a touchscreen, select **Settings**, select **Accounts**, and then select your email account. In the account pane that appears, use the **Download Email From** list to select a longer time frame, such as **The Last Month** or **Any Time**.

Figure 12.1 *When Mail is looking for new messages sent to you, it displays* Syncing *in the upper-right corner of the screen.*

Each new message that arrives is stored in the Inbox folder's message list and appears in a bold font. To view the contents of any message, select it in the message list, and Mail displays the message text in the preview pane on the right, as shown in Figure 12.2.

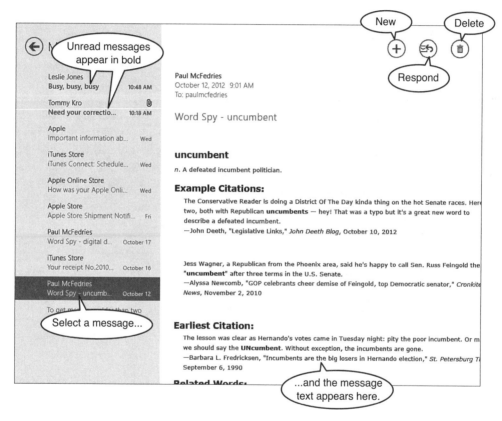

Figure 12.2 *Select a message to read its contents.*

Note

Mail Accounts are Web-Based

Mail supports only IMAP accounts, which are Web-based email accounts, so you can also use Internet Explorer to log in to your account and work with it online (see your provider to learn the address). It's important to remember that anything you do to your messages on the Web is also reflected in the Mail app (and vice versa). For example, if you delete a message on the Web, that message is also deleted from the Mail app.

When you have a message selected, you can do plenty of things with it (in addition to reading it, of course). You can print it, move it to another folder, reply to it, forward it to someone else, delete it, and more. The next few sections take you through these and other message tasks.

Handling Message Attachments

A message *attachment* is a file that the sender has included with her email message. It might be a photo she wants you to view or a document she wants you to read. You'll know when a message arrives with an attachment because Mail displays a paperclip icon, as pointed out in Figure 12.3. When you select the message, you also see an icon for the file as well as the filename and size, as shown in Figure 12.3.

Note

Handling Large Attachments

If the attachment is large, Mail might not show the icon right away. If so, click the **Get the Rest of This Message** link.

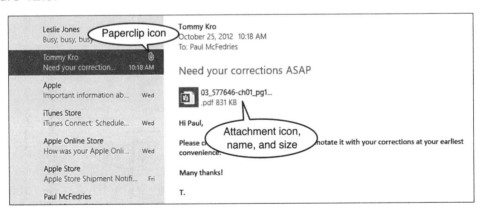

Figure 12.3 *A message with an attached file.*

To handle the attachment, you have two choices:

- **Open the attachment**—Select the attachment's icon and then select **Open**.

- **Save the attachment to your PC**—Select the attachment's icon, select **Save**, select **Files**, choose a folder into which you want to save the attachment, and then select **Save**.

Replying to a Message

Some of the emails you receive will be information-only messages that require you only to read the message. However, many emails will require you to respond in some way—for example, to answer a question, confirm an appointment, or provide feedback.

Mail gives you two options for replying to a message:

- **Reply to message author**—This option sends the reply only to the person who sent the original message. To use this option, select the message, select **Respond** (pointed out earlier in Figure 12.2), and then select **Reply**. Mail creates a reply message, as shown in Figure 12.4. Type your response and then select **Send**.

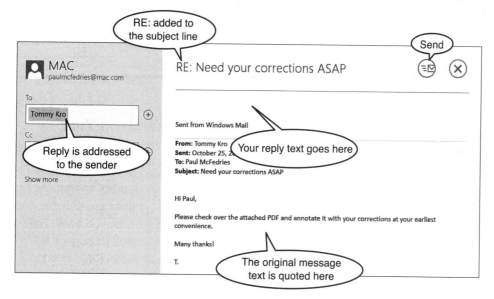

Figure 12.4　*A message reply.*

- **Reply to all message recipients**—This option sends the reply not only to the original author but also to anyone else who was copied on the original message. To use this option, select the message, select **Respond**, and then select **Reply All**. When Mail creates the reply message, type your response and then select **Send**.

Forwarding a Message

If you want someone else to take a look at a message you've received, you can send a copy of the message to that person, which is called *forwarding* the message. Follow these steps to forward a message using Mail:

1. Select the message.

2. Select **Respond** and then select **Forward**. Mail creates the forward message, which includes the original message text as well as the original subject line with FW: appended.

3. Use the **To** box to type the email address of the person you want to view the message.

4. If you want to include your own text (say, to introduce the message or explain why you're forwarding it), select **Add a Message** and then type your text.

5. Select **Send**. Mail sends the forward to the recipient.

Printing a Message

If you want a hard copy of a message, follow these steps to print it out:

1. Select the message you want to print.

2. Display the Charms menu by pressing **Ctrl+C** or swiping left from the right edge of a touchscreen.

3. Select **Devices**.

4. Select your printer. Mail displays the printer options.

5. Select your printer option (such as the number of copies you want).

6. Select **Print**. Mail sends the message to your printer.

Tip

Searching Your Messages

If your Inbox contains a large number of messages, you might have trouble finding individual emails. Rather than scroll through a long list of messages, use the **Search** feature to find the one you're looking for. Display the Charms menu by pressing **Ctrl+C** or swiping left from the right edge of a touchscreen, select **Search**, type a word or phrase that identifies the message you want, and then press **Enter** or click **Search**. Mail displays a list of messages that match your search text.

Moving a Message to a Different Folder

If you want to keep a message, it's best not to let it clutter your Inbox folder. Instead, follow these steps to move it to another folder:

1. Select the message you want to move.

2. Right-click the screen or swipe up from the bottom edge of a touchscreen.

3. Select **Move**. Mail displays a list of available folders.

4. Select the folder. Mail moves the message to that folder.

Deleting a Message

If you no longer need a message, you should delete it to reduce Inbox clutter. To delete a message, select it and then select **Delete** (pointed out earlier in Figure 12.2).

If you delete a message by accident, follow these steps to recover the message:

1. Select the left-pointing arrow beside **Inbox**. Mail displays a list of folders associated with your account.

2. Select **Deleted**. Mail displays a list of messages you've deleted.

3. Select the message you want to restore.

4. Right-click the screen or swipe up from the bottom edge of a touchscreen and then select **Move**. Mail displays a list of available folders.

5. Select **Inbox**. Mail restores the message to the Inbox folder.

Sending a Message

When you're ready to send a message of your own using the Mail app, follow these steps:

1. Select **New** (pointed out earlier in Figure 12.2). Mail displays a new message.

2. Use the **To** box to type the address of your recipient. You can add more than one address, if necessary, by pressing **Enter** after you type each address.

3. If you want someone else to receive a copy of the message, type that person's address in the **Cc** (Courtesy Copy) box. Again, you can add multiple addresses here.

4. Use the **Add a Subject** field to type a short description of the message.

5. Use the big box below that field to type your message. With the cursor inside the message area, right-click the screen (or swipe up from the bottom edge of a touchscreen) to bring up the app bar, which has all kinds of buttons for formatting your text (see Figure 12.5).

Tip

Creating a Signature

By default, Mail includes the text Sent from Windows Mail in the message. Text that is added to a message automatically is called a *signature,* and you can create your own. Display the Charms menu by pressing **Ctrl+C** or swiping left from the right edge of a touchscreen, select **Settings**, select **Accounts**, and then select your account. Make sure the **Use an Email Signature** switch is set to **Yes** and then use the text box below it to type your signature text. Be sure to select and delete **Sent from Windows Mail** if you don't want this text to appear at the end of each message.

Tip

Saving a Draft

If you can't send your message right away (for example, you're waiting for more information), you can save your work and then return to the message later. Select **Close** (see Figure 12.5) and then select **Save Draft**. Mail moves the message to your Drafts folder. To return to the message, select the left-pointing arrow beside Inbox to display the folder list, select **Drafts**, select the message, and then select **Edit** (the pencil icon).

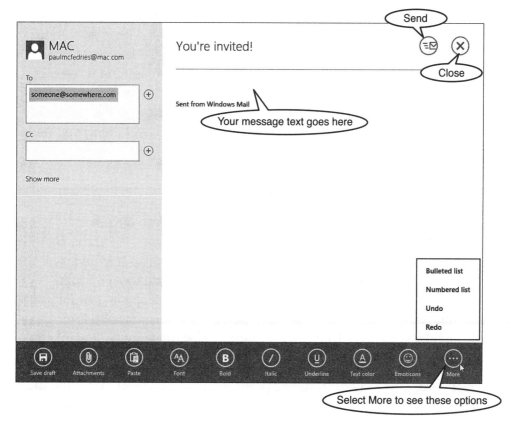

Figure 12.5 *Click inside the message area and then right-click the screen to see the formatting options.*

6. If you want to include a file, select **Attachments**, locate and select the file you want to send, and then click **Attach**.

7. When your message is complete, select **Send**.

Minding Your Email Manners

One of the first things you notice when you're drifting around the Internet is that it attracts more than its share of bohemians, non-conformists, and rugged individualists. And despite all these people surfing to the beat of a different drum, the Internet resolutely refuses to degenerate into mere anarchy. Oh sure, you get the odd every-nerd-for-himself hurly-burly, but civility reigns the vast majority of the time.

Usually most folks are just too busy with their researching and rubbernecking to cause trouble, but there's another mechanism that helps keep everyone in line: it's called *netiquette* (a blend of *network etiquette*). Netiquette is a collection of suggested behavioral norms designed to grease the wheels of online social discourse. Scofflaws who defy the netiquette rules can expect to see a few reprimands in their email inbox. To help you stay on the good side of the Internet community, the next few sections tell you everything you need to know about the netiquette involved in sending email.

The Three B's of Composing Email

Back in the long-gone days when I was a good corporate citizen, my boss used to call his secrets for successful presentations "the three Bs": be good, be brief, begone. These simple prescriptions also form a small chunk of the basic netiquette landscape. Being good means writing in clear, understandable prose that isn't marred by sloppy spelling or flagrant grammar violations. Also, if you use some facts or statistics, cite the appropriate references to placate the Doubting Thomases who'll want to check things for themselves.

Being brief means getting right to the point without indulging in a rambling preamble. Always assume your addressee is plowing through a stack of email and so has no time or patience for verbosity. State your business and then practice the third "B": begone!

DON'T SHOUT!

When writing with your high-end word processor, you probably use italics (or, more rarely, underlining) to emphasize important words or phrases. But because email appears to use just plain vanilla text (since the fancy formatting options are hidden away), you might think that, in cyberspace, no on can hear you scream. That's not true, however. In fact, many email scribes add emphasis to their epistles by using UPPERCASE LETTERS. This works, but please use uppercase sparingly. AN ENTIRE MESSAGE WRITTEN IN CAPITAL LETTERS FEELS LIKE YOU'RE SHOUTING, WHICH IS OKAY FOR USED-CAR SALESMAN ON LATE-NIGHT TV, BUT IS INAPPROPRIATE IN THE MORE SEDATE WORLD OF EMAIL CORRESPONDENCE.

on the other hand, you occasionally see e-mail messages written entirely in lowercase letters from lazy susans, toms, dicks, and harrys who can't muster the energy to reach out for the shift key. this, too, is taboo because it makes the text quite difficult to read. Just use the normal capitalization practices (uppercase for the beginning of sentences, proper names, etc.), and everyone'll be happy.

Take Your Subject Lines Seriously

Busy email readers often use the contents of the Subject line to make a snap judgment about whether or not to bother reading a message. (This is especially true if the recipient doesn't know you from Adam.) The majority of email mavens *hate* Subject lines that are either ridiculously vague (such as, "Info required" or "Please help!"), or absurdly general (such as, "An e-mail message" or "Mail"), and they'll just press their email software's Delete button without giving the message a second thought. (In fact, there's a kind of illicit thrill involved in deleting an unread message, so don't give the person any excuse to exercise this indulgence.) Give your Subject line some thought and make it descriptive enough so the reader can tell at a glance what your dispatch is about.

More Snippets of Sending Sensitivity

Here, in no particular order, are a few more netiquette gems that'll help make sure you always put your best sending foot forward:

- If you receive private email correspondence from someone, it's considered impolite to quote them in another message without the author's permission.

- When replying to a message, include quotes from the original message for context. Few things are more frustrating in e-mail than to receive a reply that just says "Great idea, let's do it!" or "That's the dumbest thing I've ever heard." Which great idea or dumb thing are they talking about? To make sure the other person knows what you're responding to, include the appropriate lines from the original message in your reply. You'll need to use some judgment here, though. Quoting the entire message is usually wasteful (especially if the message was a long one). Just include enough of the original to put your response into context.

- When you want to respond to a message, make sure you use the Reply feature. This feature provides you with three advantages: It automatically addresses the reply to the original sender; it adds "Re:" to the Subject line so the original sender knows which message is being responded to; and it gives you the option of including some or all of the original message in the reply.

- Be careful when using the Reply All command. If your response is only relevant to the person who sent the message, use the Reply command to send your response just to that person. On the other hand, some email exchanges become a kind of group conversation that applies to all the people who were sent the original message. In this case, it's okay to use Reply All so that everyone stays in the loop.

- Resist the temptation to forward to your friends and family members every knock-knock joke, sensational news story, or cute kitten picture that graces your Inbox. Believe me, they've all seen way more than their share of these things, so think twice (or, really, three times) before hitting that Forward button. If you honestly believe that the forwarded message will be relevant, important, or truly entertaining to the recipient, then go for it.

- Forgive small mistakes. If you see a message with spelling mistakes, incorrect grammar, or minor factual blunders, resist the urge to scold the perpetrator. For one thing, the international flavor of email just about guarantees a large percentage of participants for whom English isn't their primary language. For another, I hope you have better things to do than nitpick every little slip of the keyboard that comes your way.

Chapter 13

Maximizing Internet Security and Privacy

As more people, businesses, and organizations establish a presence online, the world becomes an increasingly connected place. And the more connected the world becomes, the more opportunities arise for communicating with others, doing research, sharing information, and collaborating on projects. The flip side to this new connectedness is the increased risk of connecting with a remote user whose intentions are less than honorable. The person at the other end of the connection could be a fraud artist who sets up a legitimate-looking website to steal your password or credit card number, or a cracker (that is, a hacker who has succumbed to the Dark Side of the Force) who breaks into your Internet account. It could be a virus programmer who sends a Trojan horse attached to an email, or a website operator who uses web browser security holes to run malicious code on your machine.

Fortunately, these aren't threats that you have to constantly fend off as you make your way around the Internet. They're relatively rare, but that rarity is no excuse not to keep up your guard full-time while you're online. This chapter shows you how to do just that.

Avoiding Viruses

A *virus* is a malevolent program that installs itself on your PC without your permission. After it's done that, the virus might then steal your data, record your passwords, trash your files, or turn your PC into a *zombie computer* that the virus forces into attacking other PCs. Viruses are nasty bits of business no matter how you slice it, so they're to be avoided like the plague that they are.

The best way to inoculate your PC against virus infections is to use an *antivirus program.* This special software application is designed to detect, block, and if necessary, remove viruses. The company that offers the antivirus program maintains a list of known viruses, and the software uses this list to keep your PC safe. This list is distressingly long—it likely contains thousands of viruses—and it's constantly growing (because virus writers seem to be a creative and energetic lot), so all good antivirus programs update themselves frequently.

The good news is that your Windows 8 PC already comes with an antivirus program called Windows Defender. If you're not using Windows 8, here are some popular antivirus programs and suites for your consideration:

- Avast! Antivirus (www.avast.com)
- AVG Internet Security (http://free.avg.com/)
- McAfee Internet Security Suite (www.mcafee.com)
- Microsoft Security Essentials (www.microsoft.com/security/pc-security/mse.aspx)
- Norton Internet Security (http://us.norton.com/)

Note that Avast!, AVG Internet Security, and Microsoft Security Essentials are free, but the others require annual payments to keep their virus lists up to date.

Avoiding Viruses on the Web

Having an antivirus program installed is a good (and necessary) thing, but it doesn't mean you can let your guard down while you surf the Web. You should avoid tempting fate by following these simple precautions:

- **Look for—and do *not* click—links to programs or scripts.** Some nasty websites attempt to install a virus by setting up an innocuous-looking link that actually connects you to a program or script that installs a virus on your PC. To be safe, point at each link before you click it and take a look at the address displayed by the web browser. Don't click the link if the filename ends with any of the following extensions: `.bat`, `.cmd`, `.com`, `.doc`, `.exe`, `.js`, `.ppt`, `.reg`, `.vb`, `.vbs`, `.wsh`, or `.xls`.

- **Avoid downloading files from websites that you don't know or trust.** Downloading files from the Web to your PC is a common task and one that you generally don't have to worry about because files from reputable websites are almost certainly virus-free. However, if you're using a website that you don't know or don't trust, it's probably best to avoid the download altogether. If you need the file, be sure to use your antivirus software to scan the file for infection before opening it.

- **Ignore online ads that make wild or too-good-to-be-true claims.** As you surf the Web, you'll come across sites that display ads claiming that "you have messages waiting" or that "you've won a prize." Believe me, you have no messages and you haven't won anything. Most of these ads are just annoying come-ons, but some of them have a hidden virus payload that activates when you click the ad.

- **Don't allow pop-up windows.** A *pop-up window* is a web page that appears in a separate browser window. Some sites use pop-ups for activities such as logging in, but this is relatively rare nowadays. Most pop-ups are just intrusive advertisements, but some are more nefarious and will trigger a virus download if you click anything within the pop-up. Windows 8's Internet Explorer browser is aware of all this, and it automatically blocks pop-ups when it detects them. You'll know when this is happening because you'll see an information bar similar to the one shown in Figure 13.1. Click **Close** to keep the pop-up at bay.

Caution

Avoid These Ads

The main ads to avoid are those that display realistic-looking "dialog boxes" that tell you "Your PC Is Infected" or "Potential Threats Detected" and offer a button that you're urged to click to solve the problem. Don't do it! The most likely scenario is that you'll trigger a virus installation that really *will* leave your PC infected!

Figure 13.1 *When Internet Explorer detects a pop-up, be sure to click Close.*

Avoiding Viruses in Email

Although malicious websites are a common cause of virus infections, in recent years the most productive method for viruses to replicate has been the humble email message. The virus arrives as a message attachment, usually from someone you know. When you open the attachment, the virus infects your computer and then, without your knowledge, uses your email program and your address book to ship out messages with more copies of itself attached. The nastier versions also mess with your computer by deleting data or corrupting files.

You can avoid infection from one of these viruses by implementing a few commonsense procedures:

- Never open an attachment that comes from someone you don't know.

- Even if you know the sender, check the message: If it's vague or extremely short (or just doesn't sound like the sender), you should be immediately suspicious about the attachment. Otherwise, if the attachment isn't something you're expecting, assume that the sender's system is infected. Write back and confirm that the sender emailed the message.

- Some viruses come packaged as scripts hidden within messages that use the HTML format (the same format that underlies most web pages). This means that the virus can run just by the message being viewed! If a message looks suspicious, don't open it; just delete it.

Keeping Spyware at Bay

Viruses are an example of the general category known as *malware*, short for "malicious software." The worst malware offender by far these days is *spyware*, a program that surreptitiously monitors a user's computer activities—particularly the typing of passwords, PINs, and credit card numbers—or harvests sensitive data on the user's computer and then sends that information to an individual or a company via the user's Internet connection without the user's consent.

All this means that you need to buttress your PC with an antispyware program that can watch out for spyware and prevent it from getting its hooks into your system. Fortunately, Windows 8 comes with its own antispyware program called Windows Defender (yes, the same program that also defends your PC against viruses), which protects your PC from spyware in two ways: It can scan your system for evidence of installed spyware programs (and remove or disable those programs, if necessary), and it can monitor your system in real time to watch for activities that indicate the presence of spyware.

Follow these steps in Windows 8 to make sure the real-time protection feature of Windows Defender is turned on:

1. Switch to the **Start** screen, type **defender**, and then click **Windows Defender** in the search results.

2. Click the **Settings** tab.

3. Click **Real-Time Protection**.

 Tip

Install Multiple Antispyware Programs

Many security experts recommend installing multiple antispyware programs on the premise that one program may miss one or two examples of spyware, but two or three programs are highly unlikely to miss any. So, in addition to Windows Defender, you might also consider installing antispyware programs such as Lavasoft Ad-Aware (www.lavasoft.com) and PC Tools Spyware Doctor (www.pctools.com). Note, however, that you might find this slows down your PC considerably. If so, uninstall the second antispyware utility and just stick with Windows Defender.

4. Make sure that the **Turn On Real-Time Protection** check box is activated, as shown in Figure 13.2.

5. Click **Save Changes**.

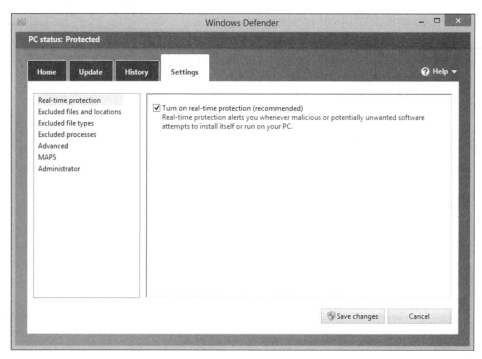

Figure 13.2 *Open Windows Defender and ensure that its real-time protection feature is turned on.*

For the scanning portion of its defenses, Windows Defender supports three different scan types:

- **Quick Scan**—This scan checks just those areas of your system where it is likely to find evidence of spyware. This scan usually takes just a couple of minutes. It is the default, and you can initiate it at any time by selecting the **Home** tab and then clicking **Scan Now**.

- **Full Scan**—This scan checks for evidence of spyware in system memory, all running processes, and the system drive (usually drive C), and it performs a deep scan on all folders. This scan might take 30 minutes or more, depending on your system. To run this scan, select the **Home** tab, activate the **Full** option, and then click **Scan Now**.

- **Custom Scan**—This scan checks just the drives and folders you select. The length of the scan depends on the number of locations you select and the number of objects in those locations. To run this scan, select the **Home** tab, activate the **Custom** option, and then click **Scan Now**. In the dialog box that appears, activate the check boxes for the drives and folders you want scanned and then click **OK** to start the scan.

Listening to User Account Control

Each Windows user account comes with a predefined set of *privileges* that specify the types of tasks the user can perform on the system. In Windows 8, there are two types of user accounts:

- **Administrator account**—This is the account you set up when you first started Windows 8. It's an "administrator" account in the sense that you use it to administer certain things on your PC, such as creating other user accounts. Note that Windows 8 allows only a single user account in the administrators category.

- **Standard account**—All other accounts you create in Windows 8 are members of this group, and these accounts can't perform as many tasks as the administrator account.

The main point of all this from a security perspective is that any malware that insinuates itself onto your system is also capable of operating with the same privileges as your user account. If you're using the administrator account, that could spell big trouble because now the virus (or whatever) wreaks havoc on the PC and just about anything connected to it.

With that worst-case scenario in mind, Windows implements a security feature called User Account Control (UAC). With your main Windows 8 user account (which, again, is a member of the administrators category), you run with the privileges of a standard user for extra security. When you attempt a task that requires administrative privileges, Windows 8 prompts for your consent by displaying a User Account Control dialog box similar to the one shown in Figure 13.3. Click **Yes** to permit the task to proceed. If this dialog box appears unexpectedly instead of in response to an action you've just taken, it's possible that a malware program is trying to perform some task that requires administrative privileges; you can thwart that task by clicking **No** instead.

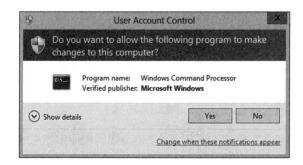

Figure 13.3 *When your main Windows 8 administrative account launches a task that requires elevated privileges, Windows 8 displays this dialog box to ask for consent.*

If you're running as a standard user and attempt a task that requires administrative privileges, Windows 8 uses an extra level of protection. That is, instead of just prompting you for consent, it prompts you for the password of the main administrative account, as shown in Figure 13.4. Type the password for the main administrative account and then click **Yes**. Again, if this dialog box shows up unexpectedly, it might be malware, so you should click **No** to prevent the task from going through.

Figure 13.4 *When a standard user launches a task that requires administrative privileges, Windows 8 displays this dialog box to ask for administrative credentials.*

Note, too, that in both cases Windows switches to secure desktop mode, which means that you can't do anything else with Windows until you give your consent or credentials or cancel the operation. Windows indicates the secure desktop by darkening everything on the screen except the User Account Control dialog box.

Creating Secure Online Passwords

Many websites require a password to access the site's content. For example, on some sites you must log in to access restricted content that's available only to registered users or paid subscribers. On retail sites, you often have an account that's password-protected so that you can place orders and track shipments. Finally, a password is a must for secure sites such as online banking and online investing pages.

Each of these scenarios has a different level of security, but in each case you don't want an unauthorized person to log in using your account. The best way to prevent unauthorized access is to protect your account with a strong password.

Lots of books suggest absurdly fancy password schemes (I've written some of those books myself!), but there are really only three things you need to know to create strong-like-bull passwords:

- **Use passwords that are at least 8 characters long.** Shorter passwords are susceptible to programs that just try every letter combination. You can combine the 26 letters of the alphabet into about 12 million 5-letter word combinations, which is no big deal for a fast program. If you bump things up to 8-letter passwords, however, the total number of combinations rises to 200 *billion,* which would take even the fastest computer quite awhile. If you use 12-letter passwords, as many experts recommend, the number of combinations goes beyond mind-boggling: 90 *quadrillion,* or 90,000 trillion!

- **Mix up your character types.** The secret to a strong password is to include characters from the following categories: lowercase letters, uppercase letters, numbers, and symbols. If you include at least one character from three (or even better, all four) of these categories, you're well on your way toward a strong password.

- **Don't be too obvious.** Because forgetting a password is inconvenient, many people use meaningful words or numbers so their password will be easier to remember. Unfortunately, this means that they often use extremely obvious things such as their name, the name of a family member or colleague, their birth date, their Social Security number, or even their site username. Being this obvious is just asking for trouble.

Speaking of passwords, after you sign in to a site, Internet Explorer might display a message like the one shown in Figure 13.5, asking whether you want it to store the password that you just typed.

Note

Checking Your Password Strength

How will you know whether the password you've come up with fits the definition of strong? One way to find out is to submit the password to an online password complexity checker, such as the Microsoft Password Checker available at https://www.microsoft.com/security/pc-security/password-checker.aspx. Type your password in the Password box, and make sure the Strength indicator says either Strong or BEST.

Do you want to store the password for twitter.com?   Yes   No   Don't Ask Again

Figure 13.5 *Internet Explorer sometimes asks whether it can save a site password.*

Should you click Yes or No? The answer is: It depends. Let me explain:

- **Yes**—This is certainly the convenient way to go because it means that Internet Explorer enters your password automatically the next time you access the login portion of the site. Clicking **Yes** can save a bit of time.

- **No**—This is often the safer way to go because if a malicious user managed to sit down in front of your computer while it's logged on to Windows, that person could access any website where you've saved the password. Clicking **No** ensures that unauthorized users can't access your account on that site.

To help make the choice, ask yourself a simple question: What is the worst thing that could happen if an unauthorized person accesses my account? If the answer is that you could lose money, have private data exposed, or suffer some other harm, you should definitely click **No** to avoid having your password stored. On the other hand, if the answer is that the risk is minimal (and it often is), you can feel safe clicking **Yes** to have the password stored.

Avoiding Online Scams

If all we had to worry about online were viruses and spyware, life on the Web wouldn't be too bad because these and other forms of malware are relatively rare. Unfortunately, the online world mirrors the offline world in being home to a significant population of scam artists and fraudsters, particularly ones who tend to prey on older folks. The rest of this chapter gives you a few tips to help avoid getting fleeced while online.

Giving Out Your Credit Card Information Safely

If you want to purchase anything online, you can use a payment system such as PayPal (www.paypal.com) to shield your payment info from the vendor. However, not all online retailers support PayPal, so in those cases you're basically stuck with having to give the merchant your credit card info. Is it safe to do that?

The answer in many cases is yes, but that depends entirely on whether the website you're using is secure. That is, you must be able to see the following on your screen:

- **An address beginning with https instead of http**—The extra "s" stands for "Secure," and it tells you that the website is using a secure communications channel to receive your credit card data.

- **A lock icon to the right of the address**— This tells you that the website has been verified as legitimate and is using a secure connection.

Note

You Don't See the Security Features All the Time

Bear in mind that legitimate sites don't display these security features full time. In almost all cases, you only see the security features when the site requires sensitive data from you, such as your credit card info.

Both of these features tell you that the website is secure enough to keep your credit card information safe. If you don't see these features when a site is asking for your credit card details, do *not* give them out. Figure 13.6 shows an example of a website that has these features.

Figure 13.6 *An example of a secure web page.*

Understanding Phishing Scams

Phishing refers to creating a replica of an existing web page or using false emails to fool you into submitting personal information, financial data, or a password. It's a whimsical word for a serious bit of business, but the term comes from the fact that Internet scammers are using increasingly sophisticated lures as they "fish" for your sensitive data.

The most common ploy is to copy the web page code from a major site—such as America Online or eBay—and use that code to set up a replica page that appears to be part of the company's site. You receive a fake email with a link to this page, which solicits your credit card data or password. When you submit the form, it sends the data to the scammer while leaving you on an actual page from the company's site so you don't suspect a thing.

A phishing message is a junk email message that appears to come from a legitimate organization, such as a bank, a major retailer, or an Internet service provider. The message asks you to update your information or warns you that your account is about to expire. In most cases, the message offers a link to a bogus website that tries to fool you into revealing sensitive or private data.

Never trust any email message or website that asks you to update or confirm sensitive data, such as your bank account number, credit card information, Social Security number, or account password. It's important to remember that no legitimate company or organization will ever contact you via email to update or confirm such information online.

A phishing scammer can easily craft an email message that looks like it came from a legitimate organization. However, there are ways to recognize a phishing message:

- If the message is addressed to an individual but you see something like "Undisclosed recipients" in the To line, you know something's wrong right off the bat.

- The message appears to come from a major corporation or organization, but the text contains numerous spelling and grammatical errors—or even misspells the name of the company!

- Position the mouse pointer over any links in the message and examine the address that appears in the status bar. If the address is clearly one that is not associated with the company, the message is almost certainly a phishing attempt.

A phishing page looks identical to a legitimate page from the company because the phisher has simply copied the underlying source code from the original page. However, no spoof page can be a perfect replica of the original. Here are four things to look for:

- **Wrong page address**—A legitimate page has the correct domain— such as aol.com or ebay.com—whereas a spoofed page has only something similar, such as aol.whatever.com or blah.com/ebay.

- **Wrong link addresses**—Most links on the page probably point to legitimate pages on the original site. However, the page may have some links that point to pages on the phisher's site.

- **Text or images not associated with the trustworthy site**—Many phishing sites are housed on free Web-hosting services. However, many of these services place an advertisement on each page, so look for an ad or other content from the hosting provider.

- **No lock icon**—A legitimate site would only transmit sensitive financial data using a secure connection, which Internet Explorer indicates by placing a lock icon in the Address box, as described earlier. If you don't see the lock icon with a page that asks for financial data, the page is almost certainly a spoof.

Preventing Identity Theft

Identity theft is the unauthorized and unlawful use of information that personally identifies a person, including that person's name, address, Social Security number, and credit card data. Identity thieves use that information to commit fraud in the victim's name, so it's important to take steps to prevent your identity from falling into the wrong hands.

We're talking here about staying safe online, but first you should know that you can take some easy steps offline to help prevent identity theft. They include shredding unneeded financial documents and papers that contain personal information; keeping a close eye on your finances to look for suspicious activity, such as credit card charges for goods or services you didn't purchase; obtaining a copy of your credit report and scouring it for unusual activities or inaccurate information; and watching out for missed bills and account statements (identity thieves often use change-of-address forms to divert bills and statements to a different address).

ID thieves use plenty of offline methods to gather personal information (such as going through your trash or stealing your wallet or purse), but these days much of the action is online. Here are a few things you can do to help keep your information safe and out of the grubby paws of identity thieves:

- Never give out your Social Security number (or the equivalent in your country, such as the Social Insurance Number in Canada). Yes, it uniquely identifies you, but any reputable site will take some other form of ID. If a site insists, take your business elsewhere.

- Give your name, address, and phone number only to reputable sites or to sites that you know are legit. The same goes for information about your relatives, including personal data for your spouse, siblings, children, and grandchildren.

- Don't expose too much personal information on social networking sites such as Facebook. Also, if you use any social networking sites, make sure you crank up your security settings to the highest level to avoid strangers seeing too much of your info.

- Never give out data related to your vehicle, including its make and model, license plate number, vehicle identification number (VIN), your insurance company and account details, loan information, and your driver's license number.

- Learn to recognize phishing email messages and websites, as described earlier in this chapter, because phishing is now a very common method that identity thieves use to gather personal data.

- Use strong passwords for all websites and email accounts, as described earlier. Those few letters, numbers, and symbols are often the only things that stand between you and a would-be thief, so it's not hyperbole to say that your financial health and personal reputation depend on them.

- Just say "No" when a website asks you to provide your credit history or credit rating. No site needs to know this stuff.

Protecting Yourself from "419" Scams

Many junk email messages are scams that advertise nonexistent products, services, and money-making opportunities. The most common of these is the so-called *advance fee fraud,* in which a person is asked for money to help secure the release of a much larger sum with the promise of sharing the riches in return for that help. These scams often originate in Nigeria, so they're sometimes called *Nigerian letter scams* or *419 scams,* because 419 is the section number of the Nigerian penal code that covers this sort of fraudulent behavior.

These 419 scams almost always originate as email messages, and the details vary but the overall story is the same:

- The writer has access to lots of money—typically, several million dollars. In most of these scams, the writer needs to shield the money from a corrupt government, has won a lottery or inheritance, needs helping converting the currency, or wants to give the money to charity.

- The writer creates an impressively detailed persona and situation to sound plausible.

- For arcane and complex reasons, the writer needs help getting the money out of his home country.

- You, as a person of outstanding character and honesty, are just the person to help.

Of course, "helping" means first sending some cash to cover "transfer" fees or "account" fees. Then an even larger sum is required to pay for a lawyer or an accountant. Then hundreds of dollars are needed for bribing certain government or law-enforcement officials. Finally, thousands of dollars are requested for airfare or other transportation costs. The result: You're out a few thousand dollars or more, and you never hear from the scammer again.

If you receive an apparently all-too-sincere email from a polite and well-connected foreigner who needs to liberate millions of dollars and is offering you a large chunk of that fortune to help, there's only one thing you should do: Hit the **Delete** key!

Chapter 14

Securing Your PC

Some folks claim that you can never be too thin or too rich. Other folks might give you an argument about one or both assertions, but I doubt anyone would take you to task if you added a third item to the list: Your PC can never be too secure. There are just too many threats out there, and too many ways that the defenses in Windows can be breached.

With that in mind, this chapter focuses on general PC security, including basic precautions that everyone should take, a review of your computer's security settings, and more.

Thwarting Snoops and Crackers

Let's begin with a look at protecting your PC from direct and indirect attacks. A direct attack occurs when an unauthorized *cracker* (which I define as a hacker who has succumbed to the Dark Side of the Force) sits down at your keyboard and tries to gain access to your system. Sure, it may be unlikely that a malicious user would gain physical access to the computer in your home or office, but it's not impossible.

An indirect attack is one that occurs via the Internet. Crackers specialize in breaking into systems ("cracking" system security, hence the name), and at any given time hundreds, perhaps even thousands, of crackers roam cyberspace looking for potential targets. If you're online right now, the restless and far-seeing eyes of the crackers are bound to find you eventually.

Sounds unlikely, you say? You wish. The crackers are armed with programs that automatically search through millions of IP addresses (the addresses that uniquely identify any computer or device connected to the Internet). The crackers are specifically looking for computers that aren't secure, and if they find one, they'll pounce on it and crack their way into the system.

Again, if all this sounds unlikely or that it would take them forever to find you, think again. Tests have shown that new and completely unprotected systems routinely get cracked within 20 minutes of connecting to the Internet!

Taking Some Basic Precautions

So how do you thwart the world's crackers? I often joke that it's easy if you follow a simple four-pronged plan:

- Don't connect to the Internet. Ever.

- Don't install programs on your PC. No, not even that one.

- Don't let anyone else work with, touch, glance at, talk about, or come within 20 feet of your PC.

- Burglarproof your home or office.

The point here is that if you use your PC (and live your life) in an even remotely normal way, you open up your machine to security risks. That's a bleak assessment, for sure, but fortunately it doesn't take a lot of effort on your part to turn your PC into a maximum security area. The security techniques in this chapter (and in Chapter 13, "Maximizing Internet Security and Privacy") will get to that goal, but first make sure you've nailed down the basics:

- **Leave User Account Control turned on**. Yes, I know UAC is a hassle, but it's the best thing that's happened to Windows security in a long time, and it's a fact of life that your computer is much more secure when UAC has got your back. See "Making Sure User Account Control is Turned On," later in this chapter.

- **Be paranoid**. The belief that everyone's out to get you may be a sign of trouble in the real world, but it's just common sense in the computer world. Assume someone will sit down at your desk when you're not around; assume someone will try to log on to your computer when you leave for the night; assume all uninvited email attachments are viruses; assume unknown websites are malicious; assume any offer that sounds too good to be true probably is.

- **Keep to yourself**. We all share lots of personal info online these days, but there's sharing and then there's asking-for-trouble sharing. Don't tell anybody any of your passwords. Don't put your email address online unless it's disguised in some way (for example, by writing it as `username at yourdomain dot com`). Don't give out sensitive personal data such as your Social Security number, bank account number, or even your address and phone number (unless making a purchase with a reputable vendor). Give your credit card data only to online vendors that you trust implicitly or, even better, get a secure PayPal account and use that instead.

- **Test the firewall**. A firewall's not much good if it leaves your computer vulnerable to attack, so you should test the firewall to make sure it's doing its job. I show you several ways to do this, later in this chapter (see the section "Making Sure the Firewall Is Up to Snuff").

- **Update, update, update**. Many crackers take advantage of known Windows vulnerabilities to compromise a system. To avoid this, keep your PC updated with the latest patches, fixes, and service packs, many of which are designed to plug security leaks.

- **Assume the worst**. Back up your data regularly, keep your receipts, keep all email correspondence, and read the fine print.

Locking Your PC

Many of Windows' built-in security features have a small flaw: They rely on the assumption that after you've entered a legitimate username and password to log on to your Windows user account, only *you* will use your computer. This means that after you log on, you become a "trusted" user and you have full access to your files.

This assumption is certainly reasonable on the surface. After all, you wouldn't want to have to enter your account credentials every time you want to open, edit, create, or delete a document. So while you're logged on and at your desk, you get full access to your stuff.

But what happens when you leave your desk? If you remain logged on to Windows, any other person who sits down at your computer can take advantage of your trusted-user status to view and work with your files (including copying them to a USB flash drive inserted by the snoop). This is what I mean by Windows' security having a flaw, and it's a potentially significant security hole in large offices where it wouldn't be hard for someone to pull up your chair while you're stuck in yet another meeting or you dash out to the store.

One way to prevent this situation would be to turn off your computer every time you leave your desk. That way, any would-be snoop would have to get past your login to get to your files. This approach, obviously, is wildly impractical and inefficient.

Is there a better solution? You bet: You can lock your system before leaving your desk. Anyone who tries to use your computer must enter your password to access the Windows desktop.

Locking Your PC Manually

Windows 8 gives you three ways to lock your computer before heading off:

- On the Start screen, click your user account tile and then click **Lock**.

- Press **Windows Logo+L**.

- Press **Ctrl+Alt+Delete** and then click **Lock**.

Whichever method you use, you end up at the Lock screen. Click the screen or press **Enter** to switch to the Windows sign-on screen, shown in Figure 14.1. Note that it says Locked under the username.

Figure 14.1 *You see a screen similar to this when you lock your Windows 8 PC.*

Locking Your PC Automatically

The locking techniques from the preceding section are easy enough to do, but the hard part is *remembering* to do them. If you're late for a meeting or a rendezvous, locking up your machine is probably the last thing on your mind as you dash out the door. The usual course of events in these situations is that just as you arrive at your destination you remember that you forgot to lock your PC, and you then end up fretting about your defenseless computer.

To avoid the fretting (not to mention the possible intrusion), you can configure your computer to lock automatically after a period of inactivity. Here's how it's done:

1. Press **Windows Logo+W**, type **personalize**, and then click **Personalize Your Computer** in the results to open the Personalization window.

2. Click **Screen Saver**.

3. If you want to have a screen saver kick in after your PC is inactive for a while, choose one from the **Screen Saver** list.

4. Use the **Wait** spin box to set the interval (in minutes) of idle time that Windows 8 waits before locking your PC.

5. Activate the **On Resume, Display Logon Screen** check box.

6. Click **OK**.

Checking Your Computer's Security Settings

Windows comes with four security features enabled by default:

- Windows Firewall is turned on.

- Windows Defender protects your computer against spyware in real-time and by scanning your PC on a schedule.

- User Account Control is turned on.

- The Administrator account is disabled.

However, even though these are the default settings, they're important enough not to be left to chance. The following sections show you how to check that these crucial security settings really are enabled on your PC.

Making Sure Windows Firewall Is Turned On

By far the most important thing you need to do to thwart crackers is to have a software firewall running on your computer. A *firewall* is a security feature that blocks unauthorized attempts to send data to your computer. The best firewalls completely hide your computer from the Internet, so those dastardly crackers don't even know you're there! Windows Firewall is turned on by default, but you should check this, just to be safe:

1. Press **Windows Logo+W** to display the Settings search pane.

2. Type **firewall** and then click **Windows Firewall** in the search results. The Windows Firewall window appears. Check the **Windows Firewall State** value. If it says **On**, you're fine; if it says **Off**, as shown in Figure 14.2, continue to step 3.

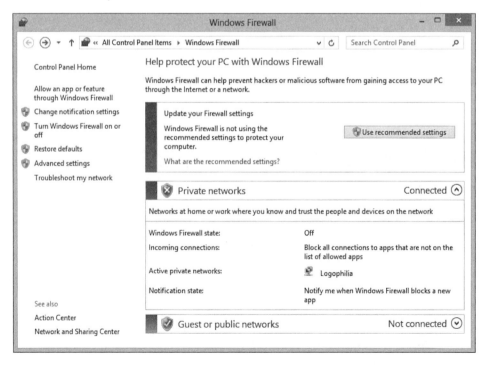

Figure 14.2 *You need to take immediate action if you see that the Windows Firewall State is Off, as shown here.*

3. Click **Turn Windows Firewall On or Off**. The Customize Settings window appears.

4. In the Private Network Settings section, activate the **Turn On Windows Firewall** option.

5. In the Public Network Settings section, activate the **Turn On Windows Firewall** option.

6. Click **OK**.

Making Sure Windows Defender Is Turned On

I've been troubleshooting Windows PCs for many years. It used to be that users accidentally deleting system files or making ill-advised attempts to edit the Registry or some other important configuration file caused most problems. Recent versions of Windows (particularly XP) could either prevent these kinds of PEBCAK (*problem exists between chair and keyboard*) issues or recover from them without a lot of trouble. However, I think we're all too well aware of the latest menace to rise in the past few years, and it has taken over as the top cause of desperate troubleshooting calls I receive: *malware*, the generic term for malicious software such as viruses and Trojan horses. And, as I described in Chapter 13, *spyware* is the worst of these.

You might think that having a robust firewall between you and the bad guys would make malware a problem of the past. Unfortunately, that's not true. These programs piggyback on other legitimate programs that users actually *want* to download, such as file sharing programs, download managers, and screen savers. A *drive-by download* is the download and installation of a program without a user's knowledge or consent. This relates closely to a *pop-up download*—the download and installation of a program after the user clicks an option in a pop-up browser window, particularly when the option's intent is vaguely or misleadingly worded.

To make matters even worse, most spyware embeds itself deep into a system, and removing it is a delicate and time-consuming operation beyond the abilities of even experienced users. Some programs actually come with an Uninstall option, but it's nothing but a ruse, of course. The program appears to remove itself from the system, but what it actually does is a *covert reinstall*—it reinstalls a fresh version of itself when the computer is idle.

Fortunately, Windows 8 comes with Windows Defender, an antispyware program, which can help keep spyware out of your system. If the real-time protection feature of Windows Defender is turned off, you usually see the Action Center message shown in Figure 14.3 when you access the Desktop. Click that message to launch Windows Defender and turn on real-time protection as described in Chapter 13.

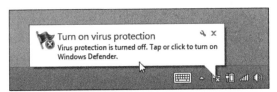

Figure 14.3 *The Windows Action Center lets you know if Windows Defender isn't monitoring your system in real-time for spyware.*

Making Sure User Account Control Is Turned On

I described User Account Control in detail in Chapter 13. For now, let's just make sure it's enabled on your system:

1. Press **Windows Logo+W** to open the Settings search pane.

2. Type **user** and then click **Change User Account Control (UAC) Settings** in the search results. The User Account Control Settings dialog box appears.

3. Use the slider to choose one of the following three UAC settings (I'm ignoring the **Never Notify** setting at the bottom of the slider because that turns off UAC):

   - **Always Notify**—This is the top level, and it means that you're prompted for elevation when you change Windows settings, and when programs try to change settings and install software. This keeps your PC super-safe, but it also means you get pestered by Windows a lot, so it might get annoying after a while.

   - **Default**—This is the second highest level, and it prompts you for elevation only when programs try to change settings and install software. This level uses secure desktop mode to display the UAC dialog box. This setting offers the best trade-off between security and convenience.

- **No Secure Desktop**—This is the second lowest level, and it's the same as the Default level (that is, it prompts you for elevation only when programs try to change settings and install software), but this level doesn't use secure desktop mode when displaying the UAC dialog box. This makes your PC slightly less safe, but given that it doesn't make UAC all that much more convenient, I don't recommend this setting.

4. Click **OK**. The User Account Control dialog box appears.

5. Enter your UAC credentials to put the new setting into effect.

Making Sure the Administrator Account Is Disabled

One of the confusing aspects about Windows 8 is that the Administrator account seems to disappear after the setup is complete. It does so, for security reasons, because Windows 8 doesn't give you access to this all-powerful account. However, there are ways to activate this account, so it pays to take a second and make sure it's still in its disabled state.

You can do this in several ways, but here's a quick look at two of them:

- **Using the Local Security Policy Editor**—At the Start screen, type **secpol. msc** and then press **Enter**. In the Local Security Policy editor, open the **Local Policies, Security Options** branch and then double-click the **Accounts: Administrator Account Status** policy. Click **Disabled** and then click **OK**.

- **Using the Local Users and Groups snap-in**—Select **Start**, type **lusrmgr. msc**, and then press **Enter**. In the Local Users and Groups snap-in, click Users and then double-click **Administrator**. In the Administrator Properties dialog box, activate the **Account Is Disabled** check box and then click **OK**.

Making Sure the Firewall Is Up to Snuff

If you want to see just how vulnerable your computer is, several good sites on the Web will test your security:

- **Gibson Research (Shields Up)**—www.grc.com/default.htm

- **DSL Reports**—www.dslreports.com/secureme_go

- **HackerWhacker**—www.hackerwhacker.com

The good news is that Windows includes the Windows Firewall tool, which is a personal firewall that can lock down your ports and prevent unauthorized access to your machine. In effect, your computer becomes *invisible* to the Internet (although you can still surf the Web and work with email normally). Other firewall programs exist out there, but Windows Firewall does a good job.

Chapter 15

Maintaining Your PC

Computer problems, like the proverbial death and taxes, seem to be one of those constants in life. Whether it's a hard disk giving up the ghost, a power failure that trashes your files, or a virus that invades your system, the issue isn't *whether* something will go wrong, but rather *when* it will happen. Instead of waiting to deal with these difficulties after they've occurred (what I call *pound-of-cure mode*), you need to become proactive and perform maintenance on your system in advance (call it *ounce-of-prevention mode*). Doing so not only reduces the chances that something will go wrong, but also sets up your system to recover more easily from any problems that do occur. This chapter shows you various Windows tools and techniques that can help you do just that. At the end of the chapter, I give you a step-by-step plan for maintaining your system and checking for the first signs of problems.

Checking Free Disk Space

Hard disks with capacities measured in the hundreds of gigabytes are standard even in low-end systems nowadays, and multiterabyte hard disks are now commonplace. This means that disk space is much less of a problem than it used to be. Still, you need to keep track of how much free space you have on your disk drives.

Follow these steps to check the free disk space on your PC's drives:

1. On the Windows 8 Start screen, type **computer** and then select **Computer** in the search results. Windows opens the File Explorer program and displays the contents of the Computer folder, which displays icons for the disk drives on your PC.

2. Select the **View** tab.

3. In the Layout list, select **Tiles**. File Explorer displays the disk drive icons as shown in Figure 15.1.

4. Examine the icons for your disk drives:

   • Each icon has a caption of the form X free of Y, where X is the number of gigabytes (GB) or megabytes (MB) of free space and Y is the total capacity of the drive.

   • Each icon displays a horizontal bar that uses a color strip to give you a visual indication of how full the drive is. If the colored portion of that bar is blue, it means the drive still has plenty of free space; if it's red, instead, it means the drive is running low on disk space.

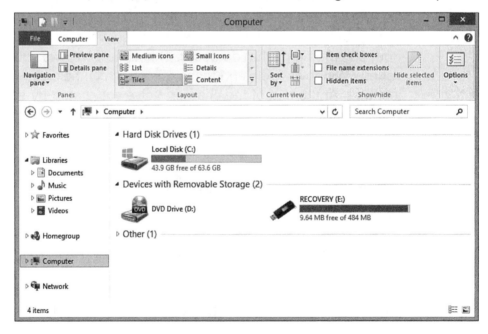

Figure 15.1 *In File Explorer, the Computer folder tells you the total size and free space on your system's disks.*

Deleting Unnecessary Files

If you find that a hard disk volume is getting low on free space, you should delete any unneeded files and programs. Windows 8 comes with a Disk Cleanup utility that enables you to remove certain types of files quickly and easily. Before using this utility, you should first uninstall programs (see Chapter 5, "Learning Windows Basics") you don't use, which should free up quite a bit of space.

You should next run the Disk Cleanup utility, which can automatically remove various categories of files that your system no longer needs, including the following:

- **Downloaded program files**—Small web page programs downloaded onto your hard drive.

- **Temporary Internet files**—Copies of web pages that Internet Explorer keeps on hand so the pages view faster the next time you visit them. Deleting these files slows down some of your web surfing slightly but also rescues lots of disk space.

- **Offline web pages**—Web page copies stored on your hard drive for offline viewing.

- **Recycle Bin**—The files that you've deleted recently. Windows 8 stores them in the Recycle Bin just in case you delete a file accidentally. If you're sure you don't need to recover a file, you can clean out the Recycle Bin and recover the disk space.

- **Temporary files**—"Scratch pad" files that some programs use to doodle on while they're up and running. Most programs toss out these files, but a program or computer crash can prevent that from happening; delete these files at will.

- **Thumbnails**—Copies of picture files used by Windows 8 to quickly display thumbnail versions of those files. If you delete them, Windows 8 will re-create them as needed.

Here's how the process works:

1. On the Windows 8 Start screen, type **computer** and then select **Computer** in the search results. Windows opens the File Explorer program and displays the Computer folder.

2. Right-click the drive you want to clean up and then click **Properties**. The drive's Properties dialog box appears.

3. Click **Disk Cleanup**. Disk Cleanup scans the drive to see which files can be deleted.

4. Click **Clean Up System Files**. Disk Cleanup displays an expanded list of file types, as shown in Figure 15.2.

Figure 15.2 *Disk Cleanup can automatically and safely remove certain types of files from a disk drive.*

5. In the **Files to Delete** list, activate the check box beside each category of file you want to remove. If you're not sure what an item represents, select it and read the text in the **Description** box below. Note, too, that for most of these items you can click **View Files** to see what you'll be deleting.

6. Click **OK**. Disk Cleanup asks whether you're sure that you want to delete the files.

7. Click **Yes**. Disk Cleanup deletes the selected files.

Defragmenting Your Hard Disk

Windows 8 comes with a utility called Defragment and Optimize Drives that's an essential tool for tuning your hard disk. The job of Defragment and Optimize Drives is to rid your hard disk of file fragmentation.

File fragmentation is one of those terms that sounds scarier than it actually is. It simply means that a file is stored on your hard disk in scattered, noncontiguous bits. Having files stored this way is a performance drag because it means that when Windows 8 tries to open such a file, it must make several stops to collect the various pieces. If a lot of files are fragmented, even the fastest hard disk can slow to a crawl.

The good news with Windows 8 is that it configures Defragment and Optimize Drives to run automatically; the default schedule is once a week. This means you should never need to defragment your system manually. However, you might want to run a defragment before loading a particularly large software program.

Before using Defragment and Optimize Drives, you should delete any files from your hard disk that you don't need, as described in the "Deleting Unnecessary Files" section earlier in this chapter. Defragmenting junk files only slows down the whole process.

Follow these steps to use Defragment and Optimize Drives:

1. In the Start screen, press **Windows Logo+W** to open the Settings search pane, type **defrag**, and then click **Defragment and Optimize Your Drives** in the search results. The Optimize Drives window appears, as shown in Figure 15.3.

2. Click the disk you want to defragment.

3. Click **Optimize**. Windows 8 defragments your hard drives.

4. When the defragment is complete, click **Close**.

 Tip

Double Defragment

In some cases, you can defragment a drive even further by running Defragment and Optimize Drives on the drive twice in a row. (That is, run the defragment, and when it's done, immediately run a second defragment.)

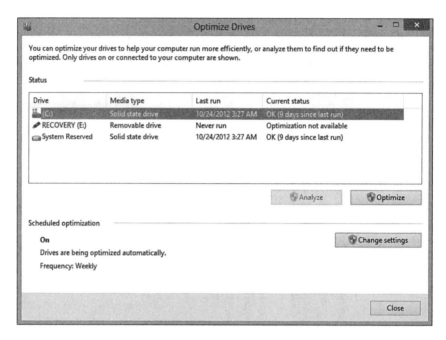

Figure 15.3 *Use Defragment and Optimize Drives to eliminate file fragmentation and improve hard disk performance.*

Preparing for Trouble

A big part of ounce-of-prevention mode is the unwavering belief that someday something *will* go wrong with your computer. That might sound unduly pessimistic, but hey, this is a *PC* we're talking about here, and it's never a question of *if* the thing will go belly up one day, but rather *when* that day will come.

With that gloomy mindset, the only sensible thing to do is prepare for that dire day so that you're ready to get your system back on its feet. So part of your Windows 8 maintenance chores should be getting a few things ready that will serve you well on the day your PC decides to go haywire on you. Besides performing a system image backup (which I describe a bit later), you should be backing up your files, setting system restore points, and creating a recovery drive. The next few sections cover all these techniques.

Backing Up File Versions with File History

Windows 8 has the capability to store previous versions of files and folders, where a "previous" version is defined as a copy of an object that has subsequently changed. For example, suppose that you make changes to a particular document each day for three days in a row. This means that you'll end up with three previous versions of the document: the original, the one with yesterday's changes, and the one with today's changes.

Taken together, these previous versions represent the document's *file history*, and you can access and work with previous versions by activating the File History feature. When you turn on File History and specify an external drive to store the data, Windows 8 begins monitoring your libraries, your desktop, your contacts, and your Internet Explorer favorites. Once an hour, Windows 8 checks to see whether any of this data has changed since the last check. If it has, Windows 8 saves copies of the changed files to the external drive.

When you have some data saved, you can then use it to restore a previous version of a file, as described later in this chapter.

To start, connect an external drive to your PC. The drive should have enough capacity to hold your user account files, so an external hard drive is probably best. Now you need to set up the external drive for use with File History.

The easiest way to do this is to look for the notification that appears a few moments after you connect the drive. Click the notification and then click **Configure This Drive for Backup**.

If you miss the notification, follow these steps instead:

1. In the Windows 8 Start screen, press **Windows Logo+W** to open the Settings search pane, type **history**, and then click **File History**. The File History window appears.

2. Examine the **Copy Files To** section of the window. If you see your external hard drive listed, as shown in Figure 15.4, you can skip the rest of these steps.

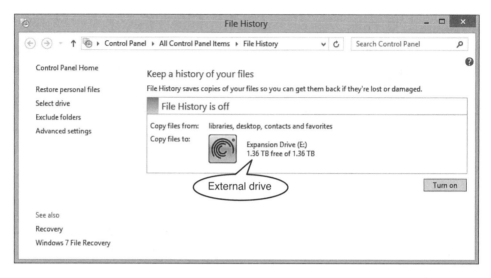

Figure 15.4 *Windows 8 should recognize your external drive and add it to the File History window.*

3. Click **Select Drive**. The Change Drive window appears.

4. Select the drive you want to use and then click **OK**. Windows 8 displays the external drive in the File History window.

At long last, you're ready to start using File History. In the File History window, click **Turn On**. If Windows 8 asks whether you want to recommend the drive to your homegroup, click **Yes** or **No**, as you see fit. File History immediately goes to work saving the initial copies of your files to the external drive or network share.

Restoring a Previous Version of a File

When you activate File History on your PC, as described earlier in this chapter, Windows 8 periodically—by default, once an hour—looks for files that have changed since the last check. If it finds a changed file, it takes a "snapshot" of that file and saves that version of the file to the external drive that you specified when you set up File History. This gives Windows 8 the

Note

Previous Versions of Folders

Windows 8 also keeps track of previous versions of folders, which is useful if an entire folder becomes corrupted because of a system crash.

capability to reverse the changes you have made to a file by reverting to an earlier state of the file. An earlier state of a file is called a *previous version*.

Why would you want to revert to a previous version of a file? One reason is that you might improperly edit the file by deleting or changing important data. In some cases, you may be able to restore that data by going back to a previous version of the file. Another reason is that the file might become corrupted if the program or Windows 8 crashes. You can get back a working version of the file by restoring a previous version.

Follow these steps to restore a previous version of a file:

1. In the Start screen, press **Windows Logo+W**, type **history**, and then click **File History** to open the File History window.

2. Click **Restore Personal Files**. The File History window appears.

3. Double-click the library that contains the file you want to restore.

4. Open the folder that contains the file.

5. Click **Previous Version** (see Figure 15.5) or press **Ctrl+Left arrow** until you open the version of the folder you want to use. If you'd prefer a more recent version, click **Next Version** or press **Ctrl+Right arrow**.

6. Click the file you want to restore.

7. Click **Restore to Original Location** (pointed out in Figure 15.5). If the original folder has a file with the same name, File History asks what you want to do.

8. Select an option:

   - **Replace the File in the Destination Folder**—Click this option to overwrite the existing file with the previous version.

   - **Skip This File**—Click this option to skip the restore and do nothing.

   - **Compare Info for Both Files**—Click this option to display the File Conflict dialog box (see Figure 15.6), which shows the original and the previous version side by side, along with the last modification date and time and the file size. Activate the check box beside the version you want to keep and then click **Continue**. To keep both versions, activate both check boxes. File History restores the previous version with (2) appended to its filename.

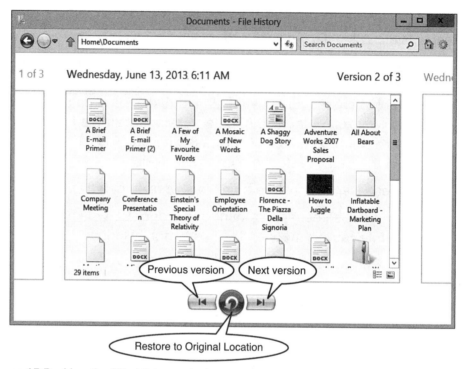

Figure 15.5 *Use the File History window to choose which previous version you want to restore.*

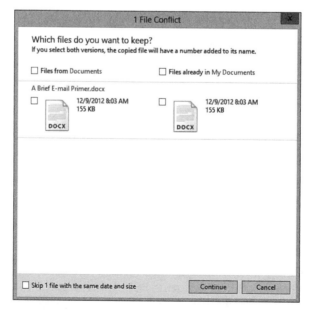

Figure 15.6 *If the original folder has a file with the same name and you're not sure which one to keep, use the File Conflict dialog box to decide.*

Setting System Restore Points

One of the biggest causes of Windows instability in the past was the tendency of some newly installed programs simply to not get along with Windows. The problem could be a program that didn't mesh with the Windows system or a settings change that caused havoc on other programs or on Windows. Similarly, hardware installations often caused problems by adding faulty device drivers to the system or by corrupting some Windows files.

To help guard against software or hardware installations that bring down the system, Windows 8 offers the System Restore feature. Its job is straightforward yet clever: to take periodic snapshots—called *restore points* or *protection points*—of your system, each of which includes the currently installed program files, system settings, and other crucial system data. The idea is that if a program or device installation causes problems on your system, you use System Restore to revert your system to the most recent restore point before the installation (I show you how to do this in Chapter 16, "Troubleshooting Your PC").

System Restore automatically creates restore points under certain conditions. For example, it creates an automatic restore point (called a *system checkpoint*) once a week, and it creates a restore point before installing certain programs and devices.

You also are able to create a restore point manually using the System Protection feature, which is a good idea if you're installing a large program or an older device that might not work properly with Windows 8. Here are the steps to follow:

1. Press **Windows Logo+W** to open the Settings search pane, type **restore point**, and then click **Create a Restore Point** in the search results. This opens the System Properties dialog box with the System Protection tab displayed, as shown in Figure 15.7.

2. Click **Create** to display the Create a Restore Point dialog box.

3. Type a description for the new restore point and then click **Create**. System Protection creates the restore point and displays a dialog box to let you know.

4. Click **Close** to return to the System Properties dialog box.

5. Click **OK**.

Figure 15.7   *Use the System Protection tab to set a restore point.*

Creating a Recovery Drive

We all hope our computers operate trouble-free over their lifetimes, but we know from bitter experience that this is rarely the case. Computers are incredibly complex systems, so it is almost inevitable that a PC will develop glitches. If your hard drive is still accessible, you can boot to Windows 8 and access the recovery tools, as I describe in Chapter 16.

If you can't boot your PC, however, you must boot using some other drive. If you have your Windows 8 installation media, you can boot using that drive. If you don't have the installation media, you can still recover if you've created a USB recovery drive. This is a USB flash drive that contains the Windows 8 recovery environment, which enables you to refresh or reset your PC, use System Restore, recover a system image, and more.

Before you can boot to a recovery drive, such as a USB flash drive, you need to create the drive. Follow these steps:

1. Insert the USB flash drive you want to use. Note that the drive must have a capacity of at least 256MB. Also, Windows 8 will erase all data on the drive, so make sure it doesn't contain any files you want to keep.

2. In the Start screen, press **Windows Logo+W**, type **recovery**, and then click **Create a Recovery Drive**. User Account Control appears.

3. Click **Yes** or enter administrator credentials to continue. The Recovery Drive Wizard appears.

4. Click **Next**. The Recovery Drive Wizard prompts you to choose the USB flash drive, as shown in Figure 15.8.

Note

Ignore the Notification

You might see a notification a few moments after you insert the flash drive. If so, you can ignore it.

Figure 15.8 *Select the flash drive that you inserted in step 1.*

5. Click the drive, if it isn't selected already, and then click **Next**. The Recovery Drive Wizard warns you that all the data on the drive will be deleted.

6. Click **Create**. The wizard formats the drive and copies the recovery tools and data.

7. Click **Finish**.

Remove the drive, label it, and then put it someplace where you'll be able to find it later, just in case.

Creating a System Image Backup

The worst-case scenario for PC problems is a system crash that renders your hard disk or system files unusable. Your only recourse in such a case is to start from scratch with either a reformatted hard disk or a new hard disk. This usually means that you have to reinstall Windows 8 and then reinstall and reconfigure all your applications. In other words, you're looking at the better part of a day or, more likely, a few days, to recover your system. However, Windows 8 has a feature that takes most of the pain out of recovering your system. It's called a *system image backup,* and it's part of the system recovery options that I discuss in Chapter 16.

Tip

Test Your Recovery Drive

To make sure your recovery drive works properly, you should test it by booting your PC to the drive. Insert the recovery drive and then restart your PC. How you boot to the drive depends on your system. Some PCs display a menu of boot devices, and you select the USB drive from that menu. In other cases, you see a message telling you to press a key.

The system image backup is actually a complete backup of your Windows 8 installation. Creating a system image takes a long time (at least several hours, depending on how much stuff you have), but doing so is worthwhile for the peace of mind. Here are the steps to follow to create the system image:

1. Press **Windows Logo+W**, type **file recovery**, and then click **Windows 7 File Recovery**. The Windows 7 File Recovery window appears.

2. Click **Create a System Image**. The Create a System Image Wizard appears.

3. The wizard asks you to specify a backup destination. You have three choices, as shown in Figure 15.9. (Click **Next** when you're ready to continue.)

    *   **On a Hard Disk**—Select this option if you want to use a disk drive on your computer. If you have multiple drives, use the list to select the one you want to use.

- **On One or More DVDs**—Select this option if you want to use DVDs to hold the backup. Depending on how much data your PC holds, you might need to use dozens of discs for this (at least!), so I don't recommend this option.

- **On a Network Location**—Select this option if you want to use a shared network folder. Either type the address of the share or click **Select** and then click **Browse** to use the Browse for Folder dialog box to choose the shared network folder. Make sure it's a share for which you have permission to add data. Type a username and password for accessing the share and then click **OK**.

Figure 15.9 *You can create the system image on a hard drive, on DVDs, or on a network share.*

4. The system image backup automatically includes your internal hard disk in the system image, and you can't change that. However, if you also have external hard drives, you can add them to the backup by activating their check boxes. Click **Next**. Windows Backup asks you to confirm your backup settings.

5. Click **Start Backup**. Windows Backup creates the system image. When the backup is complete, Windows 8 asks whether you want to create a system repair disc.

6. You don't need a system repair disc if you already created a recovery drive, so click **No**. If you don't have a recovery drive and don't have a USB flash drive to create one, click **Yes** and follow steps 2–5 in the next section.

7. Click **Close**.

8. Click **OK**.

If you used a hard drive and you have multiple external drives lying around, be sure to label the one that contains the system image so you'll be able to find it later.

Caution

Refresh Your System Image

Many people make the mistake of creating the system image once and then ignoring it, forgetting that their systems aren't set in stone. Over the coming days and weeks, you'll be installing apps, tweaking settings, and, of course, creating lots of new documents and other data. This means that you should periodically create a fresh system image. Should disaster strike, you'll be able to recover most of your system.

Setting Up a Maintenance Schedule

Maintenance is effective only if it's done regularly, but there's a fine line to be navigated. If maintenance is performed too often, it can become a burden and interfere with more interesting tasks; if it's performed too seldom, it becomes ineffective. How often should you perform the maintenance chores listed in this chapter? Here's a maintenance plan:

1. Check free disk space. Do this about once a month. If the free space is getting low on a drive, check it approximately once a week.

2. Delete unnecessary files. If free disk space isn't a problem, run this chore once every two or three months.

3. Defragment your hard disk. How often you defragment your hard disk depends on how often you use your computer. If you use it every day, then you're fine using the default Defragment and Optimize Drives schedule of once a week. If your computer doesn't get heavy use, you probably need to run Defragment and Optimize Drives only once a month or so.

4. Set restore points. Windows already sets regular system checkpoints, so you need to create your own restore points only when you're installing a program or device or making some other major change to your system.

5. Create a system image backup. You should create a system image backup once a month or any time you make major changes to your system.

Chapter 16

Troubleshooting Your PC

In Chapter 15, "Maintaining Your PC," you learned a few techniques that can help stave off problems, such as deleting unnecessary files and defragmenting your hard drive. That chapter also pessimistically included a section on preparing for trouble because, well, stuff happens in the PC world. If you find yourself in a bit of a pickle because your PC is acting wonky (or not acting at all), you've come to the right place. This chapter provides you with a number of strategies and techniques for not only diagnosing the problem, but also for fixing whatever's gone haywire with your PC.

Determining the Source of a Problem

One of the ongoing mysteries that all Windows users experience at one time or another is what might be called the "now you see it, now you don't" problem. This is a glitch that plagues you for a while and then mysteriously vanishes without any intervention on your part. (This situation also tends to occur when you ask a nearby user or someone from the IT department to look at the problem. Like the automotive problem that goes away when you take the car to a mechanic, computer problems often resolve themselves as soon as a knowledgeable user sits down at the keyboard.) When this happens, most people just shake their heads and resume working, grateful to no longer have to deal with the problem.

Unfortunately, most computer ills aren't resolved so easily. For these more intractable problems, your first order of business is to hunt down the source of the glitch. This is, at best, a black art, but it can be done if you take a systematic approach. Over the years, I've found that the best approach is to ask a series of questions designed to gather the required information or to narrow down what might be the culprit. The next few sections take you through these questions.

Did You Get an Error Message?

Unfortunately, most computer error messages are obscure and do little to help you resolve a problem directly. However, error codes and error text can help you down the road, either by giving you something to search for in an online database or by providing information to a tech support person. Therefore, you should always write down the full text of any error message that appears.

 **Tip**

Capture the Error Screen

If the error message is lengthy and you can still use other programs on your computer, don't bother writing down the full message. Instead, while the message is displayed, press **Windows Logo+Print Screen** to place an image of the current screen as a file in your Pictures library.

Did You Recently Change Any Windows Settings?

If the problem started after you changed your Windows configuration, try reversing the change. Even something as seemingly innocent as activating a screensaver can cause problems, so don't rule out anything. If you've made a number of recent changes and you're not sure about everything you did, or if it would take too long to reverse all the changes individually, use System Restore to revert your system to the most recent checkpoint before you made the changes. See "Recovering Using System Restore," later in this chapter.

Did You Recently Change Any Application Settings?

If you've recently changed an application setting, try reversing the change to see whether doing so solves the problem. If that doesn't help, here are three other things to try:

- Check the developer's website to see whether an upgrade or patch is available.

- Run the application's Repair option (if it has one), which is often useful for fixing corrupted or missing files. To see whether a program has a Repair option, press **Windows Logo+W**, type **uninstall**, and then click **Change or Remove a Program**. In the Programs and Features window, click the problematic application and then look to see whether there is a Repair item in the taskbar (see Figure 16.1).

- Reinstall the program.

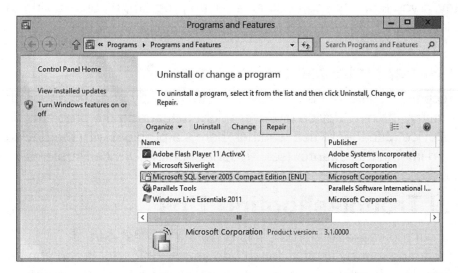

Figure 16.1 *In the Programs and Features window, click the program and look for a Repair option in the taskbar.*

Note

Shutting Down a Stuck Program

If a program freezes, you won't be able to shut it down using conventional methods. If you try, you might see a dialog box warning you that the program is not responding. If so, click **End Now** to force the program to close. If that doesn't work, right-click the taskbar and then click **Task Manager**. You should see your stuck application listed. Click the program and then click **End Task**.

Did You Recently Install a New Program?

If you suspect a new program is causing system instability, restart Windows 8 and try operating the system for a while without using the new program. If the problem doesn't reoccur, the new program is likely the culprit. Try using the program without any other programs running.

You should also examine the program's readme file (if it has one) to look for known problems and possible workarounds. It's also a good idea to check for a Windows 8–compatible version of the program. Again, you can also try the program's Repair option (if it has one), or you can reinstall the program.

Similarly, if you recently upgraded an existing program, try uninstalling the upgrade.

Did You Recently Install a New Device?

If you recently installed a new device or if you recently updated an existing device driver, the new device or driver might be causing the problem. Check Device Manager to see whether there's a problem with the device, as described later in this chapter (see "Troubleshooting Device Problems").

General Troubleshooting Tips

Figuring out the cause of a problem is often the hardest part of troubleshooting, but by itself it doesn't do you much good. When you know the source, you need to parlay that information into a fix for the problem. I discussed a few solutions in the preceding section, but here are a few other general fixes you need to keep in mind:

- **Close all programs.** You can often fix flaky behavior by shutting down all your open programs and starting again. This is a particularly useful fix for problems caused by low memory or low system resources.

- **Log off Windows 8.** Logging off clears the memory and thus gives you a slightly cleaner slate than merely closing all your programs.

- **Reboot the computer.** If you have problems with some system files and devices, logging off won't help because these objects remain loaded. By rebooting the system, you reload the entire system, which is often enough to solve many computer problems.

- **Turn off the computer and restart.** You can often solve a hardware problem by first shutting off your machine. Wait for 30 seconds to give all devices time to spin down, and then restart.

- **Check connections, power switches, and so on.** Some of the most common (and some of the most embarrassing) causes of hardware problems are the simple physical things. Therefore, make sure that a device is turned on, check that cable connections are secure, and ensure that insertable devices are properly connected.

Troubleshooting Device Problems

Windows 8 has excellent support for most newer devices, and most major hardware vendors have taken steps to update their devices and drivers to run properly with Windows 8. If you use only recent, Plug and Play–compliant devices that qualify for the Designed for Windows 8 logo, you should have a trouble-free computing experience (at least from a hardware perspective). Of course, putting *trouble-free* and *computing* next to each other is just asking for trouble. Hardware is not foolproof—far from it. Things still can, and will, go wrong, and when they do, you'll need to perform some kind of troubleshooting. (Assuming, of course, that the device doesn't have a physical fault that requires a trip to the repair shop.) Fortunately, Windows 8 also has some handy tools to help you both identify and rectify hardware ills.

Troubleshooting with Device Manager

Device Manager (press **Windows Logo+X** and then click **Device Manager**) not only provides you with a comprehensive summary of your system's hardware data, but also doubles as a decent troubleshooting tool. To see what I mean, check out the Device Manager window shown in Figure 16.2. See how the **Other Devices** branch has an **Unknown Device** item that has an exclamation mark superimposed on its icon? This icon tells you that there's a problem with the device.

If you double-click the problem device to open its properties, as shown in Figure 16.3, the **Device Status** area tells you a bit more about what's wrong. As you can see in Figure 16.3, the problem here is that the device drivers aren't installed. Device Manager usually offers a suggested remedy (such as the **Update Driver** button shown in Figure 16.3).

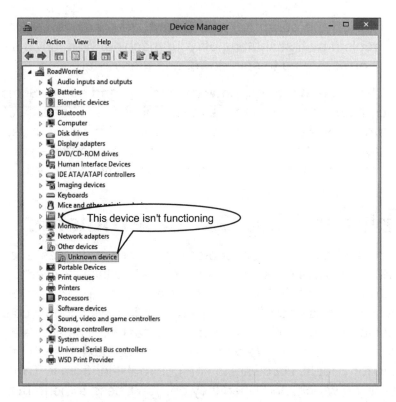

Figure 16.2 *The Device Manager uses icons to warn you there's a problem with a device.*

Figure 16.3 *The Device Status area tells you if the device isn't working properly.*

Device Manager uses three different icons to give you an indication of the device's current status:

- A black exclamation mark (!) on a yellow field tells you that there's a problem with the device.

- A red X tells you that the device is disabled or missing.

- A blue i on a white field tells you that the device's **Use Automatic Settings** check box (on the Resources tab) is deactivated and that at least one of the device's resources was selected manually. Note that the device might be working just fine, so this icon doesn't indicate a problem. If the device isn't working properly, however, the manual setting might be the cause.

If your system flags a device, but you don't notice any problems, you can usually get away with just ignoring the flag. I've seen lots of systems that run perfectly well with flagged devices, so this falls under the "If it ain't broke..." school of troubleshooting. The danger here is that tweaking your system to try to get rid of the flag can cause other—usually more serious—problems.

Troubleshooting Device Driver Problems

Other than problems with the hardware itself, device drivers are the cause of most device woes. This is true even if your device doesn't have one of the problem icons mentioned in the preceding section. That is, if you open the device's properties sheet, Windows 8 may tell you that the device is "working properly," but all that means is that Windows 8 can establish a simple communications channel with the device. So if your device isn't working right, but Windows 8 says otherwise, suspect a driver problem. Here are a few tips and pointers for correcting device driver problems:

- **Reinstall the driver.** A driver might be malfunctioning because one or more of its files have become corrupted. You can usually solve this problem by reinstalling the driver. Just in case a disk fault caused the corruption, you should check the partition where the driver is installed for errors before reinstalling.

- **Upgrade to a signed driver.** Unsigned drivers—that is, device drivers that don't come with a signature from Microsoft that verifies the drivers are safe to install—are accidents waiting for a place to happen in Windows 8, so you should upgrade to a signed driver, if possible. How can you tell whether an installed driver is unsigned? Open the device's properties sheet and then display the Driver tab. Signed driver files display a name beside the Digital Signer label, whereas unsigned drivers display "Not digitally signed" instead.

- **Disable an unsigned driver.** If an unsigned driver is causing system instability and you can't upgrade the driver, try disabling it. In the Driver tab of the device's properties sheet, click **Disable**.

- **Try the manufacturer's driver supplied with the device.** If the device came with its own driver, either try updating the driver to the manufacturer's or try running the device's setup program.

- **Download the latest driver from the manufacturer.** Device manufacturers often update drivers to fix bugs, add new features, and tweak performance. Go to the manufacturer's website to see whether an updated driver is available.

- **Roll back a driver.** If the device stops working properly after you update the driver, try rolling it back to the old driver. (See the next section.)

Rolling Back a Device Driver

If an updated device driver is giving you problems, you have two ways to fix things:

- If updating the driver was the last action you performed on the system, restore the system to the most recent restore point.

- If you've updated other things on the system in the meantime, a restore point might restore more than you need. In that case, you need to roll back just the device driver that's causing problems.

Follow these steps to roll back a device driver:

1. Press **Windows Logo+X** and select **Device Manager**.

2. Double-click the device to open its **Properties** dialog box.

3. Display the Driver tab.

4. Click **Roll Back Driver** and then click **OK**.

Recovering from a Problem

Ideally, solving a problem requires a specific tweak to the system: a Registry setting change, a driver upgrade, a program uninstall. But sometimes you need to take more of a "big picture" approach to revert your system to some previous state in the hope that you'll leap past the problem and get your system working again. Fortunately, Windows 8 comes with a boatload of tools that can help in both scenarios, and I use the rest of this chapter to tell you about these tools.

Accessing the Recovery Environment

Windows 8 offers a revamped Recovery Environment (RE) that gives you a simple, easily navigated set of screens that offer a number of troubleshooting tools and utilities. In previous versions of Windows, you could access the advanced startup options by pressing **F8** during startup— that is, after your PC completed its Power On Self Test (POST). That technique no longer works, but Windows 8 offers many other ways to get to the RE and its advanced startup options, including the following:

- Use the PC Settings app from within Windows 8.
- Boot to a recovery drive.
- Boot to your Windows 8 installation media.

The next few sections discuss each method in more detail.

Accessing the RE via PC Settings

If you're having trouble with your PC, but you can still start Windows 8, you can use the PC Settings app to access the RE. Follow these steps to boot to the RE using the PC Settings app within Windows 8:

1. Press **Windows Logo+W** to open the Settings search pane.

2. Type **advanced** and then click **Advanced Startup Options** in the search results. Windows 8 opens the PC Settings app and displays the General tab.

3. In the Advanced Startup section, click **Restart Now**. The Choose an Option screen appears, as shown in Figure 16.4.

4. Click **Troubleshoot**.

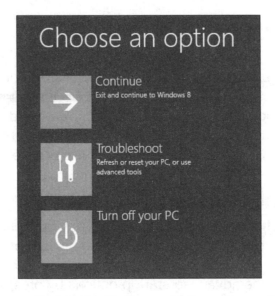

Figure 16.4 *When you boot to the Choose an Option screen, click Troubleshoot to see the Recovery Environment tools.*

Accessing the RE via a Recovery Drive

If you're having a problem with your system and are unable to start Windows 8 and can't even access your hard drive, you can still access a version of the RE if you created a recovery drive (see "Creating a Recovery Drive" in Chapter 15).

Follow these steps to boot to the RE using the recovery drive:

1. Insert the recovery drive.

2. Restart your PC and boot to the USB flash drive:

   - If you have a newer PC, Windows 8 should recognize the flash drive automatically and display the Use a Device screen. Click your flash drive in the list that appears.

   - If you have an older PC, you need to access your PC's settings and configure them to boot to the flash drive. Look for a message right after you turn on the PC that says something like "Press Del to access BIOS/Start settings." Press the key and then use the settings for the boot options to configure your PC to boot to the USB flash drive.

3. Click a keyboard layout. The Choose an Option screen appears.

4. Click **Troubleshoot**.

Accessing the RE via Windows 8 Install Media

If you didn't create a recovery drive, but you have your Windows 8 installation media, follow these steps to boot to the RE using the install media:

1. Insert your Windows 8 install media.

2. Restart your PC and boot to the install drive.

3. When the Windows Setup dialog box appears, click **Next**.

4. Click **Repair Your Computer**. The Choose an Option screen appears.

5. Click **Troubleshoot**.

Navigating the Recovery Environment

In the previous few sections, each procedure dropped you off at the Troubleshoot screen, shown in Figure 16.5.

From here, you can refresh or reset your PC (we discuss these options later in this chapter; see "Refreshing Your PC" and "Resetting Your PC"). You can also click **Advanced Options** to display the Advanced Options screen, shown in Figure 16.6.

From here, you can run **System Restore** (see "Recovering Using System Restore," later in this chapter), recover a system image (see "Restoring a System Image"), and more.

Tip

Adjusting Your Boot Settings

If your system doesn't boot from the Windows 8 install media (or the system repair disc), you need to adjust the system's settings to allow it to boot. Restart the computer and look for a startup message that prompts you to press a key or key combination to modify the PC's settings (which might be called Setup or something similar). Find the boot options and either enable a media drive–based boot or make sure that the option to boot from the media drive comes before the option to boot from the hard disk. If you use a USB keyboard, you may also need to enable an option that lets the system recognize keystrokes after the POST but before Windows starts.

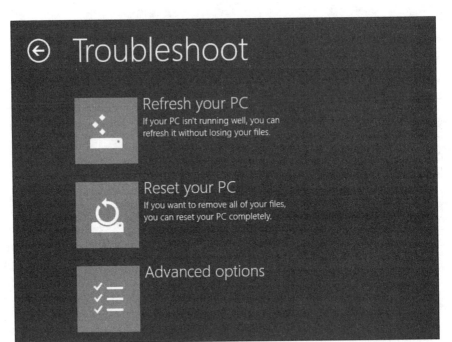

Figure 16.5 *The new Troubleshoot screen offers a few troubleshooting tools.*

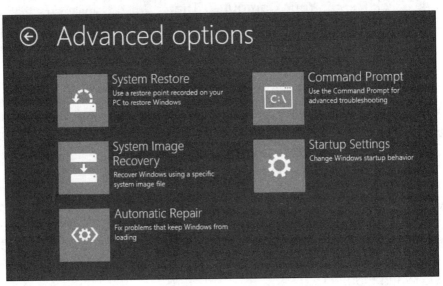

Figure 16.6 *The new Advanced Options screen offers even more troubleshooting tools.*

In most cases, you can also click **Startup Settings** and then click **Restart** to access even more startup settings. (Note that you don't see the Windows **Startup Settings** option if you boot to a recovery drive or the Windows 8 install media.) Windows 8 restarts your PC and displays the Startup Settings screen, shown in Figure 16.7.

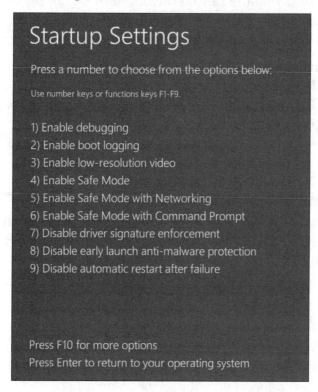

Startup Settings

Press a number to choose from the options below:

Use number keys or functions keys F1-F9.

1) Enable debugging
2) Enable boot logging
3) Enable low-resolution video
4) Enable Safe Mode
5) Enable Safe Mode with Networking
6) Enable Safe Mode with Command Prompt
7) Disable driver signature enforcement
8) Disable early launch anti-malware protection
9) Disable automatic restart after failure

Press F10 for more options
Press Enter to return to your operating system

Figure 16.7 *The Startup Settings screen offers several startup options.*

Press **Enter** to load Windows 8 in the usual fashion. You can use the other options to control the rest of the startup procedure. Here are the most useful of these options:

- **Enable Low-Resolution Video**—This option loads Windows 8 with the video display set to 640×480 and 256 colors. This capability is useful if your video output is garbled when you start Windows 8. For example, if your display settings are configured at a resolution that your video card can't handle, boot in the low-resolution mode and then switch to a setting supported by your video card.

- **Safe Mode**—The three Safe mode options enable you to run a barebones version of Windows 8 for troubleshooting. See "Booting Up in Safe Mode," next.

- **Disable Driver Signature Enforcement**—This item prevents Windows 8 from checking whether device drivers have digital signatures. Choose this option to ensure that Windows 8 loads an unsigned driver, if failing to load that driver is causing system problems.

- **Disable Early Launch Anti-Malware Protection**—This option prevents Windows 8 from scanning device drivers for malware during startup. If Windows 8 doesn't start, it's possible that the anti-malware scan is messing with a driver.

Booting Up in Safe Mode

If you're having trouble with Windows 8—for example, if a corrupt or incorrect video driver is mangling your display, or if Windows 8 doesn't start—you can use the **Safe Mode** option to run a stripped-down version of Windows 8 that includes only the minimal set of device drivers that Windows 8 requires to load. Using this mode, you could, for example, reinstall or roll back the offending device driver and then load Windows 8 normally.

When you start in Safe mode, Windows 8 uses the all-powerful Administrator account, which is the account to use when troubleshooting problems. However, caution is required when doing so.

When Windows 8 finally loads, as shown in Figure 16.8, the desktop reminds you that you're in Safe mode by displaying "Safe Mode" in each corner. (Also, Windows Help and Support appears with Safe mode–related information and links.)

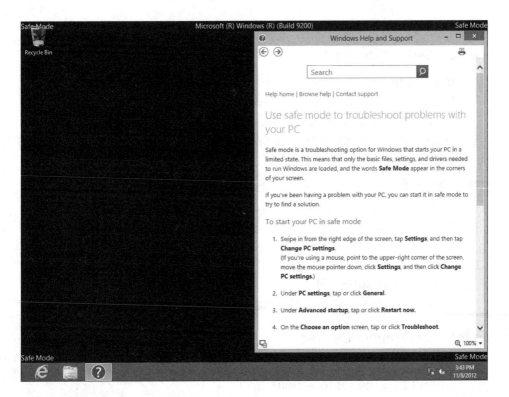

Figure 16.8 *Windows 8 in Safe mode.*

Recovering Using System Restore

If you make a change to your system—such as adding new hardware, updating a device driver, installing a program, or modifying some settings—and then find that the system doesn't start or acts weirdly, it's a good bet that the change is the culprit. In that case, you can tell Windows 8 to revert to an earlier configuration that worked. (That is, a configuration that doesn't include your most recent change.) The theory is that by using the previous working configuration, you can make your problem go away because the system is bypassing the change that caused the problem.

You revert Windows 8 to an earlier configuration by using System Restore. I showed you how to use System Restore to set restore points in Chapter 15.

To revert your system to a restore point, follow these steps:

1. Launch System Restore:

   - **If you can boot Windows 8**—In the Start screen, press **Windows Logo+W**, type **recovery**, click **Recovery**, and then click **Open System Restore**.

   - **If you can't boot Windows 8**—Boot to the Recovery Environment, as described earlier (see "Accessing the Recovery Environment"), click **Advanced Options**, and then click **System Restore**. Click your user account, type your account password, and then click **Continue**.

Tip

Restoring Via Safe Mode

System Restore is available in Safe mode. Therefore, if Windows 8 doesn't start properly, perform a Safe mode startup and run **System Restore** from there.

2. In the initial System Restore dialog box, click **Next**. System Restore displays a list of restore points.

3. If you don't see the restore point you want to use, click to activate the **Show More Restore Points** check box, which tells Windows 8 to display all the available restore points.

4. Click the restore point you want to use.

5. Click **Next**. If other hard disks are available in the restore point, Windows 8 displays a list of the disks. Activate the check box beside each disk you want to include in the restore and then click **Next**.

Note

Showing More Restore Points

By default, Windows 8 displays only the restore points from the previous five days. When you activate the **Show More Restore Points** check box, you tell Windows 8 to also show the restore points that are more than five days old.

6. Click **Finish**. Windows 8 asks you to confirm that you want your system restored.

7. Click **Yes**. System Restore begins reverting to the restore point. When it's done, it restarts your computer and displays a message telling you the results of the restore.

8. Click **Close**.

Refreshing Your PC

If the System Restore feature didn't solve your problem, the next recovery step to try is Refresh Your PC. This new tool reinstalls a fresh copy of Windows 8 while keeping your data, settings, and Windows 8 apps intact. When you refresh your PC, the computer boots to the Recovery Environment, gathers up your data, copies it to another part of the hard drive, reinstalls Windows 8, and then restores your data.

Here's what gets saved when you refresh your PC:

- The files in your user account

- Your personalization settings, wireless network connections, mobile broadband connections, and drive letter assignments

- Any Windows 8 apps you've installed

Here's what does *not* get saved during the refresh:

- All other PC settings (which are reverted to their defaults).

- Any desktop programs you installed. However, Windows 8 does generate a list of these programs for you.

Here are the steps to follow to refresh your PC:

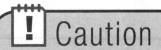

! Caution

Check Your Free Space

Because the refresh first makes a copy of your data and settings, you must have enough free space on your hard drive to hold this data. If you don't have the space, you can't refresh your PC.

1. Launch Refresh Your PC:

   - **If you can boot Windows 8**—In the Start screen, press **Windows Logo+W**, type **refresh**, and then click **Refresh Your PC**.

   - **If you can't boot Windows 8**—Boot to the Recovery Environment's Troubleshoot screen, as described earlier (see "Accessing the Recovery Environment"), and click **Refresh Your PC**. Windows 8 reboots the PC and asks you to choose your user account. Click your user account, type your account password, and then click **Continue**.

2. Click **Next**. Refresh Your PC prompts you to insert your installation media or a recovery drive.

3. Insert the media. Refresh Your PC validates the media and prompts you to start the process.

4. Click **Refresh**. Refresh Your PC reboots the computer and runs the refresh.

Resetting Your PC

Refreshing your PC should solve most problems. If it doesn't for some reason, or if you don't have enough room on your hard drive to perform the refresh, your next option is to completely reset your PC. (However, you should first consider restoring a system image, if you have one, as described in the next section.) This procedure completely erases your data, reformats your hard drive, and then reinstalls Windows 8, so it's a fairly drastic step.

Reset Your PC If You're Giving It Away

Resetting your PC is perfect if you're going to be giving your PC to someone else or selling it. This way, you don't have to worry about the new owner seeing any of your data or programs.

Follow these steps to reset your PC:

1. Launch Reset Your PC:

   - **If you can boot Windows 8**—In the Start screen, press **Windows Logo+W**, type **reset**, and then click **Remove Everything and Reinstall Windows**.

   - **If you can't boot Windows 8**—Boot to the Recovery Environment's Troubleshoot screen, as described earlier (see "Accessing the Recovery Environment"), and click **Reset Your PC**.

2. Click **Next**. Windows 8 reboots the PC and prompts you to insert your installation media or a recovery drive.

3. Insert the media. Reset Your PC asks how you want to remove your personal files.

4. Make your choice:

- **Thoroughly**—Choose this route if you're resetting your PC to give or sell to someone else. This option erases your personal data by overwriting it with random data at the sector level, but the process can take a few hours to complete.

- **Quickly**—Choose this option if you're keeping your computer and want to get it back on its feet as soon as possible.

5. Click **Reset**. Reset Your PC begins the recovery. Along the way you need to enter your Windows 8 product key, accept the license terms, name your PC, sign in with your Microsoft account, and perform a few other setup chores.

! Caution

Thorough Isn't *That* Thorough

The thorough data removal option is indeed thorough, but it is *not* 100% secure. Reset Your PC erases your data with a single pass of random data, but that's not enough to prevent someone with extremely sophisticated (and expensive) equipment from recovering some of your data. The thorough option is fine for the vast majority of us, but consider more robust erasure methods if your PC contains extremely sensitive or secret data. I suggest a free program called Eraser, which you can download from http://eraser.heidi.ie/.

Restoring a System Image

If you can't reset your PC because you don't have your Windows 8 install media or a recovery drive, you can still get your system back on its feet if you created a backup system image, as I described in Chapter 15.

Follow these steps to restore a system image:

1. If you saved the system image to an external hard drive, connect that hard drive. If you used DVDs, insert the last DVD in the set.

2. Boot to the Recovery Environment, as described earlier (see "Accessing the Recovery Environment").

3. Click **Advanced Options**. The Advanced Options screen appears.

4. Click **System Image Recovery**. Windows 8 asks you to choose a target operating system.

5. Click Windows 8. System Image Recovery prompts you to select a system image backup and offers two options:

   - **Use the Latest Available System Image**—Activate this option to restore Windows 8 using the most recently created system image. This is almost always the best way to go because it means you'll restore the maximum percentage of your data and programs. If you choose this option, click **Next** and skip to step 8.

   - **Select a System Image**—Activate this option to select from a list of restore points. This is the way to go if you saved a system image to your network, or if the most recent system image includes some change to your system that you believe is the source of your system problems. Click **Next** and continue with step 6.

6. Click the location of the system image and then click **Next**.

7. Click the system image you want to use for the restore and then click **Next**. If you want to use a system image saved to a network share, click **Advanced** and then click **Search for a System Image on the Network**.

8. If you replaced your hard drive, activate the **Format and Repartition Disks** check box.

9. Click **Next**. System Image Recovery displays a summary of the restore process.

10. Click **Finish**. System Image Recovery asks you to confirm.

11. Click **Yes**. System Image Recovery begins restoring your computer and then reboots to Windows 8 when the restore is complete.

Chapter 17

Repairing Your PC

Upgrading and repairing a desktop PC are arts that anybody can master. If you can wield a knife and fork without poking yourself in the eye, you have the requisite dexterity to perform any PC upgrade or repair task. If you can dress yourself in the morning, you have the needed organizational abilities to coordinate any PC upgrade and repair project.

That's not to say that working on the innards of a PC is trivial work—far from it. It's just that installing and configuring components such as an expansion card and memory module *seem* like tasks that require an advanced electrical engineering degree. The reality is that PC repair is a craft that falls somewhere in the middle of that spectrum, making it accessible to everyone. Accessible, that is, to everyone who's willing to learn a few basic skills that lie at the heart of the PC fixer's craft. Those skills are the subject of this chapter, where you learn about the tools you need; how to set up your work area; how to work safely; and fundamental techniques such as opening the case, connecting cables, and installing expansion cards.

What Tools Do You Need?

These days, you can almost get away with repairing a PC without requiring *any* tools at all! This is mostly thanks to the "toolless" designs of many modern computer cases, which enable you to install expansion cards, hard drives, and other internal drive bay components such as optical drives and memory card readers using clips (or variations on the clip theme) instead of screws.

I said *almost* because you still need a Phillips-head screwdriver to install a few components. In other words, you can perform probably 99% of all PC upgrade and repair chores using just an average Phillips screwdriver (see Figure 17.1)!

Figure 17.1 *The simplest PC-builder's toolkit: a single Phillips screwdriver!*

Of course, if you're anything like me, the tools are almost as much fun as the components themselves, so a single screwdriver doth not a toolkit make. If you're just starting out, one option is to buy a preassembled computer toolkit. For example, Figure 17.2 shows a toolkit that includes almost everything a budding PC repairer could want: a couple of Phillips- and flat-head screwdrivers, tweezers, pliers, extra screws, and more.

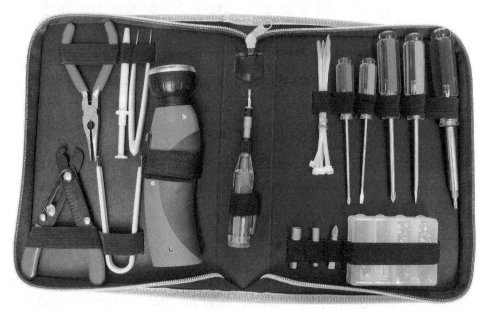

Figure 17.2 *A preassembled computer toolkit.*

The problem with almost all preassembled toolkits is that they're never perfect. For example, the kit shown in Figure 17.2 originally included a cheap soldering iron that's simply not going to be useful for most people. If they'd asked me, I'd have told them to replace the soldering iron with a decent flashlight, which is what I've done in Figure 17.2. So if you want to assemble your own toolkit (which is much more fun, anyway), here are my recommendations, more or less in descending order of importance:

- **Phillips-head screwdrivers**—This is the only essential computer tool. Note that not all Phillips screws are the same size, so I suggest getting several sizes of Phillips heads. At a minimum, get a #2 and a #1, and throw in a #0 if your budget permits it. (The smaller the number, the smaller the head; see Figure 17.3.)

Figure 17.3   *Several Phillips-head screwdrivers.*

- **Flashlight**—Although your work area should be well lit (see "Setting Up Your Work Area," later in this chapter), computer cases can have dark areas where it's tough to see what you're doing. A good flashlight can help illuminate these areas.

- **Tweezers**—You'll be surprised how often you have to manipulate tiny parts such as screws that have fallen into one nook or another. Trying to maneuver these parts with your fingers is an exercise in frustration. The solution is a good pair of tweezers. I like to keep around both a regular pair of tweezers and a screw grabber, which is often easier to maneuver into tight spots (see Figure 17.4). Instead of tweezers, you can use needle-nose pliers, particularly a pair with a long nose.

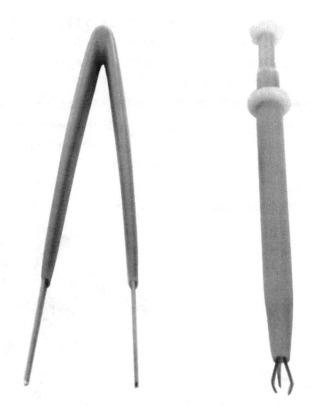

Figure 17.4 *Regular tweezers and a screw grabber often come in handy when manipulating small objects.*

- **Nut driver**—A 1/4-inch (or 7mm) nut driver is useful for screws that need to be inserted into or removed from tight spaces.

- **Cable ties**—To improve the air flow in your case, you need to combine cables and move them out of the way. Nylon cable ties make this easy.

- **Canned air**—A can of compressed air is great for thoroughly cleaning the dust off any component you've scavenged from an old PC.

- **Spare parts box**—A small plastic box provides a handy way to store extra screws, washers, jumpers, and other teensy parts that will get lost in five minutes unless you have a place to store them.

- **Flat-head screwdrivers**—These are also called slotted screwdrivers because the screws they work with include a slot across the top. You don't see these screws very often when working with PCs, but they sometimes come in handy with Phillips screws that also include a slot.

- **TORX screwdrivers**—You use these screwdrivers to manipulate tiny screws with star-shaped slots (see Figure 17.5). You'll never need a TORX screwdriver when installing PC components, but they're often used in the components themselves. So, for example, if one day you decide you want to see what the inside of a hard drive looks like, chances are you'll need a TORX screwdriver to remove the cover.

Figure 17.5 *Some TORX bits.*

! Caution

Avoid Power Tools

The inside of a PC case is no place for a power screwdriver (corded or cordless). The risk of overtightening a screw is just too great with these otherwise-useful tools, so you can easily break your motherboard or some other component. Also, power screwdrivers are bulky beasts that can easily slip off the screw and damage the board circuits.

What Software Do You Need?

Upgrading and repairing a PC are hardware-based tasks, but you'll still eventually need some software to animate the hardware and make it do something useful. In particular, many components require a *device driver*, which is a small piece of software that Windows uses to interact with (or "drive") a device such as a video card or network card.

Most new components ship with the device driver on a CD, but if you're using a used part or if Windows just doesn't recognize your device, you might need to manually load the device driver. In this case, it's a good idea to download the device's most recent driver from the manufacturer's website and place it on a CD or flash drive for later use.

Finding device drivers on the Web is an art in itself. I can't tell you how much of my life I've wasted rooting around manufacturer websites trying to locate a driver. Most hardware vendor sites seem to be optimized for sales rather than service, so although you can purchase, say, a new printer with just a mouse click or two, downloading a new driver for that printer can take a frustratingly long time. To help you avoid such frustration, I've included some tips here from my hard-won experience:

- If the manufacturer offers different sites for different locations (these are called mirror sites), always use the company's "home" site. Most mirror sites aren't true mirrors, and (Murphy's Law still being in effect) a mirror site is usually missing the driver you're looking for.

- The temptation when you first enter a site is to use the search feature to find what you want. This approach works only sporadically for drivers, and the site search engines almost always return marketing or sales material first.

- Instead of the search engine, look for an area of the site dedicated to downloads. The good sites have links to areas called Downloads or Drivers, but it's far more common to have to go through a Support or Customer Service area first.

- Don't try to take any shortcuts to where you think the driver might be hiding. Trudge through each step the site provides. For example, it's common to have to select an overall driver category, then a device category, then a line category, and then the specific model you have.

This process is tedious, but it almost always gets you where you want to go.

- If the site is particularly ornery, the preceding method might not lead you to your device. In that case, try the search engine. Note that device drivers seem to be particularly poorly indexed, so you might have to try a lot of search text variations. One thing that usually works is searching for the exact filename. How can you possibly know that? A method that often works for me is to use Google (www.google.com) or Google Groups (groups.google.com) or some other web search engine to search for your driver. Chances are someone else has looked for your file and will have the filename (or, if you're really lucky, a direct link to the driver on the manufacturer's site).

- Still no luck finding the file you need? See if the manufacturer has a tech support line (phone or chat) and, if so, tell a support engineer what you're looking for. More often than not, the engineer will be able to tell you the filename you seek and might even send you the exact URL.

- When you get to the device's download page, be careful which file you choose. Make sure that it's a driver written for your operating system, and make sure that you're not downloading a utility program or some other nondriver file.

- When you finally get to download the file, be sure to save it to your computer—ideally on removable media such as a USB flash drive, CD, or external hard drive—rather than opening it. If you reformat your system or move the device to another computer, you'll be glad you have a local copy of the driver so you don't have to wrestle with the whole download rigmarole all over again.

Setting Up Your Work Area

Repairing a PC doesn't require a high-tech workshop, but it's not a task you should perform on the living room carpet, either. A proper PC-repair area is one that makes the job easier, so here are a few considerations to help you set up the perfect construction zone:

- **You need lights, lights, and more lights.** When it comes to cobbling together a PC, you simply can't have too much light. Some of the tasks you face take place in dim corners of the case or require you to make fairly precise connections. All this is much easier if you have a lot of light. A bright overhead light is great, but I also suggest a table lamp with some kind of adjustable neck so you can concentrate the light where you need it.

- **You need power!** Your area must have at least one power outlet nearby to plug in any lamps you use.

- **Get up off the floor.** A hardwood floor or other noncarpeted surface makes a nice even surface, but it's not a comfortable place for most people over a certain age. It's also more of a problem if dogs, cats, children, and other pets (kidding!) come along. It's better to build your new machine on a table or some other surface.

Tip

Use a Hat Light

A good flashlight helps you illuminate even the murkiest corners of a case, but when it comes time to work in those corners, you almost always need two hands, so you have to put down the flashlight and try to angle it just so, which rarely works. Technology rides to the rescue here, too, by offering hat lights (sometimes called cap lights) that clip to the brim of a hat for hands-free illumination.

- **Give yourself plenty of elbow room.** Speaking of a table, be sure you use one that has a reasonable amount of room. It should be big enough to hold your case lying flat and still give you plenty of room around the case to hold your tools and parts.

- **Set up a work area of your own.** The ideal work surface is one you can claim as your own for the duration of your repair. That way, you can leave things as they are until you get a chance to resume the job. If you use a kitchen table, coffee table, or dining room table, chances are you're going to have to clear out to let others use it at some point, and you run the risk of losing things or just forgetting where you left off.

Playing It Safe

We live in a world where concerns for our personal safety have become borderline absurd: An iron-on transfer for a T-shirt comes with a piece of paper that warns, "Do not iron while wearing shirt," and a letter opener has a label that says, "Caution: Safety goggles recommended." I'm hip to this over-the-top concern, so when I tell you that you need to observe a few safety precautions when working inside a PC, remember that I'm coming at this from necessity, not paranoia.

Keeping Yourself Safe

So just how dangerous is it to work inside a PC? The answer depends on the PC's current state:

- **The PC has never been turned on, or it has been off for a long time.** This is the safest state because you have to worry about only one thing: cutting or scratching yourself on something sharp. Many PC components are quite sharp. The solder points under most motherboards and expansion cards are nasty little daggers; devices such as power supplies and hard drives often have sharp, metal edges; and the cooling fins on some CPU coolers are razor thin. Handle all PC components carefully to avoid getting a nasty cut or abrasion.

- **The PC has only recently been turned off.** In this state, you still have to worry about sharp objects, but you also have two other things to watch out for:

  Heat—Components such as the processor, power supply, and hard drive work hard while the computer is on and so build up a tremendous amount of heat. Give everything a few minutes to cool down before diving into the case to prevent getting burned.

  Electricity—Most electronic components use capacitors to store electricity, and that voltage often drains out of the capacitors slowly after you turn off the PC and yank out the power cord. Because you're waiting a few minutes to let the PC's components cool down anyway, that's also enough time for most capacitors to drain. The exception is the power supply and its massive capacitors, which can retain life-threatening amounts of voltage for quite a while after you shut off the power. This is a concern only if you're going to open the power supply casing and, because you shouldn't ever do that, it's not a problem.

- **The PC is powered up.** This is the PC at its most dangerous because the components remain sharp (duh), parts such as the processor and power supply can heat up to burn-inducing levels within a few minutes, and electricity is everywhere. Not only that, but a running PC has a fourth danger: spinning fans on the case, CPU cooler, and often the video card, too. The danger here isn't so much that you might stick a finger in a fan (that would be unlikely to cause you much harm), but that you might get something caught in a fan, such as clothing, a bracelet, hair, and so on. Because of all this, the inside of a running PC is definitely a "hands-off" area. Feel free to open the case and look around, but touching things is just asking for trouble.

Keeping Your Components Safe

Keeping yourself out of harm's way when working inside a PC is important, obviously, but it's not the only safety concern. Without proper precautions, you can also damage sensitive computer components, which means your PC either might run erratically or might not run at all. It also means you might have wasted good money. Fortunately, keeping your components safe takes only a few sensible precautions:

- **Discharge static electricity.** If you walk across a carpeted floor, or if your clothes rub together as you walk, your body builds up static electricity, perhaps as much as a few thousand volts! If you were to touch a sensitive component such as a processor or motherboard, the resulting electrical discharge could easily damage or destroy the part. To prevent

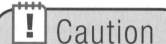

Caution

Disconnect the Power Cable

Let me reiterate that when you shut down your computer and are going to open it to work inside, *always* disconnect the power cable. Doing so ensures that the computer has no incoming electricity, so the chances of electrocution are virtually nil.

Caution

Case Safety

To be safe, open the case before you turn on the computer, and don't close the case until after you shut down the computer. Also, the open case wrecks the airflow inside the PC, so components can run hotter than usual; therefore, don't leave the computer running for an extended time with the case open.

this, after you open the PC case, you first should should ground yourself by touching the chassis, the power supply unit, or some other metal object. Doing so discharges your static electricity and ensures that you won't damage any of the computer's sensitive electronic components. Ideally, you shouldn't walk around the room until you've finished working inside the PC. If you need to walk away from the computer for a bit—particularly if you're wearing socks on a carpeted surface—be sure to ground yourself again when you're ready to resume working.

- **Avoid liquids in your work area.** Liquids and computer components definitely don't mix, and spilling almost any amount of liquid on a part could damage the part or render it inoperable. Therefore, keep all liquids well away from your work surface.

- **Don't touch electrical connectors.** Many parts have electrical connectors that serve as conduits for data or power. The natural oils that reside on even the cleanest of hands can reduce the conductivity of these contacts, resulting in the part acting erratically. Therefore, never touch the connectors.

- **Handle all components with care.** This means not only avoiding the contacts but also leaving components in their electrostatic discharge (ESD) bags (if they come with one) when not being used, carefully removing parts from their packaging to avoid breaking them, handling components with exposed electronics (such as resistors and capacitors) by the edges, setting down parts carefully, and allowing cold parts to heat up to room temperature before using them.

Get an Antistatic Wrist Strap

If you find that you always forget to ground yourself, you can take the matter out of your hands, literally, by using an antistatic wrist strap. This is a device with a wrist strap on one end and a metal clip at the other. You attach the clip to a metal object to ground yourself full-time. However, if you move away from the computer, be sure to check that the clip hasn't fallen off before continuing to work with the PC.

Cleaning Contacts

If you do touch a contact, you can clean it either by using isopropyl alcohol (also called rubbing alcohol) and a cotton swab or with an unused pencil eraser.

> ## ! Caution
>
> **Avoid the Outside of an ESD Bag**
>
> After you take a component out of its ESD bag, if you need to put the component back down, don't lay it on the ESD bag because the outside of those bags can draw static electricity! Put the component back inside the bag.

Opening the Computer Case

All PC upgrade and repair jobs begin with an apparently simple task: opening the computer case, usually by removing a side panel. (If you're facing the case from the front, you almost always remove the left side panel.) Why is this an "apparently" simple task? Because the technology case manufacturers use to secure the side panel isn't universal. That wasn't the case a few years ago. In those days, the vast majority of side panels were attached using two or three screws, and removing the panel was a straightforward matter of removing the screws and sliding or lifting the panel away from the case. Figure 17.6 shows an example.

Figure 17.6 *A case side panel attached with screws.*

Those days are long gone. Yes, most cases still connect their side panels with screws, but this method is no longer even remotely universal. Nowadays case manufacturers have come up with an endless variety of ways to attach side panels. The goal in almost all cases is "tool-free access." That is, the older method required the use of a screwdriver, although many cases now use thumbscrews. In modern case designs, tools are verboten. Instead, you usually have to press a button or hold down a latch, sometimes while sliding the side panel at the same time!

My favorite case opening mechanism by far is the one that appears on some models of Cooler Master cases. As you can see in Figure 17.7, the back of the case contains a simple lever. Lift that lever up, and the side panel slides open as slowly and deliberately as if it were mechanized. Beautiful! To close the side panel, you simply snap it into place. Bliss!

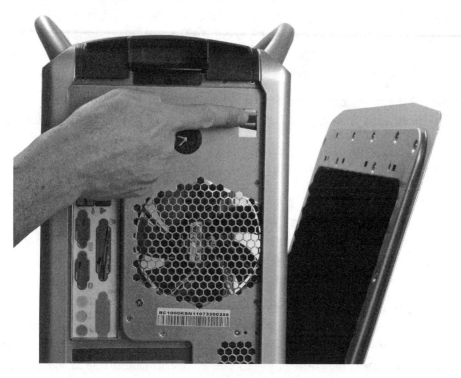

Figure 17.7   *Some Cooler Master cases open with the lift of a simple latch.*

Making Cable Connections

Great chunks of your PC repair time will be taken up connecting cables either to provide components with power or to provide a conduit along which the device can send and receive data. There are many cable types, and at first blush you might think this is just the computer industry's way of confusing novice upgraders. In fact, the opposite is the case: There are so many types because that's the only way to ensure that the connections you make are pretty close to foolproof. In other words, because each cable connector has a unique shape and configuration, it's nearly impossible for you to insert the cable in the wrong port or to insert the cable incorrectly in the right port.

Before going any further with all this, I should establish some terminology:

- **Connector**—This is a generic term for any piece of hardware that enables one thing to connect to another. So, the hardware at the end of a cable is a connector, as is the corresponding hardware on the other device to which you want the cable attached.

- **Male**—This is a connector that has protruding pins. Each pin corresponds to a wire in the cable. A male connector is also called a header or plug.

- **Female**—This is a connector that has holes, and it's also called a jack or port.

The key issue here is that on a proper connection, each pin on a male connector maps to a corresponding hole in a female connector. (There are some exceptions to this, such as female connectors with more holes than there are pins on a male connector.)

For example, older hard drives connect to the motherboard using a 40-pin ribbon cable. In Figure 17.8, you can see that the cable has a 40-hole female connector, the motherboard has a 40-pin male connector, and the holes and pins match up perfectly. However, if you place the same cable beside a floppy drive connector, which uses a 34-pin male connector as shown in Figure 17.9, it's obvious that the two don't match. In other words, it isn't possible to insert this style of hard drive cable in a floppy drive connector, even though they look similar.

Figure 17.8 *The holes on an ATA hard drive ribbon cable connector match up perfectly with the pins on the motherboard's ATA cable connector.*

Figure 17.9 *The pin configuration on a motherboard's floppy drive header doesn't match the ATA hard drive connector.*

So, your first clue when deciding where to insert a cable is to look for a connector that has the corresponding number of pins (or holes). Next, you often have to decide which way to insert the cable connector. As you can see in Figure 17.8, you can either insert the cable as shown or turn the cable 180° and try it that way. The pin configuration is the same both ways, so how do you know which is correct?

In this particular case, you need to look for the notch that appears in the back of the plastic shroud that surrounds the pins. That notch corresponds with a protrusion that appears on one side of the cable connector (you can see it in Figure 17.9). The only way to insert the cable is to match up the protrusion and the notch.

Another way system designers help you orient a cable connector correctly is by using a nonsymmetrical pin layout. For example, a motherboard's USB header has nine pins: five in one row and four in another. The case's USB jack has nine holes: five in one row and four in another. As you can see in Figure 17.10, there's only one way to match up the holes and pins, so there's only one way to connect the header and jack.

Figure 17.10 *The arrangement of the pins on a USB header matches the arrangement of the holes on the USB jack, so there's only one way to make the connection.*

A third way system designers ensure that you don't insert a connector incorrectly is to use a nonsymmetrical shape for the connector. For example, the 4-pin Molex power jack is designed to connect to a 4-pin Molex power header on a device. As you can see in Figure 17.11, two of the jack's four corners are rounded, and they match the rounded corners on the header. Again, there's only one way to make the connection.

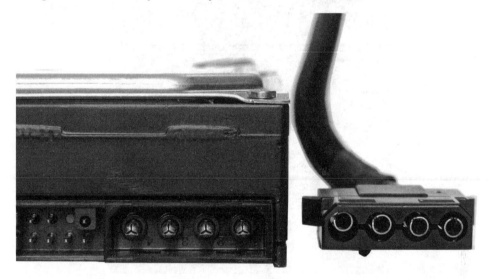

Figure 17.11 *The rounded corners of the 4-pin Molex power jack match the rounded corners of the 4-pin Molex power header, so there's only one way to make the connection.*

All this rigmarole of matching the numbers of pins, notches, and connector shapes is a complex business, so there has been a movement of late to reduce the complexity. System designers are accomplishing this by making connectors with a unique shape, period. With such connectors, you don't have to worry about pins or any other physical characteristics of the connector because there's only one kind of matching connector and only one way to insert the cable.

A good example is the newer hard drive data interface called SATA (Serial Advanced Technology Attachment). As you can see in Figure 17.12, the unique shape of the cable connector has a corresponding match on the hard drive. There's no danger here of inserting the cable in the wrong device or in the wrong way.

Figure 17.12 *The unique shape of a SATA hard drive data cable connector matches the corresponding SATA hard drive data header for an unambiguous connection.*

Installing an Expansion Card

Expansion cards are circuit boards that provide extra functionality such as networking, video, and sound. You install them by inserting them into slots inside your PC. So if you're having trouble with one of these internal components, you can usually fix the problem by taking out the old expansion card and replacing it with a new one.

Note, however, that you can't install any type of card into any type of slot. The various card types use different slot configurations. That's good news for you as a system repairer because it means you can't insert a card into the wrong slot, and you can't insert a card into the correct slot with the wrong orientation.

System designers ensure foolproof expansion card connections by using two configuration parameters:

- **Length**—The various slot types all use different lengths. For example, a PCI slot is larger than a PCI Express x4 slot, but smaller than a PCI Express x16 slot. This ensures that you can't install a card in the wrong type of slot. For example, Figure 17.13 shows a PCI card next to a PCI Express x1 slot. As you can see, the PCI card is much too long to fit into the slot.

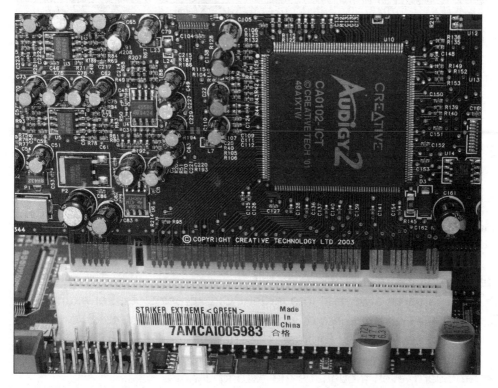

Figure 17.13   *The length of an expansion card's connectors must match the length of the motherboard slot, unlike the PCI card and PCI Express x1 slot shown here.*

- **Slot ridges**—Each slot type has one or more ridges that correspond to notches in the expansion card's connector area. This ensures that you can't install a card with the incorrect orientation. For example, Figure 17.14 shows a PCI Express x16 card next to a PCI Express x16 slot. As you can see, the notches in the card match up perfectly with the ridges in the slot.

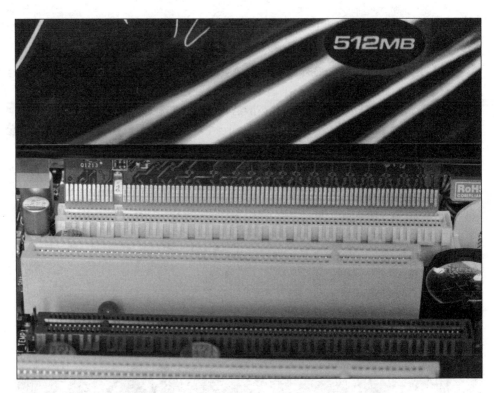

Figure 17.14   *The notches in an expansion card's connectors must match the ridges in the motherboard slot, as shown here with a PCI Express x16 card and slot.*

Note that PCI Express provides certain exceptions to all this. That is, smaller PCI Express cards always fit into larger PCI Express slots. For example, a PCI Express x1 card fits into any other PCI Express slot (x4, x8, or x16). Figure 17.15 shows a PCI Express x1 card next to a PCI Express x16 slot. The card's notches match the slot's first two ridges, so you can successfully insert the card, even though it's the "wrong" length.

In days of yore (the 1990s), all case slot covers were attached using a screw. Now, as with case side panels, manufacturers have been experimenting with various tool-free slot covers—latches, levers, and so on—so there's no longer a universal way to either remove a slot cover or attach an expansion card to the slot. You need to consult your case manual to see how things work.

Figure 17.15 *You can always insert smaller PCI Express cards into larger PCI Express slots, such as the x1 card into the x16 slot shown here.*

With that in mind, here are the generic steps to follow to install an expansion card:

1. Make sure the computer is turned off and the power cable is disconnected.

2. Remove the computer's side panel.

3. Touch something metal to ground yourself.

4. Locate the slot you want to use (see Figure 17.16).

5. Remove the slot cover. If the slot cover is held in place with a screw, use a Phillips screwdriver to remove the screw and then place the screw in a handy place.

Tip

Removing a Slot Cover

When the screw is out, the slot cover should come out easily; it might even fall out on its own, so it's a good idea to hold onto the slot cover with your free hand to ensure that it doesn't fall onto the motherboard and damage a component. If the slot cover doesn't budge, it's probably being held in place by the slot cover above it (or, less often, the slot cover below it). Loosen—but don't remove—the screw on the other slot cover. Doing so should give you enough slack to remove the cover for the empty slot. When that slot cover is out, you can tighten the screw on the other slot cover.

Figure 17.16 *An empty PCI slot with an increasingly old-fashioned screw-on slot cover.*

6. Place the expansion card so that its bracket is flush with the open slot cover, and slowly slide the card toward the slot.

7. When the card's connectors are touching the slot and are perfectly aligned with the slot opening, place your thumbs on the edge of the card and press the card firmly into the slot (see Figure 17.17).

8. Attach the bracket to the case, as shown in Figure 17.18.

Tip

Inserting a Card

How do you know whether the card is completely inserted into the slot? The easiest way to tell is to look at the portion of the bracket that attaches to the case. If that portion isn't flush with the case, the card isn't fully inserted.

Figure 17.17 *Press the card firmly into the slot.*

Figure 17.18 *Screw (or whatever) the expansion card's bracket to the computer chassis.*

Chapter 18

Upgrading Your PC

We live in a world of rapid and relentless obsolescence: A car is worth a fraction of the selling price as soon as you drive it off the lot; our cell phones come and go like streetcars; a computer is practically obsolete after the first boot. Faced with this inevitable decay, most people chuck the old and ring in the new: The lease is up? Great, let's start a new one! My cell phone's dead? No problem, I'll get another! Our computer is yesterday's technology? Let's get today's instead!

If there's a problem with this disposable lifestyle, it's that it tends to be awfully hard on the planet because new things require new resources and old things have to rot *somewhere*. Plus, constantly replacing our gadgets is expensive. Finally, although buying new things can be exhilarating, the thrill wears off soon after each new gadget is up and running.

Many people are saying "Enough!" to all this. They'd rather save the planet's resources, avoid contributing to landfills, save a few bucks, and take on a project that's satisfying and interesting. They want, in short, not to toss their old technology, but to *upgrade* it to make it better and give it a longer life. You might have a tough time upgrading a cell phone, but a PC is upgradeable and then some. It might need some extra RAM, a bigger hard drive, or even both. However far you're willing to go, it doesn't take much effort or cash to give an old computer a new lease on life, as you see in this chapter.

Like all things related to PCs, a proper upgrade doesn't proceed willy-nilly. You need to get your bearings and get a sense both of what needs to be done and, perhaps more importantly, what *can* be done. To do that, I always begin an upgrade by doing five things:

- Look inside the computer to check out the existing hardware.

- Access the system's configuration program to gather information about the machine.

- If the computer is currently running Windows, launch the **Device Manager** and **System Information** utilities, which provide oodles of information about the system.

- If the computer was built by a mainstream manufacturer, look for the system manual online.

- Use the online system manual to gather information about specific components.

I talk about each of these techniques in this chapter.

Looking Inside the Computer

Before you begin your PC renovations, it's best to take stock of what you're dealing with so that you can better tell what needs to be replaced and what you can replace it with. So, the first thing I always do is go under the hood and see what I've got to work with inside the computer.

In this chapter, I take a Dell computer I bought nearly five years ago and see whether I can spruce it up. To begin, I removed the side panel of the Dell. Figure 18.1 shows what I saw: lots of dust!

So, my first chore was to tidy things up a bit:

- I cleaned the inside to get rid of the dust.

- I disconnected the interface and power cables and stuffed them out of the way so that I could take a good look at things.

- I moved the processor's airflow shroud out of the way.

Figure 18.2 shows the results.

Figure 18.1 *The PC's innards revealed: what a mess!*

Figure 18.2 *This PC actually cleaned up not too bad.*

I immediately saw three things that made me very confident that I could upgrade this computer significantly:

- The memory sockets contain just a single module. This gives us lots of room to improve the memory by adding at least one other module. Also, I pulled out the existing module, and the sticker on the side told me it contained 512MB of RAM, which is low, and that the RAM is PC2-3200 (DDR2-400). I explain all this RAM stuff in Chapter 22, "Adding More Memory."

- The PC includes an empty expansion card slot, which means we could add a better graphics card, add a sound card, and so on (see "Installing an Expansion Card" in Chapter 17, "Repairing Your PC").

- The PC has a couple of ports for fast SATA hard drives, so there's room for a good hard drive upgrade (see Chapter 20, "Replacing the Hard Drive").

Accessing the System Configuration Program

Although you can glean some specific information by physically examining the inside of the PC (such as the memory data that I got from the module), we're going to need a lot more data if we hope to perform a successful and useful upgrade. A great source for this extra data is the PC's built-in configuration program, which you access at system startup. For the Dell machine (I had to press F2 after power-up but before Windows started loading), the utility told me the following:

- The processor type and speed: Intel Pentium 4 processor running at 2.8GHz

Note

Getting to the PC's Setup Program

If you're not sure which key to press to access the setup program on your old PC, look for a message such as `Press F2 to Enter Setup` soon after the computer starts up, but before you see the Windows logo. If you don't see such a message, the most common access keys are F2, Delete, F1, F10, and Esc.

- The chipset used by the motherboard: Intel 915G Express

- The make and model of the computer: Dell Dimension 4700

The utility also confirmed that the system did indeed have a single 512MB memory module.

Knowing the motherboard's chipset is crucial because that will give us some idea of what the board is capable of. A quick Google search for "Intel 915G Express" brought up the Intel product page for this chipset as the first result (see Figure 18.3). This page is a gold mine of information for our upgrade (see Figure 18.4): supported processors, CPU socket, bus slot types, memory, hard drive interfaces, and more. (I get into some of these details when I discuss specific upgrades a bit later.)

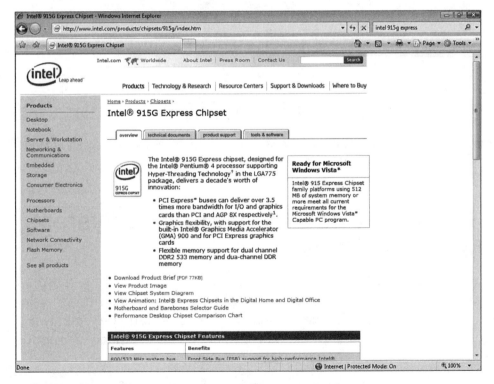

Figure 18.3 *The Intel product page for the 915G Express chipset.*

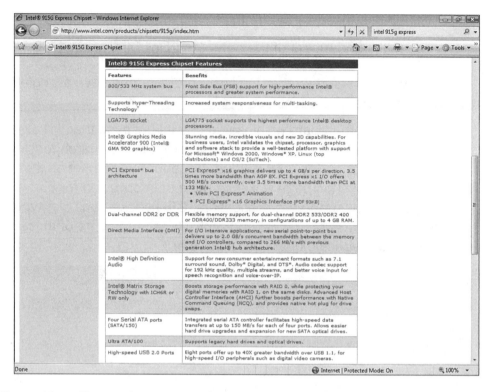

Figure 18.4 *The 915G Express chipset's product page gives detailed information on the features and capabilities of the chipset.*

Running the Device Manager and System Information Utilities

If you can't access the system's configuration program for some reason, but you can boot into Windows, you can still find out a lot of information using various Windows tools. For the purposes of most upgrade projects, two tools supply you with most of the data you need: Device Manager and the promisingly named System Information.

To run Device Manager, use one of the following techniques, depending on your version of Windows:

- **Windows 8**—Open the **Charms** menu, select **Search**, select **Settings**, type **device**, and then select **Device Manager** in the search results.

- **Windows 7 or Vista**—Click **Start**, type **device** in the Search box, and then click **Device Manager** in the search results. Enter your User Account Control (UAC) credentials to continue.

- **Windows XP**—Select **Start, Run**; type **devmgmt.msc**; and then click **OK**.

In the Device Manager window, the following branches contain information pertinent to upgrading your PC (see Figure 18.5):

- **Disk drives**—This branch tells you the hard drive that's installed, albeit a bit cryptically. In Figure 18.5, you see WDC WD800JB-00JJC0 ATA Device. This tells you that the drive was manufactured by Western Digital and its model number is WD800JB.

- **Display adapters**—This branch tells you the video devices that are installed.

- **Processors**—This branch tells you the type and speed of the PC's processor.

- **System devices**—This branch gives you a hint about the chipset in the Processor to I/O Controller item, which in Figure 18.5 shows Intel 915G/P/GV/PL/910GE/GL.

To run System Information, use one of the following techniques, depending on your version of Windows:

- **Windows 8**—Open the **Charms** menu, select **Search**, type **msinfo32**, and then select **msinfo32** in the search results.

- **Windows 7 or Vista**—Click **Start**, type **system** in the Search box, and then click **System Information** in the search results.

- **Windows XP**—Select **Start, Run**; type **msinfo32**; and then click **OK**.

In the System Information window (see Figure 18.6), the **System Summary** shows various bits of useful data, particularly the System Manufacturer, System Model, Processor, BIOS Version/Date, and Total Physical Memory.

Figure 18.5 *Device Manager contains lots of data about your PC's hardware.*

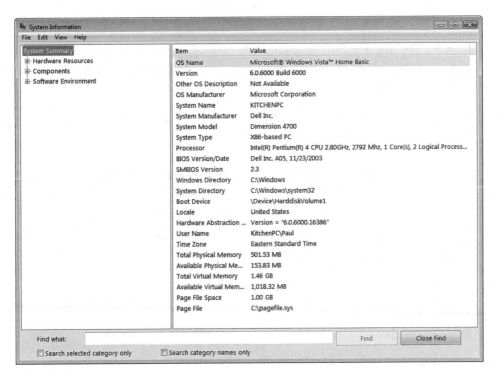

Figure 18.6 *System Information gives you some good basic information about your system.*

Searching for the System Manual Online

If you purchased your old PC from a system manufacturer, particularly a larger company such as Dell or HP, chances are you can find the computer's original manual online. (I'm assuming, of course, that the manual that came with the computer is long lost.) Even better, you can sometimes find more in-depth documentation for a machine. Dell, for example, usually offers a "service manual" that shows the motherboard's components, power supply watts (important if you'll be adding more components to your old PC), system settings, and instructions for removing and installing parts.

To look for the manual online, you have a couple of ways to proceed:

- Head for the manufacturer's site, find the Support section, look up your old PC's make and model number, and then look for a link named Manual or Documentation.

- Head for Google and run a search on the manufacturer's name, the PC's make and model, and the word manual.

In my case, I Googled "Dell Dimension 4700 manual" and was rewarded with a direct link to the Dell Dimension 4700 Series Service Manual as the first result. Figure 18.7 shows the first page of the manual.

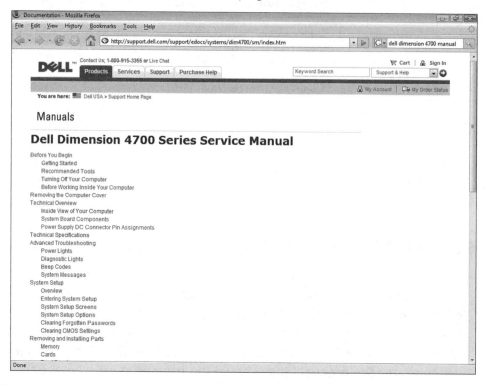

Figure 18.7 *The service manual for my Dell Dimension 4700.*

This service manual is a gold mine of useful information for the upgrader. For example, clicking the System Board Components link takes me to a really useful map of the PC's internal components, as shown in Figure 18.8.

Note

Use the Correct Version of the Manual

The manual is useful only if it applies to the specifications of your computer. Manufacturers often update a model's specs, so they update the manual to reflect those changes. Make sure the manual you find applies to your computer and not some later iteration. If it doesn't, either keep searching for the correct version of the manual, or contact the manufacturer to see whether one is available.

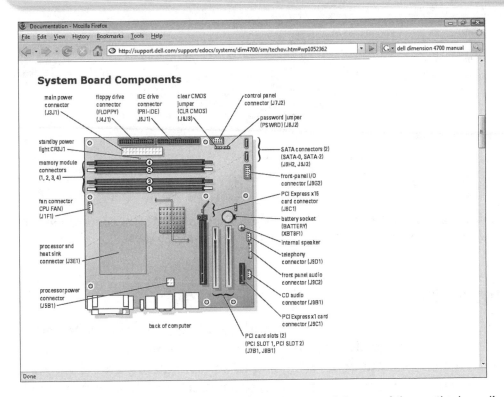

Figure 18.8 *The service manual includes a useful map of the motherboard's components.*

Even better, clicking the Technical Specifications link takes me to a page chock full of great data about the machine and its capabilities (see Figure 18.9).

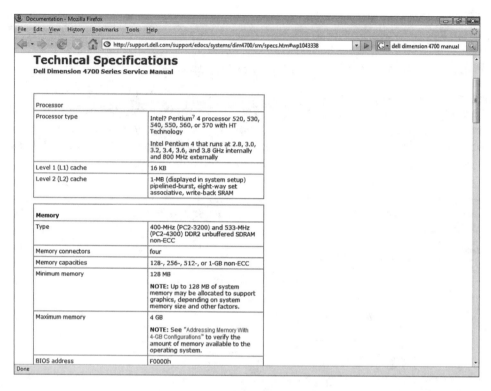

Figure 18.9 *The service manual's Technical Specifications page contains tons of great information on the machine's components and capabilities.*

Making the Old PC Run Faster

Although there are many ways to upgrade an old PC—put in quieter fans, replace the power supply, and update all the device drivers, to name a few—in the chapters to come I'm going to concentrate my efforts where I'm sure most people would want to spend the upgrade time and money: making an old PC run a bit faster. There's nothing like an extra dose of speed to make a machine a more useful member of your PC family. Better performance enables you to run more programs, upgrade to the latest operating system, or just provide a better hand-me-down machine for the kids to use.

Chapter 19

Buying PC Components

Over the next few chapters, I'm going to provide you with various "buying guides" for components such as the hard drive, optical drive, and memory. My aim in each of those guides will be to give you a few pointers to help you get the right part for your PC repair project. However, savvy fixers know that it's not enough to think just about *what* components you need: you also need to think about *how* you buy those components. Can you research components online? Which online retailers have what you need? Are all online stores the same? What about things such as refurbished parts, open boxes, and extended warranties? My goal in this chapter is to answer all these questions (and quite a few more) so that by the end you'll have all the information you need to purchase parts like a pro.

Researching Parts Online

Sure, we use the Internet to communicate, connect, and have fun, but its main use for most of us is to do research. That's not only because the Web contains a vast amount of information (much of which is actually true!), but also because we can easily search and surf to the information we need. This is a boon to the PC upgrader because it makes it absurdly easy to research components to find the right product at the right price. Whatever part you're looking to add to your PC, somebody has reviewed it and somebody else is selling it.

To help you get started, the next couple of sections list the best sites for checking hardware reviews and comparing component prices.

Checking Out Product Reviews

Whether you're looking for a new hard drive or more memory, it's a lead-pipe cinch that someone has reviewed it and posted that review online for all to read. I'm not talking here about little Johnny the budding computer geek proclaiming the latest digital doodad to be "Awesome!" on his blog (although, of course, there's no shortage of that kind of thing around). Rather, I'm talking about in-depth, nonpartisan reviews by hardware professionals who really put parts to the test and tell you the pros and cons of each piece of equipment.

Hardware-related sites are a dime a dozen (if that), but a few are really good. Here are my recommendations:

- **AnandTech**—Although this site offers extras such as forums, blogs, product pricing, and hardware news, its heart—and its claim to fame—is the massive collection of incredibly in-depth reviews (see Figure 19.1). These reviews are often quite technical, but you should feel free to skim the mumbo-jumbo because there's still plenty of useful information for everyone.

  www.anandtech.com/

- **Ars Technica**—The name means "The Art of Technology," and that's an appropriate description of this deep, sprawling site aimed at computer enthusiasts. For system upgraders, the site includes buyer's guides, technology guides, how-to articles, and lots more.

  www.arstechnica.com/

- **CNET**—This massive site has a Reviews section that covers tons of products. Each review is simply laid out with headings such as Pros, Cons, Suitability, Value, and Suggestions. The layout of the site leaves something to be desired, so use the search engine to find what you want.

  www.cnet.com/

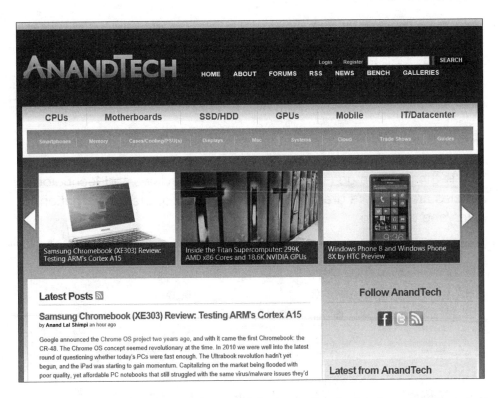

Figure 19.1 *AnandTech is one of the best sites for hardware product reviews.*

- **ExtremeTech**—This professional site (it's affiliated with *PC Magazine*) is loaded with in-depth product reviews and recommendations for the products suited to building your own PC.

  www.extremetech.com/

- **Maximum PC**—This is the Web home of the terrific print magazine *Maximum PC*. The website offers reviews of thousands of products in every conceivable category. The reviews aren't particularly exhaustive, but they give you a good overview of each product.

  www.maximumpc.com/

- **The Tech Report**—If you want your reviews to tilt more toward the obsessively detailed side of the spectrum, look no further than this site, which has some of the most in-depth reviews on the Web. It's not the best-looking website I've ever seen, but the content rules here.

  www.techreport.com/

- **Tom's Hardware**—If you want to know everything there is to know about a particular piece of technology, this jaw-droppingly impressive site is the place to go (see Figure 19.2). The reviews and technology articles are a geek's dream, and there's plenty of great information for everyone else, too.

  www.tomshardware.com/

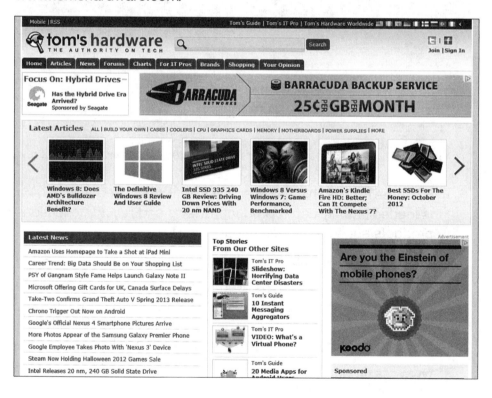

Figure 19.2   *Tom's Hardware features awesomely in-depth product reviews.*

Google Reviews

Besides checking specific sites for reviews of a particular component, you can also try running a Google search that includes the product name and the word *review*. Be sure to search not only the Web, but also Google Groups.

Read Summaries to Save Time

No time to read a long-winded review? No problem! Almost all reviews have a "summary" section at the end that recaps the highlights of the review, including the major pros and cons, the reviewer's kudos and caveats, and whether the reviewer recommends the product.

Performing Price Comparisons

After you've read the reviews and know exactly what you want, your next step as a savvy shopper is to find the best price. You could do that by jumping around to various online retailers, searching for your product, and making note of the price each time. However, plenty of sites out there will do all the hard work for you. I'm talking about the Web's price comparison sites (sometimes called *shopping portals*), where you select or specify the product you want and the site returns the product listings from a number of online retailers. You can then compare prices with just a few mouse clicks.

Here are some decent shopping portals to check out:

- **Become**—This site shows you not only the prices for each listing, but also the product's rating at each store (one to five stars, based on user reviews).

  www.become.com/

- **CNET Shopper.com**—This is the Shopper.com section of the CNET site. Its nicest feature is that for each store returned in the listings, you get the store's rating (one to five stars) and whether the store currently has stock of the item—and if you enter your ZIP code, the taxes and shipping fees are displayed (see Figure 19.3).

  http://shopper.cnet.com/

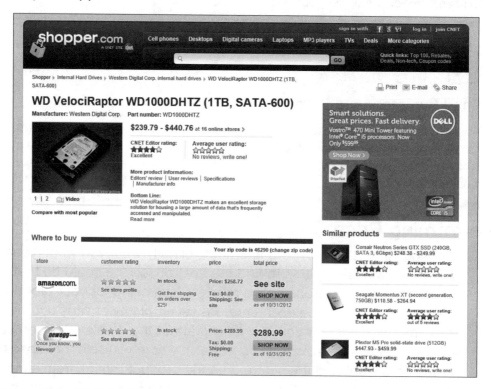

Figure 19.3 *CNET's Shopper.com site not only compares prices, but also provides each store's rating, stock, taxes, and shipping costs to your ZIP code.*

- **Google Product Search**—This site applies the awesome power of Google's search engine to online products. You search on the name of the product you want, and Google returns product listings from around the Web.

  www.google.com/shopping/

- **PriceGrabber.com**—This is one of the most popular shopping portals, and no wonder because, for each product, you get tons of information: price, stock, product details, user reviews and discussions, expert reviews, seller rating, and taxes and shipping for your ZIP code. What more could you want?

  www.pricegrabber.com/

- **Shopzilla**—This site doesn't have all the bells and whistles that you see with some of the other sites, but it often returns a broader array of listings and has all the basic information you need: price, taxes, shipping, product details, and product reviews.

  www.shopzilla.com/

- **Yahoo! Shopping**—Lots of people like this section of Yahoo! because it provides all the standard shopping portal data and gives you full product specifications, user ratings, and the ability to send listings to a mobile phone (perfect if you're doing your shopping offline).

  http://shopping.yahoo.com/

Researching Retailers Online

With hundreds of online retailers out there, how can you tell the e-commerce stars from the fly-by-night shysters? The best way is to ask your friends, family, and colleagues which retailers they've used and had good experiences with in the past. Because these are people you trust, you can rely on the information you get.

Besides that, you can also go by the ratings that online users have applied to retailers. These are usually stars (usually up to five stars, and the more stars the better). Many of the shopping portals in the previous section also include user ratings for each store. For example, Google Product Search (www.google.com/shopping/) also doubles as a retailer ratings service. When you run a product search, the name of the reseller appears below the price and below that are a rating (one to five stars) and the number of user ratings that have produced the result. As you can see in Figure 19.4, you can also sort the results by seller rating, and the site has links to restrict the results based on seller rating (for example, to show only the results for sellers with four or more stars).

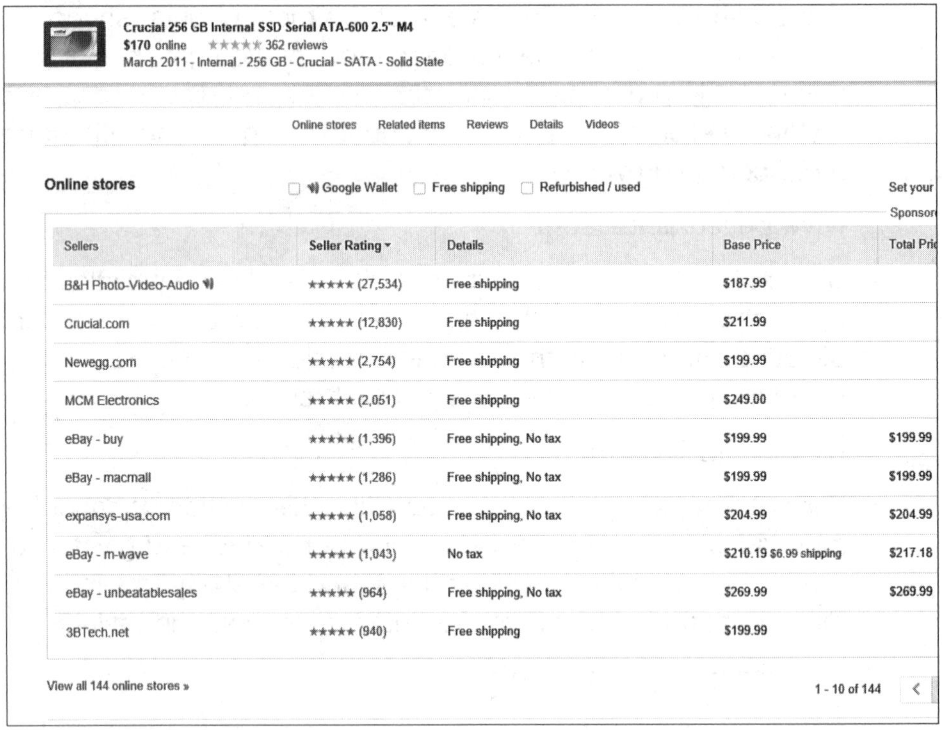

Crucial 256 GB Internal SSD Serial ATA-600 2.5" M4
$170 online ★★★★★ 362 reviews
March 2011 - Internal - 256 GB - Crucial - SATA - Solid State

Online stores Related items Reviews Details Videos

Online stores ☐ Google Wallet ☐ Free shipping ☐ Refurbished / used Set your

Sponsor

Sellers	Seller Rating ▾	Details	Base Price	Total Pri
B&H Photo-Video-Audio	★★★★★ (27,534)	Free shipping	$187.99	
Crucial.com	★★★★★ (12,830)	Free shipping	$211.99	
Newegg.com	★★★★★ (2,754)	Free shipping	$199.99	
MCM Electronics	★★★★★ (2,051)	Free shipping	$249.00	
eBay - buy	★★★★★ (1,396)	Free shipping, No tax	$199.99	$199.99
eBay - macmall	★★★★★ (1,286)	Free shipping, No tax	$199.99	$199.99
expansys-usa.com	★★★★★ (1,058)	Free shipping, No tax	$204.99	$204.99
eBay - m-wave	★★★★★ (1,043)	No tax	$210.19 $6.99 shipping	$217.18
eBay - unbeatablesales	★★★★★ (964)	Free shipping, No tax	$269.99	$269.99
3BTech.net	★★★★★ (940)	Free shipping	$199.99	

View all 144 online stores » 1 - 10 of 144

Figure 19.4 *You can sort the Google Product Search results by reseller rating.*

A site that's dedicated to rating resellers is the appropriately named ResellerRatings.com (see www.resellerratings.com/). This site uses a 1-to-10 scale, where the higher the rating, the better the store. You can use the site as a shopping portal, or you can look up an individual store to see its rating. (Usefully, you get two ratings for each store: a lifetime rating and a six-month rating; if the latter is much lower than the former, that's a sign something has gone seriously wrong at the store over the past few months and you might want to shop elsewhere.) The site also has interesting lists of the "Highest Rated Stores" (see Figure 19.5) and "Lowest Rated Stores."

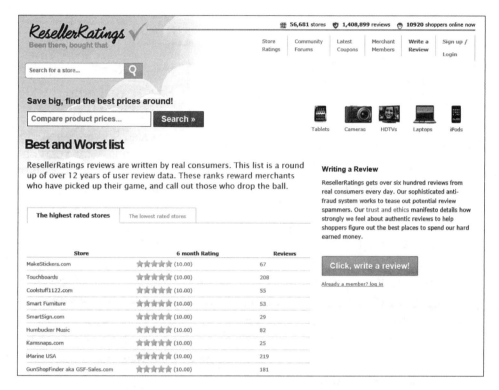

Figure 19.5 *ResellerRatings.com is a massive database of online retailer ratings and reviews.*

Buying Parts Online

Buying components online isn't the scary proposition it was a few years ago. You can choose from many reliable, reputable, and secure merchants now, so buying online is no longer a big deal. Even still, shopping online is different from buying at a retail store or via mail order. To ensure the best online transaction possible, bear in mind these few pointers:

- The three most important points to remember when buying online are compare, compare, compare. It's not at all unusual to find one store selling the same part for 10% or even 20% less than other stores, so use the shopping portals I mentioned earlier to get the best price.

- Keep an eye out for special deals. Many online retailers offer promotions on a particular day of the week or when they need to clear out inventory. Troll the sites of your favorite online retailers to watch out for these specials.

- Be wary of a price that seems too good to be true. Yes, some retailers occasionally offer a product as a loss leader—a price that's substantially lower than their competitors as a way of tempting you to buy something and thus establish a relationship with the store. (After you purchase at least one thing from a store, you're more likely to go back, particularly if the experience was a positive one.) However, it's also entirely possible for some of the shadier outfits to offer super-low prices on returned or refurbished parts without telling you what you're getting. Unless you know the store is reputable, assume really low prices are bogus and move on to the next store.

- Following on from the preceding point, note that a really cheap price might be the net price you pay after processing a mail-in rebate. Obviously, you'll payer a higher price up front, but some retailers don't tell you that, or they hide the fact in small print somewhere. Also, beware of extra "handling" charges and other fees that the retailer might try to tack on. Before committing to the sale, always give the invoice a thorough going-over so you know exactly what you're paying.

- Be sure you understand the difference between an original equipment manufacturer (OEM) version and a retail box version of a component. The OEM version of a product is the version that would normally go to a system builder. It's the same part but minus the extras that come with the retail box version, so it's often much cheaper. At best, this just means no-frills packaging, but it can also mean no manual, no device drivers, no extra parts such as hard drive data cables, and often a shorter warranty. If you just need the part itself, the OEM version can save you a few shekels, but be sure you know what you're getting.

Tip

Look for Promotion Feeds or Lists

Some sites offer RSS feeds that alert you to upcoming promotions, which can be an easier way to stay on top of things. If a site doesn't have an RSS feed, look for a mailing list.

- Buy just off the bleeding edge. It's a truism in PC component retailing that the latest-and-greatest parts cost the most. A top-of-the-line 3 terabyte (TB) internal hard drive can set you back hundreds of dollars, but a 1TB drive (which is still big enough for most people) can be had for well under $200.

- Most good online vendors will give you a chance during checkout to enter your ZIP code or postal code so you can see exactly what your shipping charges will be. Because the cost of shipping can often be extravagant, whenever possible you should find out the cost in advance before completing the sale.

- Some retailers allow you to mail a check or money order and will ship the order when they receive the payment. You should avoid these payment options like the plague because, if something goes wrong (for example, the product never shows up), getting your money back could be a challenge. If you pay by credit card, however, you always have the option of charging back the cost to the vendor.

- If the retailer offers a PayPal option, use it. Currently owned by eBay, PayPal is an online payment service that enables you to buy online without exposing your credit card data to the retailer. You sign up for a PayPal account at www.paypal. com and provide your credit card, debit card, or bank account information. (It's all super-secure and everything is verified before your account goes online.) When you buy something online with a PayPal-friendly retailer, that retailer tells PayPal the cost of the sale and PayPal charges it to

Note

OEM Terminology

The term *OEM* is pretty universal, but some retailers use alternate terminology for specific products. For example, an OEM hard drive is sometimes called a *bare drive*.

! Caution

Extra Credit Card Fees

Watch out for online retailers who charge some kind of extra fee (usually a percentage of the product price) for accepting credit card payments. This is almost always a sign of a shady dealer who's either trying to squeeze an extra few percentage points out of you or is trying to discourage you from using a credit card.

your credit card, debit card, or bank account and then passes along the money to the retailer. The retailer never sees your financial data, so you never have to worry about that data being stolen or accidentally exposed.

- When the checkout process is complete, leave the final window open on your Desktop so you have access to the order number, final total, tracking information, and other order details. After you get an email confirming the transaction and you've checked the email for accuracy, you can close the web window.

Capturing the Order Details

In the unlikely event that the retailer doesn't provide a confirmation email message, either print the screen or capture it to an image: in Windows 8, press **Windows Logo+Print Screen** (in earlier versions of Windows, just press **Print Screen**) and then paste the image into Paint.

Returning Parts Online

The arrival of a new PC part is often quite exciting, particularly for meaty components such as motherboards and cases. However, that initial excitement occasionally turns to disappointment when your new toy doesn't live up to expectations. It might be defective, incompatible, or just not what you want. Bummer. The good news is that the vast majority of the time you're not stuck with your part because almost all retailers offer returns for either refund or replacement. This process is usually fairly straightforward, but to ensure a smooth return, you need to know a few things; I detail them in this section.

Avoid No-Returns Policies

With so many vendors offering returns privileges, you should avoid retailers that don't offer them. If resellers can't stand behind their products by offering returns, there's no reason you should ever stand in front of them!

First, when you get your package, resist the temptation to tear off the cellophane and dive into the box to eyeball your new bauble. A more deliberate pace should always be the norm when building a custom PC, but it also has ramifications in the returns department:

- You run the risk of scattering teensy-but-vital bits to the nether regions of your office. When you return an item, the retailer will check to see whether all the parts are present, and if anything's missing, it might disallow your refund.

- It's a general rule that hastily liberating the contents of a box means that those contents *never* go back in as neatly, or at all! Your return stands far less chance of being rejected if you pack the contents back into the box exactly the way you found them originally.

- Don't throw anything away, even if you think you're *really*, *really* sure you're going to keep the component. First, the component might not work, which makes a return mandatory. Second, the component might not work the way you thought it would, and you can assuage your disappointment by sending the sucker back and getting something better. However, that's going to be a lot harder if you've already tossed the manual and other previously nonessential pieces.

- Open bags and containers as carefully as possible. If you just rip into things, you won't be able to put their components back in if the need for a return arises. This means either you have to leave them loose in the box (which could cause damage to other parts), or you need to improvise a new container (which is just a waste of your precious time).

- Don't remove any stickers, decals, or barcode labels. Try to keep the components as pristine as possible just in case they need to go back.

- Try the component as soon as possible. Most retailers offer returns for only a limited time—for refunds, it's sometimes as short as 14 days, but more typically it's 30 days—so give your product a whirl within that time frame.

- Check to ensure that you can send back your nondefective product. Many retailers have return exceptions for parts such as processors and memory modules, as well as for special purchases such as open-box items.

- Check to see whether the retailer charges a restocking fee. This might be something like 15% of the cost, so find out in advance so that you're not surprised when an apparently too-small refund comes through on your next credit card statement.

If, after all that, you do have something to return, you need to contact the retailer and ask for a return authorization number—usually called a return merchandise authorization (RMA) number. Most of the larger online retailers enable you to request an RMA number on their sites, usually by accessing your account. Otherwise, you need to contact the retailer's customer service department. After you have authorization, you're ready to make the return:

- Keep a box or three around for use with returns. Retailers often ship components in boxes filled with Styrofoam chips, so I keep a box of those around for safe shipping.

- If the retailer supplies you with a label, be sure to place the label on your box in a visible location. The label usually contains information—such as the retailer's address, the RMA number, and the original invoice number—that can help smooth the returns process.

- If you don't have a special label, write "RMA Number:" on the box, followed by the number the retailer supplied to you for the return. This helps steer the package to the retailer's returns department and helps the returns clerk process the package. If you want, you can also add the original invoice number to the box to help speed up processing.

- When sending back the component, use a traceable method such as registered mail or a courier. This enables you to keep track of the package. It's also a good idea to insure the contents, so you're not on the hook if the package gets lost or damaged.

- Keep an eye peeled on your credit card statement to look for the refund. (Having online access to your card statement is particularly handy here.) Most reputable retailers will process the return in just a few business days, and it shouldn't take more than another couple of business days for the credit to show up. If you don't see anything

Note

Watch the Restocking Fees

No reputable reseller will charge a restocking fee on an item you're returning for replacement. For refund returns, thumb your nose at any vendor that charges more than a 15% restocking fee. Unfortunately, fees in the 20% to 30% range aren't unheard of, so watch out for them and don't give any business to a company that would charge such an outrageous amount.

after a couple of weeks, see whether the retailer offers an option for checking the status of your return online. If not, contact the retailer's customer service department to see what the holdup is.

Buying Parts Offline

Should you buy your PC parts from a bricks-and-mortar store such as Best Buy, Circuit City, CompUSA, Costco, Fry's, Future Shop, Staples, or your local electronics store? Here's the simple answer to that question: It depends. Buying in person has its advantages, but doing so is not without its disadvantages. So the retail route you choose depends on what you need, when you need it, and a host of other factors.

Here are the main advantages of buying offline:

- **No shipping charges**—When you buy retail, the only "shipping charge" is the cost of gas for the trip to the store and back. This is particularly advantageous with large items such as computer cases and heavy items such as power supplies, which often generate exorbitant shipping charges when ordered online.

- **Faster**—If you need a part now, the only way to get it done (assuming you're not mid-repair at 3 a.m.) is to go to a store. Even the fastest online service can only offer overnight delivery (for big bucks, too).

- **Expertise**—In-store sales associates are often quite knowledgeable and can help you make a decision if you're having trouble finding the right part or choosing between two similar components. However, see also my comments below about aggressive salesmanship and the commission connection.

- **Easier returns**—If your component isn't right for whatever reason, you can drive it back to the store and get an instant refund or replacement, usually without any hassle. (Although someone will give the package a thorough going-over to ensure it's in returnable condition.) This is much easier than the online rigmarole of getting an RMA number, shipping the component (at your own expense), and waiting for the refund or replacement to show up.

- **Mail-in rebates**—Both online and offline retailers sometimes offer instant rebates that immediately reduce the price of a component. Real-world stores often go one better and also offer a mail-in rebate where you have to send a form and proof-of-purchase to a mailing address and a check comes your way a couple of weeks later.

Here are the main disadvantages of buying offline:

- **Smaller selection**—Due to the inevitable shelf space limitations, even the largest superstore can carry only a limited number of items in any one area. Even mid-size online retailers have access to many times more products.

- **More expensive**—Buying retail is almost always more expensive than buying online, although the big electronics superstores usually have fairly competitive prices. Not only that, but the retailer will have to charge you sales tax, and chances are an online retailer won't, depending on where you and the retailer are located. (Remember, however, that to compare retail apples with online apples, you also have to factor in the shipping costs that are part of most online orders.)

- **More time**—Besides the time it takes to get from your home to the store, more often than not you'll find yourself making a second or third stop at different stores to find the exact item you need.

- **Aggressive salesmanship**—Many electronics retailers put their sales staff on commission, which means the more they sell, the more money they make. That's a very simple recipe for aggressive and often annoying sales come-ons. Ask any overly insistent sales associate whether he's on commission and, if so, be sure to stick to your guns and purchase only what you need. Even better, take your business to a retailer that doesn't use commissioned sales staff.

Note

Send In Your Rebate

Truth be told, mail-in rebates are a way for the retailer to make the product appear cheaper (because they usually show the after-rebate price prominently), and the retailer is counting on people not bothering to follow through on the rebate. Don't fall into their trap: Send in those rebates! Also, to make sure the rebate is honored, keep copies of the rebate forms and send the rebate via registered mail or some other traceable method.

- **Extended warranty**—Speaking of aggressive sales, many electronics stores pay their staff big commissions for signing people up for extended warranties. As I explained in Chapter 2, "Buying a PC," these are almost always a waste of money because if you're buying components from a reputable dealer, they'll almost certainly give you years of trouble-free service. So no matter how much pressure you feel from a salesperson, just say "No, thank you" to an extended warranty.

Buying Non–Shrink-Wrapped Parts

In the same way that as soon as you drive a new car off the dealer's lot, its value immediately plummets, as soon as the shrink-wrap comes off a PC component, its value drops significantly. That can be good news for you as a consumer because you can often take advantage of this to get a good deal. Here are four possibilities:

- **Display model**—Most bricks-and-mortar stores keep items out for display so consumers can see and touch the item. This is rarely the case for sensitive PC parts such as expansion cards, but it might be true for less-sensitive components such as wireless routers. If the store has no other stock but the display model, you can often negotiate a discount. (You'll probably have to talk to the manager to get it.)

> ## ! Caution
>
> There are two main problems with purchasing a display model. First, there's a good chance it has been handled roughly, so check it over carefully to ensure that it's not damaged. (Just in case, make sure the item is returnable.) Second, if the component has multiple parts, be sure you're getting everything.

- **Open-box**—Many online retailers offer 10% or even 20% off open-box items, which are usually returns that have had their boxes opened. This is why all retailers want you to be careful when you return something because if it's in good enough shape, they can sell it. All reputable retailers carefully inspect open-box items, so they are safe to buy and you save a few dollars in the process. However, you should check the item carefully when you get it to ensure that everything's okay. (However, note that most retailers impose a shorter returns period on open-box items.)

- **Reconditioned**—These are used items the retailer has cleaned and checked, and where it has repaired or replaced any defective parts. You can often save a substantial amount on reconditioned parts, so they're a good way to go if the budget's tight. Bear in mind, however, that you're almost always getting older technology and the part won't last as long as a new one will.

- **Used**—This refers to used parts that haven't been reconditioned. Although the low prices of these components are tempting, you should probably avoid them because you can't be sure what you're getting or how long it will last.

If you do decide to purchase a display model, an open-box item, or a reconditioned part, make sure you're getting the same warranty that the manufacturer supplies for the component when it's brand-new.

Chapter 20

Replacing the Hard Drive

When I bought my first computer back in the mid-80s, its storage features were limited to a single 5.25-inch floppy drive. Yup, there was no hard drive in sight. If I wanted to run a program, I'd insert its disk into the floppy drive and run the program from there. If I wanted to save some data, I'd have to remove the program disk, swap in a data disk, save my work, and then reinsert the program disk. (A couple of years later I "upgraded" to a system with *two* floppy drives. I still didn't have a hard drive, but at least I no longer had to swap disks. Bliss!)

More than 25 years later, it's hard to even imagine trying to use a computer that way, particularly because we currently have an embarrassment of riches in the storage world, not only because capacity is as cheap as it has ever been, but also because we have a wide variety of formats to choose from.

That's good news for you because it means you have lots of choices if you need to replace your PC's hard drive. This chapter shows you what's available, gives you pointers on how to make the smartest hard drive buy, and shows you how to remove an old drive and insert a new hard drive.

How a Hard Drive Works

Hard drives are an amazing combination of speed and precision, and their inner workings are fascinating. However, I'll save all that for another book because all we're interested in here is those hard drive principles that relate to upgrading your PC. To that end, this section gives you a basic primer on how hard drives get the job done.

In simplest terms, a hard drive consists of three main parts:

- A rotating disk or platter (often more than one, but we'll ignore that complication here) that is divided into concentric areas called *tracks*.

- A *read/write head* that floats just above the surface of the platter and performs the actual reading of data to and writing of data from the disk.

- An actuator arm on which the read/write head moves back and forth. The arm itself is controlled by a highly precise motor.

Figure 20.1 points out these hard drive parts.

Figure 20.1   *The main parts of a typical hard drive.*

Here's the basic procedure the hard drive follows when it needs to write data to the disk:

1. The processor locates a free storage location (called a *sector*) on the disk and passes this information (as well as the data to be written) to the hard drive.

2. The hard drive's actuator arm moves the read/write head over the track that contains the free sector. The time it takes the hard drive to do this is called the *seek time*.

3. The hard drive rotates the disk so that the free sector is directly under the read/write head. The time it takes for the hard drive to do this is called the *latency* (or sometimes the *rotational latency*).

4. The writing mechanism on the read/write head writes the data to the free sector. The time it takes the hard drive to do this is called the *write time*.

Reading data from the disk is similar:

1. The processor determines which sector on the disk contains the required data and passes this information to the hard drive.

2. The hard drive's actuator arm moves the read/write head over the track that contains the sector to be read.

3. The hard drive rotates the disk so the sector to be read is directly under the read/write head.

4. The reading mechanism on the read/write head reads the data from the sector. The time it takes the hard drive to do this is called the *read time*.

Understanding Hard Drive Specs

Hard drives are relatively simple devices, at least from the point of view of buying them. However, in your hard drive shopping excursions, you might still come across descriptions that look something like this:

Seagate Barracuda ST310005NA1AS SATA 6.0Gb/s

3.5-inch Internal 1TB 7200 RPM

As is so often the case, these descriptions are pure gobbledygook if you're not used to seeing them. The good news is that not only is it possible to translate this apparently foreign language without much fuss, but you'll also see that the translation itself offers tons of useful information that will help you make an informed choice. Here's a quick summary of what each item in the preceding description represents, and the sections that follow expand on most of them:

Seagate	This is the name of the hard drive manufacturer.
Barracuda	This is the manufacturer's hard drive product line.
ST310005NA1AS	This is the hard drive's model number.
SATA	This is the hard drive's interface.
6.0Gb/s (or Gbps)	This is the hard drive's throughput.
3.5-inch Internal	This is the hard drive's form factor.
1TB	This is the capacity of the hard drive.
7200 RPM	This is the speed or spin rate of the hard drive.

The Hard Drive Interface and Throughput

The hard drive *interface* refers to the method by which the drive connects to the motherboard, and the *throughput* (sometimes called the *data transfer rate* or the *bandwidth*) is a measure of how much data the drive can transfer per second. A number of interfaces are available, but the five you'll come upon most often when shopping for a hard drive are PATA, SATA, USB, IEEE 1394, and eSATA.

The PATA Interface

The Parallel Advanced Technology Attachment (PATA) interface is also known as the Integrated Device Electronics (IDE) interface and is the old hard drive standard that's now pretty much extinct, but you might still come across it if you're upgrading an older PC. Before going on, I should note that to differentiate this older drive standard from the newer SATA standard (discussed next), I'm using the term *PATA* here. However, most retailers (indeed, most people) instead use the term *ATA* for the older technology and *SATA* for the newer technology. This isn't strictly accurate (both PATA and SATA are part of the ATA standard), but there you go.

The two main PATA standards you'll see are

PATA/100	This is also called ATA-6, ATA/100, or Ultra-ATA/100. In all cases, the "100" part tells you the throughput, which in this case means 100MBps.

PATA/130   This is also called ATA-7, ATA/133, or Ultra-ATA/133. Here, the "133" tells you that the throughput for this standard is 133MBps.

The back of a PATA hard drive has three sections, pointed out in Figure 20.2.

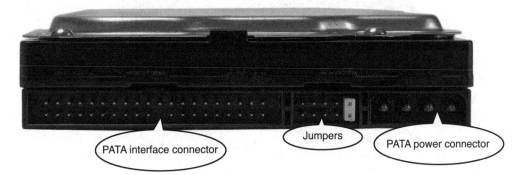

Figure 20.2 *The back of a PATA drive holds a couple of connectors and some jumpers.*

The PATA interface connector accepts a 40-pin PATA interface cable, shown in Figure 20.3, and the other side of that cable connects to a corresponding 40-pin connector on the motherboard, as shown in Figure 20.4. The PATA power connector accepts a 4-pin power cable, shown in Figure 20.3, and that cable comes from the computer's power supply. The jumpers are mostly used to determine whether the drive is the *master* (the first or only drive on the PATA cable) or a *slave* (the second drive on a PATA cable).

See the Manual for Jumper Info

See your hard drive documentation to learn which jumpers control the master/slave configurations. The docs may be available online if you no longer have them. If you don't have any documentation, many drives print a jumper diagram on the label. If you don't have that either, you can usually place a jumper on the far left pins for a master configuration and remove the jumper entirely for a slave configuration.

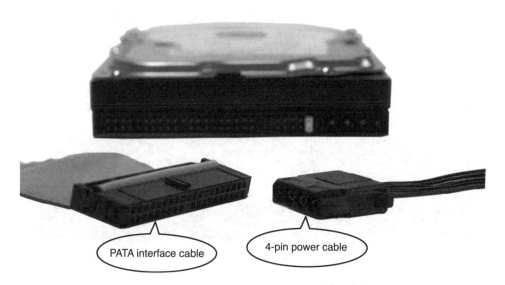

PATA interface cable

4-pin power cable

Figure 20.3 *A PATA interface cable connects the drive to the motherboard, and the PATA power cable connects the drive to the power supply.*

PATA connector

Figure 20.4 *Most PCs come with at least one PATA interface connector.*

The SATA Interface

The Serial Advanced Technology Attachment (SATA) interface is the current gold standard for PCs, and it's the only standard you should really consider for the internal hard drive (or drives) on your homebuilt system. Why? Two reasons: SATA drives cost about the same as the equivalent PATA drive, but the SATA drive will be significantly faster. How much faster? Anywhere from 1.5 times to 6 times faster! To see why, consider the three SATA standards you'll encounter:

- **SATA/150**—This is also called SATA 1. The "150" part tells you the throughput, which in this case means 150 megabytes per second (MBps). You might also see a SATA/150 drive's throughput listed as 1.5 gigabits per second (Gbps). Technically, that's the rate at which the hard drive transfers data, but some of that is overhead, so the actual rate is closer to 1.2Gbps, which is the same as 150 MBps, because there are 8 bits in a byte.

- **SATA/300**—This is also called SATA 2. The "300" part tells you the throughput, which in this case means 300MBps. Again, you sometimes see a SATA/300 drive's throughput listed as 3.0Gbps. Taking signaling overhead into account, the actual rate is closer to 2.4Gbps, which is the same as 300MBps.

- **SATA/600**—This is also called SATA 3. The "600" part tells you the throughput, which in this case means 600MBps. You sometimes see a SATA/600 drive's throughput listed as 6.0Gbps, but the actual rate is closer to 4.8Gbps, which is the same as 600MBps.

The back of a SATA hard drive usually has four sections, pointed out in Figure 20.5.

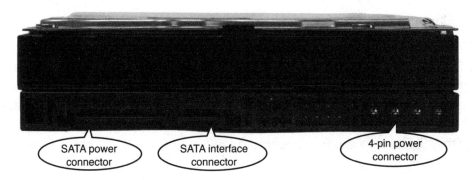

Figure 20.5 *The back of a SATA drive usually holds several connectors and some jumpers.*

The SATA interface connector accepts a 7-pin SATA interface cable, shown in Figure 20.6, and the other side of that cable connects to a corresponding 7-pin connector on the motherboard, as shown in Figure 20.7. The SATA power connector accepts a 15-pin power cable, shown in Figure 20.6, and that cable comes from the computer's power supply.

Figure 20.6 *A SATA interface cable connects the drive to the motherboard, and the SATA power cable connects the drive to the power supply.*

External Drive Interfaces

The PATA and SATA hard drive interfaces are for internal drives. If your case has room for only a small number of internal drives (or if you want to add storage to a notebook PC), the only way to augment your local storage is to add one or more external drives. Note, too, that external drives also offer portability, which lets you attach the drive to another system, take important files with you, and so on. For external drives, you have three more choices:

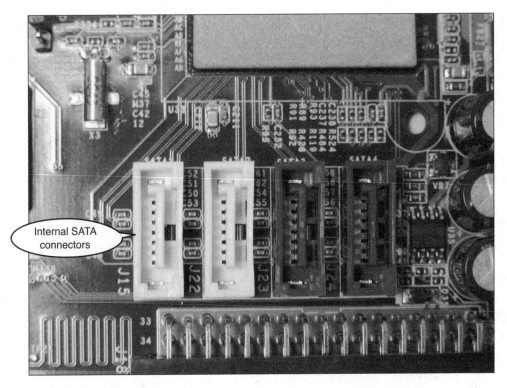

Figure 20.7 *All PCs come with two or more SATA interface connectors.*

- **USB 3.0**—These external drives attach to a USB 3.0 port. Make sure you get USB 3.0 (assuming your PC has at least one USB 3.0 port), which offers a transfer rate of 5Gbps, compared to 480Mbps for USB 2.0 and a mere 12Mbps for USB 1.1.

- **eSATA**—This is an external version of SATA (that's what the e stands for), and these drives attach to an eSATA connector. Other than the fact that it sits outside your PC, an eSATA drive is the same as an internal SATA/300 drive, which means you still get the 300MBps throughput.

- **IEEE 1394**—These external drives attach to an IEEE-1394 (also called FireWire) connector. You can get either IEEE 1394a (FireWire 400), which offers 400Mbps data throughput, or IEEE 1394b (FireWire 800), which offers 800Mbps data throughput.

For maximum flexibility, consider an external drive that offers two or more of these interfaces. For example, it's now fairly common to see external drives that offer both a USB 3.0 port and an eSATA port.

The Hard Drive Form Factor

The hard drive *form factor* refers to the dimensions of the drive—and more specifically to the approximate width of the drive. By far the most common hard drive form factor is 3.5 inches (the actual width is closer to 4 inches). Almost every case you buy will have hard drive bays that support 3.5-inch drives. The other common hard drive form factor is 2.5 inches (the actual width is closer to 2.75 inches), which is most often present in notebook drives. Figure 20.8 shows a 3.5-inch and a 2.5-inch hard drive for comparison.

The Hard Drive Speed

The hard drive *speed* is a measure of how fast the drive's internal platters spin, measured in revolutions per minute (rpm). In general, the higher the rpm value, the better the drive's performance. Most PATA and SATA hard drives spin at 7200rpm, although some older drives spin at 5400rpm. You should avoid these older drives because the performance hit is substantial, and they're not that much cheaper than the equivalent 7200rpm drive. If money is no object, you can find SATA drives that spin at 10000rpm, which offers a substantial performance boost.

> **Note**
>
> **Solid-State Hard Drives**
>
> Keep your eyes peeled on the new *solid-state* hard drives (SSDs) that are becoming quite popular. These 2.5-inch drives are made from solid-state semiconductors, which means they have no moving parts. As a result, SSDs are faster than HDDs, last longer, use less power, weigh less, and are completely silent. The downside is price. This is still bleeding-edge technology, so expect to pay around $200 for a 240GB SSD. Prices are dropping fast, however, so I'm sure it won't be long before SSDs become a viable alternative to regular drives.

3.5-inch hard drive

2.5-inch hard drive

Figure 20.8 *The two most common hard drive form factors are 3.5-inch and 2.5-inch.*

Buying a Hard Drive

Purchasing a hard drive for your PC doesn't have to be a complex exercise. In fact, you can make a smart hard drive choice by paying attention to just three numbers:

Cost/GB

This is the cost per gigabyte, which you calculate by dividing the price of the hard drive by its storage capacity. Here are some examples:

Price	Capacity	Cost/GB
$44.99	250GB	$0.18
$69.99	500GB	$0.14
$79.99	750GB	$0.11
$99.99	1TB	$0.10
$229.99	2TB	$0.12

As you can see, the low end and the high end cost more per gigabyte, and the sweet spot is the 1TB drive. Note that, from a cost/GB perspective, there's not a lot of difference between the 750GB, 1TB, and 2TB drives. So, if you have only minimal storage needs on your system, get the 750GB drive; if you need a bigger drive to store lots of media, get the 2TB drive.

Cache

The hard drive *cache* refers to a memory area embedded in the hard drive. This memory is used as a holding place for frequently used bits of data. If the CPU finds the data it needs in the hard drive cache, it saves time because the CPU can load that data directly into memory instead of asking the hard drive to fetch it from the disk. The bigger the hard drive cache, the more data it can hold, so the more likely the CPU is to find the data it needs, and thus the better the overall performance of the hard drive. So, if you're looking at two drives that are more or less the same in other respects (particularly cost/GB), choose the one that has the bigger cache.

Seek time When I explained the workings of a typical hard drive earlier (see "How a Hard Drive Works"), you learned that the four measures of hard disk read/write performance are the seek time, the latency, the write time, and the read time. Of these, the seek time is the most important. So, again, if the other factors are about equal, get the drive that has the lower seek time.

Building a hard drive that's fast, solid, reliable, quiet, and cool is a tall order, which might be why there aren't a large number of hard disk manufacturers—and of those manufacturers, only a few produce top-quality drives. In fact, I recommend only the following three hard drive companies:

Hitachi (www.hitachigst.com)

Seagate (www.seagate.com)

Western Digital (www.westerndigital.com)

Removing the Old Hard Drive

If the hard drive in your PC has become too small to store your data, or if you're having problems with the drive (or it has failed entirely), you need to remove the old drive and install a new one.

Here are the steps to remove a hard drive:

1. Make sure the computer is turned off and the power cable is disconnected.

2. Remove the computer's side panel.

3. Touch something metal to ground yourself.

4. Locate the hard drive. On most PCs, the hard drive is located near the front of the case, usually in the middle or near the bottom.

Note

Create a System Image Backup

If your existing hard drive still works, I highly recommend that you take some time now to create a system image backup, which will make it immeasurably easier to get your PC back on its feet after you've installed the new hard drive. See "Creating a System Image Backup" in Chapter 15, "Maintaining Your PC."

5. Remove the drive's power cable (see Figure 20.9).

6. Remove the drive's interface cable. Pull straight out. Don't wiggle the cable back and forth, or you risk bending the tiny pins.

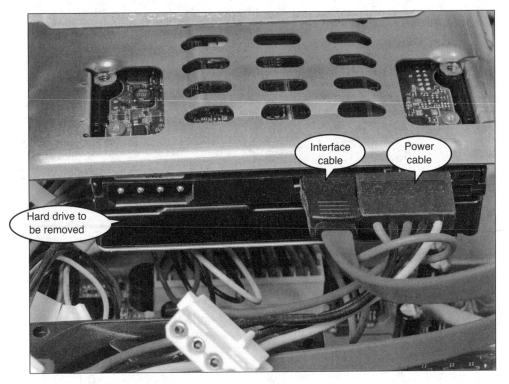

Figure 20.9 *You need to remove the power and interface cables attached to the hard drive.*

7. Get the hard drive ready to be removed. How this is done depends on the hard drive enclosure, but two scenarios are the most common:

- **The hard drive is held in place by screws.** Many hard drive enclosures use simple screws (from four to eight in most cases) to hold the hard drive in place, as shown in Figure 20.10. You need to remove these screws.

Note

Remove the Other Side Panel, If Needed

If the screws on the opposite side of the enclosure seem impossible to reach, it's most likely that you have to remove the other side panel to gain access to them.

Figure 20.10 *Many hard drives are fastened to the enclosure using several screws.*

- **The hard drive is held in place by rails.** The next most common system is to attach "rails" on either side of the hard drive and then slide the rails into special slots on the inside walls of the drive enclosure, as shown in Figure 20.11. In most cases, you pinch the rails toward each other slightly to release the hard drive.

8. Slide the drive out of the drive bay. If the hard drive has rails attached, remove them for reuse with the new drive, as described in the next section.

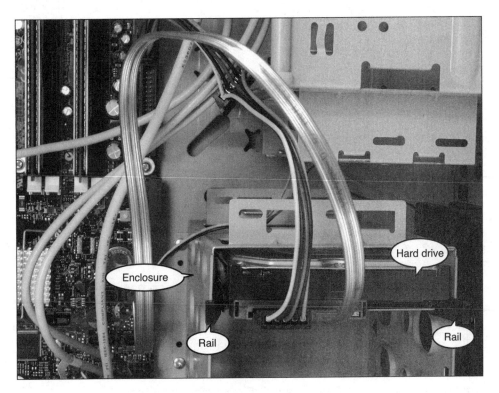

Figure 20.11 *Some hard drives are attached to the enclosure using rails that are attached to the sides of the drive.*

Installing a New Hard Drive

With the old hard drive removed from your PC, you're ready to install the new drive. Here are the steps to follow:

1. Touch something metal to ground yourself.

2. If your hard drive enclosure uses rails, orient the hard drive so the connectors are facing you and the drive label is facing up, snap a left rail into the holes on the left side of the hard drive, and snap a right rail into the holes on the right side of the hard drive. Figure 20.12 shows a hard drive fitted with rails.

Figure 20.12 *A hard drive with left and right rails attached.*

3. With the hard drive connectors facing out, slide the hard drive into a drive bay. If the hard drive is held in place with screws, slide the drive into the bay until the holes on the sides of the drive align with the holes in the enclosure. If the hard drive has rails, slide the drive until the rails click into place.

4. Run an interface cable (such as a SATA cable) from the hard drive's interface connection (such as a SATA port) inside the PC.

5. Connect a power cable from the power supply to the hard drive's power connector.

6. Reattach the side panel and plug the power cord back in.

Finishing Up

With your new hard drive installed, it's time to get your PC back up and running. Your first chore is to reinstall Windows, and then you restore your system from a system image backup (if you have one):

1. Insert the Windows installation media.

2. Restart your PC.

3. Boot to the installation media. Note that how you boot to the install media depends on your system. In some cases, you see a message telling you to press a key, whereas other systems ask you to select a boot device from a menu, as shown in Figure 20.13.

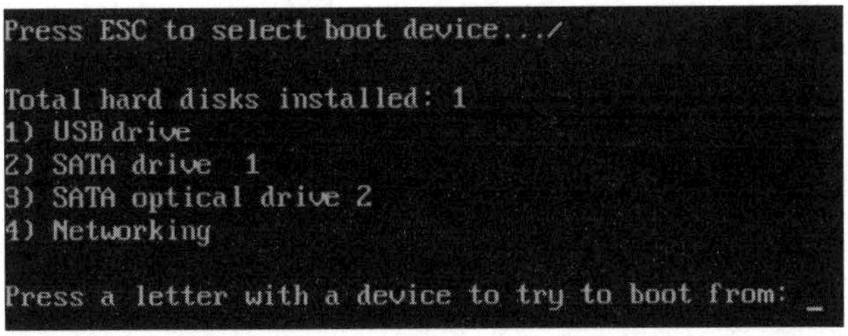

```
Press ESC to select boot device.../

Total hard disks installed: 1
1) USB drive
2) SATA drive  1
3) SATA optical drive 2
4) Networking

Press a letter with a device to try to boot from: _
```

Figure 20.13 *On some systems, you select the boot device from a menu.*

4. When the installation program starts, follow the onscreen prompts to reinstall Windows. If you need help, and if you have access to another PC, here are some online resources to check out:

    -   **Windows 8**—http://windows.microsoft.com/en-US/windows/install-upgrade-activate-help

    -   **Windows 7**—http://windows.microsoft.com/en-US/windows7/Installing-and-reinstalling-Windows-7

    -   **Windows Vista**—http://windows.microsoft.com/en-US/windows-vista/Installing-and-reinstalling-Windows-Vista

    -   **Windows XP**—http://windows.microsoft.com/en-US/windows-xp/help/setup/install-windows-xp

5. When Windows is reinstalled, restore your data from a system image backup, as described in Chapter 16, "Troubleshooting Your PC" (see the section "Restoring a System Image").

Chapter 21

Replacing the CD or DVD Drive

Any PC worth its chips should have an *optical drive*, a catchall term that includes every type of CD and DVD drive, as well as the latest Blu-ray drives. The *optical* part tells you that these drives use light—specifically, a semiconductor laser—to read data from and write data to the disc. (For example, the *Blu* in Blu-ray comes from the fact that it uses laser light with a wavelength in the blue section of the spectrum.) Among many other uses, an optical drive enables your system to play audio CDs, screen DVD movies, watch high-definition video (you need a Blu-Ray drive for that), install programs and device drivers, store data, and make backups.

In this chapter you learn about optical drives, get information on making your best purchase, and then learn how to replace your existing optical drive with a new one.

Buying a CD or DVD Drive

Optical drives are among the least expensive components you'll add to your system. For example, if all you want to do is rip and burn audio CDs, you can buy a super-fast DVD±RW drive (I'm talking about 52x write speed, 32x rewrite speed, and 52x read speed) for under $20!

There's lots of competition in this market, which is why prices are low and features are high. Quite a few manufacturers operate in the optical drive market, but here are the ones I've had good dealings with:

LG Electronics (www.lge.com)

Lite-On (www.liteonit.com)

Pioneer (www.pioneerelectronics.com)

Philips (www.philips.com)

Plextor (www.plextor.com)

Samsung (www.samsung.com)

Sony (www.sony.com)

Note

Drive Lingo

If you're scratching your head over terms such as *DVD±RW* and *write speed*, see Chapter 2, "Buying a PC," for the details.

Here are a few other pointers and notes to consider when buying an optical drive for your custom system:

- **Check the cache size**. All optical drives come with an onboard memory cache for storing bits of frequently used data. This improves performance because it's many times faster for the processor to retrieve the data it needs from the cache than from the disc. The bigger the cache, the better the performance. On burners, the cache also helps to keep the burning process running smoothly by feeding a constant supply of data to the drive. Most drives nowadays come with a 2MB cache, but some drives have a 4MB cache.

- **Check the access time**. The average time it takes the optical drive to access data on the disc is called the access time, and it's measured in milliseconds. The lower the access time, the faster the drive.

- **Check out SATA optical drives**. It used to be that optical drives came with only a PATA interface, but SATA drives started showing up a while back. Unfortunately, those drives were plagued with all kinds of problems, and the interface never took off. I'm happy to report that the manufacturers have fixed the problems, and SATA/150 optical drives are becoming quite popular. The higher bandwidth improves performance, and the SATA connector and power cables are easier to use than the larger PATA and legacy power cables.

- **Consider buying two drives**. Earlier I mentioned that the read speeds of ROM drives are faster than the read speeds of burners. Given that, a popular system configuration is to add both a ROM drive and a burner, such as a DVD-ROM drive and a DVD±RW drive. This way, you can use the DVD-ROM drive when you need read-only performance (such as when you're installing a program or accessing data on a disc), and you can use the DVD±RW drive when you need to burn data to a disc.

Note

PATA and SATA Info

See Chapter 20, "Replacing the Hard Drive," to learn about PATA and SATA connections.

Removing the Existing Optical Drive

If your PC has an existing optical drive that you're going to replace either because it no longer works or you're upgrading to a better drive, you usually need to remove the old optical drive before installing the new one. (I say *usually* because many desktop PCs have enough room to hold at least two optical drives, so if your old drive still works, consider leaving it in place.)

Here are the steps to follow to remove an optical drive:

1. Make sure the computer is turned off and the power cable is disconnected.

2. Remove the computer's side panel.

3. Remove the PC's front cover. How you do this depends on the PC, but in most cases there are several plastic tabs holding the cover in place. For example, Figure 21.1 shows a PC that has a front cover held in place by three external tabs and one internal tab.

4. Touch something metal to ground yourself.

5. Locate the optical drive. On most PCs, the optical drive is located at the front of the case, at or near the top.

6. Remove the power cable from the back of the optical drive (see Figure 21.2).

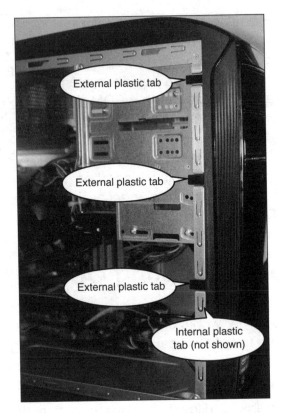

Figure 21.1 *Most desktop PCs have front covers held in place by several plastic tabs.*

7. Remove the interface cable from the back of the optical drive (see Figure 21.2).

8. Get the optical drive ready to be removed. How this is done depends on the drive enclosure, but two scenarios are the most common:

   - **The optical drive is held in place by screws.** Many optical drive enclosures use simple screws (from four to eight in most cases) to hold the hard drive in place, as shown in Figure 21.3. You need to remove these screws.

Note

Removing the Other Side Panel

If you can't see any way to remove the screws on the opposite side of the enclosure, you most likely need to remove the other side panel to get at them.

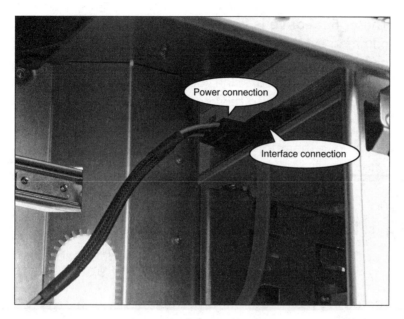

Figure 21.2 *As part of the drive removal process, you need to disconnect both the power cable and the interface cable from the back of the drive.*

Figure 21.3 *Many optical drives are fastened to the enclosure using several screws.*

- **The optical drive is held in place by rails.** The next most common system is to attach "rails" on either side of the optical drive and then slide the rails into special slots on the inside walls of the drive enclosure. In most cases, you pinch the rails toward each other slightly to release the optical drive.

9. Slide the drive out the front of the drive bay. If the optical drive has rails attached, remove them for reuse with the new drive, as described in the next section.

Installing the New Optical Drive

With the old optical drive removed from your PC, you're ready to install the new drive. Here are the steps to follow:

1. Touch something metal to ground yourself.

2. If your optical drive enclosure uses rails, orient the optical drive so the connectors are facing you and the drive label is facing up, snap a left rail into the holes on the left side of the optical drive, and snap a right rail into the holes on the right side of the optical drive.

3. Open the PC's front cover, if you haven't done so already (as described in the preceding section).

4. With the optical drive's connectors facing the inside of the case, slide the drive into a drive bay. If the optical drive is held in place with screws, slide the drive into the bay until the holes on the sides of the drive align with the holes in the enclosure. If the hard drive has rails, slide the drive until the rails click into place.

5. Run an interface cable from the optical drive's interface connection to a corresponding port inside the PC (see Figure 21.4).

Interface connection

Figure 21.4 *As part of the drive installation, you need to connect the interface cable to the back of the drive.*

6. Connect a power cable from the power supply to the optical drive's power connector.

7. Reattach the front cover.

8. Reattach the side panel. Plug in the power cable.

Chapter 22

Adding More Memory

As you see in this chapter, your computer's *random access memory (RAM)* is just an innocuous collection of chips on a special module you plug in to a slot inside your PC. But although these chips might not look like much, they perform some pretty important tasks.

Their basic purpose in life is to be used as a work area for your programs and data. These things normally slumber peacefully on your hard disk, but when you need them, the operating system rouses all of them from their spacious beds and herds the program code and data into the relatively cramped confines of memory. From there, different bits of code and data are swapped in and out of memory, as needed. Why not just work with everything from the hard disk itself? One word: *speed*. Even the highest of high-tech hard drives is a tortoise compared to the blazing memory chips.

Entire books can be (and, indeed, have been) written about the relationship between your computer and its memory. What it all boils down to, though, is quite simple: The more memory you have, the happier your PC (and the operating system and programs you run on it) will be. This chapter gives you a bit of background about memory and specific recommendations as to how much memory you might want for certain applications; then it shows you how to extract and insert memory modules.

Understanding Memory Specs

As I mentioned earlier, memory comes packaged in a special component called a *memory module* (or sometimes a *memory stick*). Figure 22.1 shows a typical memory module.

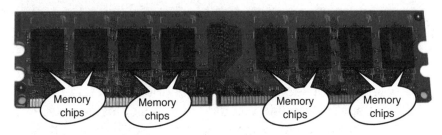

Memory chips   Memory chips   Memory chips   Memory chips

Figure 22.1 *Modern-day memory comes in the form of a memory module, where the individual memory chips are soldered into place.*

If you go online to your favorite computer parts retailer and click the Memory section, you might see a bunch of listings for memory modules that look something like this:

Corsair Vengeance 8GB PC3-12800 DDR3 1600 240-Pin

This raises computer prose to new heights of unintelligibility, but there's actually quite a bit of useful data packed ever so obscurely into just a few seemingly random characters. You need to understand only a bit of this geekspeak to buy memory modules for your system, but I'll trudge through all the terms anyway, just so you know what you're up against. This description breaks down into a dozen discrete components, some of which I discuss in more detail in the sections that follow:

Corsair
This is the name of the company that manufactures the module.

Vengeance
This is the name of the family of memory products in which the module falls in the company's hierarchy.

8GB
This is the capacity, the amount of RAM contained in the memory module.

PC3-12800
This is a code that specifies the type of memory standard used by the module.

DDR3	This tells you the memory type, which in this case is double data rate (DDR) type 3 memory.
1600	This is the effective speed of the memory chips, in megahertz (MHz).
240-Pin	This is the number of pins the memory module uses.

The Memory Module Standard

All memory modules adhere to a particular standard that specifies certain things such as the speed of the memory chips and the configuration of the module pins. The standard is indicated by a code number that takes one of the following three forms:

PC-*nnnn*	The PC part tells you that the module's chips use the double data rate (DDR) memory type (see the next section, "The Memory Type and Speed"), and the *nnnn* part is a number that tells you the theoretical bandwidth of the memory.
PC2-*nnnn*	The PC2 part tells you that the module's chips support the DDR2 memory type, and the *nnnn* part tells you the theoretical bandwidth of the memory.
PC3-*nnnn*	The PC3 part tells you that the module's chips support the DDR3 memory type, and the *nnnn* part tells you the theoretical bandwidth of the memory.

The theoretical bandwidth of the memory module is a measure of the amount of data that can pass through the module per second under ideal conditions. It's measured in megabytes per second (MBps) and, generally speaking, the higher the value, the better the memory's performance. For example, PC3-12800 implies a theoretical bandwidth of 12800MBps.

The Memory Type and Speed

Modern memory uses *synchronous dynamic RAM (SDRAM)*, which is a type of RAM that contains an internal clock that enables it to run in sync with the motherboard clock. The memory's *clock speed* is the number of ticks (or *cycles*) per second, measured in megahertz (MHz), or millions of cycles per second.

Currently, the most common memory chip type is DDR3 SDRAM, which boasts effective clock speeds ranging from 800MHz (DDR3-800) to 2800MHz (DDR3-2800).

The Memory Module Capacity

The capacity value you see in a memory module description just tells you how much RAM the module contains. If you're not sure of the capacity of a module, most have a sticker on the side that tells you, as shown in Figure 22.2.

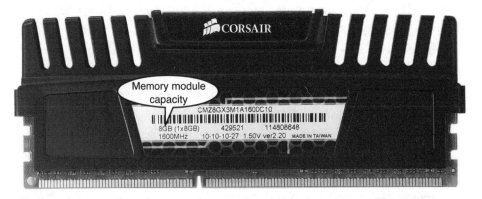

Figure 22.2 *Most RAM modules come with a sticker that tells you the module's capacity, as well as other data such as the memory type.*

Buying Memory

Buying RAM isn't nearly as complex as buying many of the other components that will make up your homebrew PC. Yes, you can obsess on obscure factors such as latency and timings (plus many other memory features I mercifully spared you from in this chapter), but when you're just starting out, there are only a few things you need to worry about. Before I talk about those things, I should mention that, as with the motherboard and processor, quality counts when it comes to RAM modules, so always buy from a major memory manufacturer. Here are a few I recommend:

Corsair (www.corsair.com)

Crucial Technology (www.crucial.com)

G.SKILL (www.gskill.com)

Kingston Technology (www.kingston.com)

Mushkin (www.mushkin.com)

OCZ Technology (www.ocztechnology.com)

Patriot (www.patriotmem.com)

Here are some pointers to think about before purchasing memory for your system:

- **Match your system**. The memory you buy should match the memory supported by your system. I discussed various ways to determine a PC's current memory in Chapter 18, "Upgrading Your PC."

- **Don't exceed you system's capacity**. All systems have a maximum RAM capacity, so you shouldn't try to install more RAM than the board can handle.

- **Match your RAM to your type of Windows**. From a memory perspective, Windows comes in two different flavors: 32-bit and 64-bit. You don't need to understand the difference, but you do need to know that for technical reasons, 32-bit versions of Windows can only use up to about 3GB of RAM, whereas 64-bit versions can use up to 128GB for Windows 8 and up to 512GB for Windows 8 Pro. (In 64-bit versions of Windows 7, the limits are 8GB for Home Basic, 16GB for Home Premium, and 192GB for Professional and Ultimate.)

Tip

Finding Your Exact Memory Type

Crucial Technology offers a handy Memory Advisor tool that enables you to look up a motherboard or computer (by manufacturer, product line, and model) and find out the exact memory you can use. See www.crucial.com.

Note

Finding Your Windows Type

To determine whether your PC uses 32-bit or 64-bit Windows 8, open the Charms menu, select **Search**, select **Settings**, type **system**, and then select **System** in the search results. For Windows 7, click **Start**, right-click **Computer**, and then click **Properties**. In the System window that appears, the **System Type** value will say either 32-bit Operating System or 64-bit Operating System.

- **Match your RAM to your needs**. The minimum amount of RAM required by Windows 7 and 8 is 1GB for a 32-bit system and 2GB for a 64-bit system, and you should consider these to be bare minimums. RAM isn't very expensive these days, so unless you're on a very tight budget, you might as well go with 3GB for a 32-bit system and 8GB for a 64-bit system.

Pulling Out the Old Memory Modules

After you purchase your memory modules, the next step in your memory upgrade is to remove the old modules. First, note that you don't necessarily have to do this. If your PC has four internal memory slots and you're just filling in the empty slots with the same type of memory that's already in the other slots, feel free to leave the old module in place.

If you're upgrading your memory, however, you should remove the old modules. Here are the steps to remove a memory module:

1. Make sure the computer is turned off and the power cable is disconnected.

2. Remove the computer's side panel.

3. Touch something metal to ground yourself.

4. Locate the memory module you want to remove.

5. Press down on one of the memory socket's ejector tabs to pivot the tab away from the module.

6. Press down on the other memory socket ejector tab to pivot the tab away from the module, as shown in Figure 22.3.

7. Remove the memory module from the socket. Take care not to bump the module against any other component.

8. Repeat steps 4–7 to remove any other module you want to salvage.

Figure 22.3 *Press down on the ejector tabs to pivot the tabs away from the module.*

Installing the New Memory Modules

The good news about installing memory modules is that they're almost impossible to install incorrectly. To understand why, Figure 22.4 shows a memory module hovering above a memory socket. Notice that the memory module has a notch in the pin area. This notch matches a corresponding ridge inside the memory socket, as pointed out in Figure 22.4. The placement of this notch prevents you from installing the module the wrong way around. Also, because the different module configurations have their notches in different places, it also prevents you from installing the wrong type of memory.

Figure 22.4 *The memory module's notch lines up with the DIMM socket ridge to ensure correct installation.*

With your new memory module in hand, here are the steps to follow to install it:

1. If the memory socket's ejector tabs are in the vertical position, open them by pivoting them away from the socket.

2. Orient the memory module over the memory socket so that the module's notch lines up with the socket's ridge, as shown in Figure 22.5.

3. On the ends of the socket, you'll see thin vertical channels. Slide the memory module into these channels, as shown in Figure 22.6.

4. Place your thumbs on the top edge of the module, one thumb on each side.

Note

Sometimes you need to use a surprising amount of force to get the module fully seated in the socket. Some sockets are just really tight fits, so you have to press really hard to get the module all the way in.

Figure 22.5 *Line up the module's notch with the socket's ridge.*

Figure 22.6 *Slide the memory module into the channels at both ends of the memory socket.*

5. Press the module into the socket. When the module is properly seated, the ejector tabs automatically snap into the vertical position.

6. Put the computer's side panel back on and plug in the power cord.

Note that it's very easy to think that you've inserted a memory module fully when in fact it's not quite seated properly. How can you tell? Check out the ejector tabs. If the module isn't fully seated in the socket, the ejector tabs are not perfectly vertical, as shown in Figure 22.7. The ejector tab should look like the one shown in Figure 22.8.

Figure 22.7 *Wrong: If the ejector tab isn't vertical, the module isn't seated.*

Figure 22.8 *Right: A vertical ejector tab tells you the module is fully seated in the socket.*

Index

Q-R

X-Y-Z